KEITH MOON
INSTANT PARTY

ALAN CLAYSON

KEITH MOON - INSTANT PARTY
Musings, Memories and Minutiae

by Alan Clayson

A CHROME DREAMS PUBLICATION

First Edition 2005

Published by Chrome Dreams
PO BOX 230, New Malden , Surrey
KT3 6YY, UK

WWW.CHROMEDREAMS.CO.UK

ISBN 1 84240 310 9

Copyright © 2005 by Alan Clayson
Editorial Director   Rob Johnstone
Editor   Rob Johnstone
Cover design   Sylwia Grzeszczuk
Interior design   Marek Krzysztof Niedziewicz

Front Cover
CAMERA PRESS

Back Cover
REX

Inside Photos
LFI
Starfile
Rex
Redferns
Barry Plummer
Alan Clayson Archive

A catalogue record for this book is available from the British Library.

Printed and bound in Great Britain by William Clowes Ltd, Beccles, Suffolk

KEITH MOON

INSTANT PARTY
MUSINGS, MEMORIES AND MINUTIAE

ALAN CLAYSON

To Peter Rowe, a Mod for all seasons

'The character I play isn't a character I put on and off like a coat. It is a part of me and a part of everything else I see'

Tony Hancock

**The author with one of Keith Moon's heroes,
Dick Dale: *King Of The Surf Guitar***

Born in Dover, England in 1951, Alan Clayson lives near Henley–on–Thames with his wife Inese. Their sons, Jack and Harry, are both at university.

A portrayal of Alan Clayson by the Western Morning News as the 'A.J.P. Taylor of the pop world' is supported by Q's 'his knowledge of the period is unparalleled and he's always unerringly accurate.' He has penned many books on music – including the best–sellers Backbeat, subject of a major film, The Yardbirds and The Beatles Box – and has written for journals as diverse as The Guardian, Record Collector, Ink, Mojo, Mediaeval World, Folk Roots, Guitar, Hello!, Drummer, The Times, The Independent, Ugly Things and, as a teen-ager, the notorious Schoolkids Oz. He has also been engaged to per-form and lecture on both sides of the Atlantic – as well as broadcast on national TV and radio .

From 1975 to 1985 he led the legendary Clayson and the Argonauts – who reformed briefly in 2005 to launch a long–awaited CD retro-spective – and was thrust to 'a premier position on rock's Lunatic Fringe' (Melody Maker). As shown by the existence of a US fan club – dating from an 1992 soiree in Chicago – Alan Clayson's following grows still as well as demand for his talents as a record producer, and the number of versions of his compositions by such diverse acts as Dave Berry (in whose backing group he played keyboards in the mid–1980s), New Age outfit, Stairway – and Joy Tobing, winner of the Indonesian version of Pop Idol. He has worked too with The Portsmouth Sinfonia, Wreckless Eric, Twinkle, The Yardbirds, The Pretty Things and the late Screaming Lord Sutch among many others. While his stage act defies succinct description, he has been labelled a 'chansonnier' in recent years for performances and record releases that may stand collectively as Alan Clayson's artistic apotheosis were it not for a promise of surprises yet to come.

Further information is obtainable from www.alanclayson.com

CALL UP THE GROUPS: *The Golden Age Of British Beat, 1962–67* (Blandford 1985)

BACK IN THE HIGH LIFE: *A Biography Of Steve Winwood* (Sidgwick and Jackson 1988)

ONLY THE LONELY: *The Life And Artistic Legacy Of Roy Orbison* (Sanctuary 1989)

THE QUIET ONE: *A LIfe Of George Harrison* * (Sanctuary 1990)

RINGO STARR: *Straight Man Or Joker?* * (Sanctuary 1991)

DEATH DISCS: *An Account Of Fatality In The Popular Song* (Sanctuary 1992)

BACKBEAT: *Stuart Sutcliffe: The Lost Beatle* (with Pauline Sutcliffe) (Pan Macmillan 1994)

ASPECTS OF ELVIS (ed. with Spencer Leigh) (Sidgwick and Jackson 1994)

BEAT MERCHANTS (Blandford 1995)

JACQUES BREL (Castle Communications 1996)

HAMBURG: *The Cradle Of British Rock* (Sanctuary 1997)

SERGE GAINSBOURG: *View From The Exterior* (Sanctuary 1998)

THE TROGGS FILE: *The Official Story Of Rock's Wild Things* (with Jacqueline Ryan) (Helter Skelter 2000)

EDGARD VARESE (Sanctuary 2002)

THE YARDBIRDS (Backbeat 2002)

JOHN LENNON * (Sanctuary 2003)

THE WALRUS WAS RINGO: *101 Beatles Myths Debunked* (with Spencer Leigh) (Chrome Dreams 2003)

PAUL McCARTNEY * (Sanctuary 2003)

BRIAN JONES (Sanctuary 2003)

CHARLIE WATTS (Sanctuary 2004)

WOMAN: *The Incredible Life Of Yoko Ono* (with Barb Jungr and Robb Johnson) (Chrome Dreams 2004)

KEITH RICHARDS (Sanctuary 2004)

MICK JAGGER (Sanctuary 2005)

*The four titles marked * are also available as THE BEATLES BOX or in edited editions as THE LITTLE BOX OF BEATLES (Sanctuary 2003)*

Prologue: 'Don't Know Myself'

'The truth as you want to know it? Oh no, dear boy. No, I'm afraid you couldn't afford me' – Keith Moon to a cameraman who asked him to 'tell the truth for a change'. [1]

This isn't a biography, but a series of essays about, well, 'aspects' of Keith Moon that have interested me, punctuated with previously untold tales about him, directly from metaphorical horses' mouths.

More than a quarter of a century after the abrupt end of his short but eventful life, mention of Moon still brings out strange stories of what people claim to have seen or heard. Yet many of the hair–raising escapades attributed to him took place under the alibi of a stage act; were elaborated by so–called 'insiders' – and then by outsiders – or were originated by others. Finally, Keith himself encouraged re–tellings of these music industry equivalents of fishermen's tall tales because he preferred folk to think him a frightful desperado and prankster rather than the mischievous but essentially authority–fearing boy he was, albeit one born without brakes. That's certainly how he's remembered by those who sat next to him at primary school; served in the same Sea Cadet Corps band in which he honked a bugle – or, as late as a matinée performance in Stockholm in October 1965, witnessed him treat with kid–gloves a kit lent by the hulking, red–fisted drummer in the parochial Mascots after Keith's own failed to materialise, owing to a flight mix–up at Heathrow.

Yet around a fortnight before, a road manager, gathering together the equipment after a show, had come across a snare drum borrowed from another support act, with a viciously torn skin and face down in a puddle of congealing vomit. If cognisant with Moon's personal history, he might have reflected then that perhaps there was a tang of significance in Keith being almost always the youngest in his class through the accident of a mid–August birth. With the same *leitmotif* of pre–emption from responsibility, the other personnel in the groups he joined – Lee Stuart and the Escorts, Clyde Burns and the Beachcombers and The Who – were two to three years older than him.

Moreover, when Moon was on the threshold of adolescence, funnymen like Bob Monkhouse, Bernard Bresslaw and Dave King were more likely focuses of adoration than pop musicians. A round–eyed twelve–year–old saw the late Bresslaw – idiotic 'Popeye' in *The Army Game*, a sitcom on the new ITV channel – passing in a triumphal Rolls–Royce through cheering streets to open a new department store along Harrow Road. Big Bernard had also come within an ace of Number One with the appositely dopey 'Mad Passionate Love' in the recently–established *New Musical Express* record sales charts – as had all the stars of *The Army Game* with its theme song a few weeks earlier.

In February 1965 however, a callow youth who'd cadged a cigarette off you the previous month was the cynosure of unseen millions of eyes on *Top Of The Pops* as Bob Monkhouse was on *Sunday Night At The London Palladium*. The Who's hits kept on coming until, with more money than sense, Keith became a personification of *hubris*, a Greek word that defies precise translation, but alludes to a resolutely foolish defiance of authority rooted in a notion that you are beyond convention and 'establishment' power.

Taken at face value alone, he was certainly the antithesis of the usual purportedly downtrodden beat group drummer, toiling over his kit in the background, ministering unobtrusively to overall effect – as Charlie Watts did in The Rolling Stones. 'Charlie was a very hermit–like guy,' estimated Michael Putland, the group's photographer, 'He didn't seem to join in the flow of it at all.' [2] As Watts had been categorised for all time as the Silent Stone in 1964, so the following year, some journalist chronicling the pandemonium surrounding The Who – Keith, vocalist Roger Daltrey, guitarist Pete Townshend and, on bass, John Entwistle – decided that Moon was their Madcap.

In professional circles, quiet Watts was thought more worthy of respect than loony Moon, for all the latter leavening a whimsical elasticity and outright craziness with intelligence, a sure touch and a subtlety of extra–rhythmic – and even tonal – shading. Yet Joe and Joanna Average didn't view it like that. They could take or leave Charlie, a crouched force hitting a plain–and–simple four–four in the Stones, but The Who would have been a far duller group without the flash personality, the off–duty antics and the general noise and crazy atmosphere that Keith, more than the others – more than just about anyone else in pop – could summon.

Johnnie Ray, a pioneer in this, hadn't liked 'the word "talent." Talent is what Einstein had. What I do is communicate with the audience.' [3]

This was at odds with the po–faced attitude of other pop idols – and that's all they were – that I could name, who intimated that what they did could be appreciated by only the finest minds.

Moon, however, was an artiste of Ray's kidney. To frantic applause in the States and delighted cheers in Britain, he seemed to imply with a wink that he wasn't a genius musician – or a genius anything – but that that didn't matter because he had an indefinable something else. What's a genius anyway? Among those blessed with that dubious title have been dart–hurling Jocky Wilson, easy–listening Horst 'A Walk In The Black Forest' Jankowski and north Middlesex's premier local hero, Screaming Lord Sutch – whose drummer, Carlo Little, guided young Moon's first attempts to keep the beat.

Sutch's pop star was waning when The Who made their stage debut in 1964, working the Home Counties circuit. Soon, the outfit was having much the same effect on their audiences as the chart–riding Beatles had had on theirs in Liverpool. With both rhythm–and–blues – R&B – credibility, teen appeal and an artful management team in Chris Stamp and Kit Lambert, their cash flow was such that, if they hadn't done so already, they were able to pack in daytime occupations – though, for a while afterwards, Keith was to amuse himself by filling in application forms and even attending interviews for mundane office posts, deriving much pleasure from first expressing doubts and then telling panels and individual bosses where they could stuff their fucking jobs.

In what was, ostensibly, an equal opportunities organisation, Moon was as much The Who's public face as any other member. Swiftly amassing a reputation as a raver like the world of pop had never known before, Keith made John Lennon's alleged antics when the pre–Ringo Beatles were in Hamburg – walking on stage clad in only underpants, say, or urinating from a balcony onto the wimples of three promenading nuns – seem like the tiny cats–cradling naughtinesses of a backward choirboy. Commenting on the popularity of the Speakeasy, a storm centre of London's pop 'in crowd' following its opening in January 1966, *Melody Maker*'s Chris Welch wrote, 'It was probably because of the tireless patience of the head waiter and the staff, who did not seem to mind too much when Mr. Moon appeared naked, letting off all the fire extinguishers.' [4]

17

Eventually, Moon felt it was almost incumbent upon him to create mayhem from nothing; the most documented – and erroneous – instance being his disruption of a party in – depending on your source – either Surrey or somewhere in America, through steering a Rolls Royce Silver Cloud into the host's swimming pool. Then there were the dynamite explosions in lavatories; breaking into a aeroplane pilot's cabin to rap his drum sticks on the control panel, and razoring his wrists at the drop of a hat. After deductions for damages he inflicted *en route*, Moon's fee for what turned out to be his last British tour with The Who was enough to buy maybe nine Chinese takeaways. On the surface, he was an appalling fellow, but 'I liked Keith very much,' smiled David Essex, 'and in his quiet moments found him to be intelligent and caring. In public, he was like a gun–slinger with a reputation for swinging on chandeliers. so rather than let people down – he did.' [5]

Sometimes, the nonsense was merely implied. Most renowned as a member of 1976 Top Twenty entrants, The Kursaal Flyers, Will Birch had been a teenage drummer in a unit supporting The Who at a provincial booking the same month as the Stockholm trip. In the dressing room, he drank in the sight of an evil–looking axe artlessly displayed on top of the toilet bag, spare underwear *et al* when an apparently nonchalant Moon opened his suitcase. It had been packed as insurance against it ever being needed – though lately he had wielded it at intrusive fans, who'd taken to their heels.

It proved useful too when the well of diversions ran dry in this Holiday Inn or that Trust House where, from a high–rise window, the sun–blanked lenses of Moon's Ray Ban Wayfarer shades flashed like twin heliographs over the concrete desolation of the car park. Within the hour, the contents of the entire room might be reduced to half–things, former things and broken things.

Off the road, he and assorted cronies – that included Screaming Lord Sutch and two of The Bonzo Dog Doo–Dah Band – once paraded round London clubland dressed in Nazi attire – with Keith as the toothbrush–moustached twentieth century Attila – carrying a knapsack containing a tape–recorder that blasted out oompah exultancies such as 'Horst Wessel Lied', 'Heil Hitler Dir' and 'Wenn Die SS Und Die SA Aufmarschiert'. For all its potential for self–publicity, Sutch for one cried off when Keith proposed protracting the exhibitionist fun when the city woke by visiting its most Jewish quarters.

Perhaps the difference between Doctor Keith and Mister Moon was similar to that between James Bond on celluloid and the more serious–minded James Bond in the original Ian Fleming novels. In a lucid moment, Moon confessed that his tomfoolery was all connected with his function as the group's headline–maker, citing examples such as the aftermath of a relatively straightforward Who show at the Stadthalle in Bremen, Germany. The following Friday, the damage he had inflicted at the city's most exclusive hotel was detailed on the front page in the local weekly newspaper

Yet, that he sustained his manic persona throughout his professional career – and behind closed doors – suggests a deeper motivation. For a start, he was such a heavy and persistent drinker that he could differentiate between brands of brandy by merely sniffing. Yet, even without artificial stimulation, his behaviour was akin to that of a schoolboy tormenting trainee teachers unable to keep order, by being endlessly disruptive as he tested how extreme a given strategy had to be before it provoked a reaction. When guitarist Link Wray, responsible for the crunching rowdiness of the 1958 instrumental million–seller 'Rumble', paid The Who a fraternal visit in the London studio where they were recording, Moon, seemingly beside himself with excitement, flung off all his clothes to cavort round the complex, arms waving. 'Rumble! Rumble!,' he kept yowling.

Then there was the time he either applied a lighter to or tore up his £150 pay packet for a day's film work (in days when £150 was worth something) – and what about the night he won a bet that he could break into Mick Jagger's eleventh floor hotel room? Clambering up the wall Spider Man–style, Moon burst through the open window to face the barrel of a revolver that Mick – heart pounding like a hunted beast – pulled from beneath a pillow. Though startled from slumber too, Bianca, the first Mrs. Jagger, subjected her spouse to a jocular scolding for so alarming the intruder, before dressing, applying make–up, and going dancing with Moon while Mick remained huddled, bemused, under the bedclothes.

Sometimes, a pet would turn into a pest, though Keith's most die-hard fans adopted an Emperor's New Clothes approach, considering the mildest censure of him as a mortal insult – just as those who supported his friend Vivian Stanshall – from the Bonzo Dog Doo–Dah Band – hailed their hero's unfunny drunken abuse and indecent exposure that passed for entertainment one unhinged pub–rock evening in 1976. In infinitely more controlled fashion, Tony Hancock, a comedian much admired by Moon – and, like him, an alcoholic – went the desperate distance on goodwill during his final concert with insultingly old and worn material as a travesty of what he'd once been.

The case for Moon's defence was freighted with statements like, 'People say to me, "Keith, you're crazy." Well, maybe I am, but I live out my fantasies, thereby getting them out of my system.' [6] At the very least, it all made work for the working man to do when he removed the screws from the furniture in his hotel suite, and left it standing perfectly still and upright but ready to collapse at an uncomprehending touch by the next occupier.

Guests who couldn't afford to buy themselves out of trouble derived vicarious enjoyment from his larks. 'Moon was a wonderful companion,' grinned actor and failed pop singer Gregory Phillips, 'He would walk down corridors, picking up fire extinguishers and bins to throw out of the window.' [7] Were more than mere inanimate objects hurled earthwards as Moon's practical jokes grew more premeditated and elaborate? Read what you like into this: during a Who tour of North America, John Entwistle, his much–tried patience exhausted, told a dithering Keith to be ready to leave for the next engagement in two minutes. Ambling down the stairs, John was open–mouthed with shock when what appeared to be a human body shot past a window outside. It looked like Moon, but by the time John completed a frenzied dash to the ground floor, the drummer was there already, relaxing in the lounge bar.

It was, nevertheless, just another incident in a harassing week which had climaxed already when a party – in which Moon had been a central figure – had got so out of hand that the entire group plus most of their entourage spent the rest of the night and half the next day in police cells. [8]

Of all The Who members, the period between one show and the next hung heaviest for Moon – as typified by the events that followed a recital at the University of Sussex. BBC Radio One presenter Anne Nightingale and her husband invited him and his chauffeur and general factotum, Peter 'Dougal' Butler, back to her Brighton home to 'chill out'. Keith, however, wasn't one for small talk, firelight and low–volume stereo. When Butler was on the point of filling a very empty stomach with the Nightingales' hospitality, his employer announced, 'We're off!', and the two vanished into the night in a lilac Rolls–Royce.

As he cruised the neon streets, Moon spread consternation like a pantomime horseman of the apocalypse; striding into the foyer of the grandest seafront hotels to demand accommodation for the two hundred passengers in the aeroplane he said he was piloting, which had been grounded by fog at Gatwick airport. Tiring of this game, he began flagging down police squad cars to ask for directions to parochial brothels. Most of the officers smiled indulgently: dear old Keith.

Finally, as milk floats wafted along the promenade, the famished Dougal made short work of the food still available at Anne Nightingale's, while Moon, still raring to go after maybe thirty–six hours without sleep, explained, 'I'm like an express train. It just takes so long to come down after a gig, I can't speak to anyone for about an hour. I always get in somewhere at some club, and then get barred for life from it. If someone tells me I can't do something, I'll go on and prove I can.' [9]

Before The Who arrived in 1965, there'd been a few precedents. Olde–tyme rock 'n' roller Jerry Lee Lewis made even Moon seem tame with turbulent years of veering fitfully between high living and destitution; tour itineraries that degenerated into subsudised booze–ups; his shooting of a bass guitarist; the accidental deaths of two sons and one of as many wives as Henry VIII; a hounding from England's shores for his marriage to a fourteen–year–old cousin, and his hammering of a – literally – blazing piano, set alight with petrol and match, after the self–styled 'Killer' was obliged to be second–billed to Chuck Berry – who, as a sexagenarian, was to issue *Sweet Little Sexteen*, a video of himself in manifold sexual activities.

In Britain, Viv Prince, drummer with The Pretty Things had set the standards for rock 'n' roll excess during the beat boom. The tip of a vast iceberg of hell–raising was his refusal to tread the boards one evening because the pub opposite the venue wouldn't serve him. 'What he forgot,' grimaced vocalist Phil May, 'was that the night before, he'd gone there with a bunch of musicians and smashed the place up.'

More insidiously, Rolling Stone Brian Jones pre–empted Moon's Nazi jape with a fashion statement whereby he was frontpaged late in

1966 in the black jack–booted uniform of a World War II stormtrooper – also grinning and stamping on a doll – in *Stern*, a glossy journal published in West Germany. This was particularly inflammable in the light of a recent election triumph by the 'new Nazis' in Bavaria.

There were also pockets of milder silliness where you'd least expect to find them. The late Chris Curtis, drummer with The Searchers – who fused Merseybeat with jingle–jangling contemporary folk – was a known practical joker, exemplified by his telephoning female acquaintances in the graveyard hours and, in a sing–song Oriental accent, demanding that they report to Waterloo Station tomorrow morning to board the chartered train for Dover and eventual incorporation into his presently depleted harem.

Curtis ended the Swinging Sixties as a withdrawn, disillusioned sociopath who'd quit showbusiness for the security of the civil service; Brian Jones drowned in his swimming pool, and The Pretty Things had cashiered the zealously unreliable Prince, who then became the generally drunken host of Knuckles, a late night watering hole in Soho. Yet Keith Moon not only kept up with but also overtook the speed of pop that dictated that each subsequent generation outdo the one before in outrage. While the likes of Jimi Hendrix, Wild Man Fischer, Ozzy Osbourne, Alice Cooper, The Damned, The Sex Pistols, The Cramps and Oasis did their worst – or best – off–stage and on, it was Moon who made the front cover of *Excess All Areas: A Who's Who Of Rock Depravity*, a slim volume given away free with a 1995 edition of the short–lived *Vox* pop periodical.

Yet, beneath it all, he was the stock Nice Lad When You Get To Know Him. 'Keith had a lot of time for those kind of gestures, which a lot of people wouldn't suspect,' Vivian Stanshall would recall, 'They hear about him smashing and breaking and being outrageous, but there was a generous and compassionate side to him that didn't get much publicity.' [10] Weighed down too with psychological pressures that the man–in–the–street couldn't begin to understand, Keith was most supportive when Stanshall's own sufferings had led to a spell in a residential clinic.

In the backstage area at 1970's Isle of Wight festival, an apprehensive Melanie, perhaps the most 'precious' of the post–Woodstock school of acoustic singer–songwriters, was befriended by a fellow who – and with no ulterior motive – invited her into his caravan for digestive and recuperative hospitality. Though they had little in common artistically, they chatted easily enough before the host was called to the stage. 'That was Keith Moon, you know,' someone remarked to Melanie later.

You'd hear murmurs too of an introspective side that rendered Moon ripe for religion. There'd been hints of this as far back as 1967 when he ascribed a spiritual dimension to the fictional Silver Cloud–in–swimming–pool matter – which, so he assured readers, actually happened – during an interview in schoolgirl comic, *Jackie*, of all places.

Conversely, there was the standpoint of the rare consumer who attended a Who extravaganza in order to talk about how 'interesting' it was afterwards. He or she reads a lot, thinks a lot, but does nothing. Perhaps the word I'm looking for is 'intellectual'. To such a person, maybe the key to Keith was that he was as earnestly superficial as pop artist Andy Warhol's soup–cans, Brillo pads and comic–strip philosophy with, agreed Warhol himself, 'nothing to explain or understand'.

Striking the healthiest balance between these opposing perspectives, *Dear Boy: The Life Of Keith Moon*, Tony Fletcher's doorstopper – nigh on six hundred pages – is an engrossing synthesis of unfamiliar anecdotes, debunking of the old yarns, and much new and rediscovered information. Yet, more than a simple 'good read', it provokes lasting thought in its in–depth estimation of motive and weighing of experience.

Fletcher's extensive work passes the litmus test of any pop life story in that it provokes a compulsion in the reader to check out the records. Moreover, it isn't aimed at fans who prefer not to know too much about what kind of people their idols are in private life. Too many illusions will be shattered, and the music may never sound the same. [11]

Me? For this volume, I ventured into many territories unexplored by even Fletcher, treating Keith like a historical figure – footnotes and all – when wading through oceans of archive material and screwing myself up to speak to complete strangers about matters that took place up to half a century ago. As his profile assumed a sharper definition, Moon surfaced as an admirable man in many ways – though some of my findings shattered further myths.

For most of my research concerning modern drumming and insight into Keith Moon's impact on same, I went to Alan Barwise, drummer and philosopher with Billy and the Conquerors, Clayson and the

Argonauts and other ventures, quixotic and otherwise, that I have instigated over the past thirty–very odd years.

Please put your hands together too for Rob Johnstone, Melanie Breen and the rest of the posse at my publishers Chrome Dreams – for patience and understanding about a deadline that I almost–but–not–quite missed.

Thanks are also in order for Ian 'Tich' Amey, Dave Dee, Dave Berry, Stuart Booth, Clem Cattini, Dick Dale, Gerry Conway, Tony Dangerfield, the late Denis D'Ell, Ray Dorset, Trevor Dunlap, Nick Garvey, Steve Gibbons, Alan Holmes, Alun Huws, Carlo Little, Kenny Lynch, Jim McCarty, Dave Munden, the late Harry Nilsson, Phil Nixon, Brian Poole, Reg Presley, Lloyd Ryan, 'Legs' Larry Smith, the late Vivian Stanshall, the late Lord David Sutch, Dick Taylor, Derrik Timms, Twinkle and Ricky West for their candour and intelligent argument.

Whether they were aware of providing assistance or not, let's have a round of applause too for these musicians: Roger Barnes, Peter Barton, Cliff Bennett, Jimmy Carl Black, Mike Cooper, Don Craine, Spencer Davis, Wayne Fontana, 'Wreckless' Eric Goulden, Keith Grant–Evans, Dave Hill, Brian Hinton, Neil Innes, the late Tony Jackson, Garry Jones, Graham Larkbey, Phil May, Tom McGuiness, Paul Samwell–Smith, Jim Simpson, John Steel, Mike and Anja Stax, John Townsend, Paul Tucker and Pete York.

It may be obvious to the reader that I have received help from sources that prefer not to be mentioned. Nevertheless, I wish to thank them – as well as Robert Cross of Bemish Business Machines, Kathryn Booth, Peter Doggett, Ian Drummond, Katy Foster–Moore, Michael Heatley, Kevin Howlett, Dave Humphries, Allan Jones, Mick and Sarah Jones, Elisabeth McCrae, Russell Newmark, Mike Ober, Mike Robinson, Anne Taylor, Warren Walters, Gina Way and Ted Woodings as well as Inese, Jack and Harry Clayson

Alan Clayson, May 2005

Notes

1. *Loose Talk* ed. L. Botts (Omnibus, 1980)
2. *Sunday Times*, 2 August 2003
3. *Daily Telegraph*, 31 March 1990
4. *London Live* by T. Bacon (Balafon, 1999)
5. *A Charmed Life* by D. Essex (Orion, 2002)
6. *NME Rock 'N' Roll Years* ed. J. Tobler (BCA, 1992)
7. *2Stoned* by A. L. Oldham (Vintage, 2003)
8. This brush with the law was encapsulated in song by John Entwistle in 'Cell Number 7' on his 1975 solo album, *Mad Dog.*
9. *Chase The Fade* by A. Nightingale (Blandford, 1981)
10. *Ginger Geezer: The Life Of Vivian Stanshall* by C. Welch (Fourth Estate, 2001)
11. *Dear Boy: The Life Of Keith Moon* by T. Fletcher (Omnibus, 1998)

'...And Now, Ladies And Gentlemen, A Nice Little Band From Shepherd's Bush' [1]

'I wouldn't pick them as friends, but I wouldn't pick anyone else as musicians to play with' – Keith Moon [2]

His membership of The Who will always remain pivotal to any consideration of Keith Moon as a figure in time's fabric. Therefore, although others have told the tale too, I proffer my own version of events.

Roger Daltrey, John Entwistle and Pete Townshend emerged from a background that, like Keith's and so many other 1960s pop stars, was solidly suburban. John and Pete were in the same year at Acton Grammar School. Before they left, John – who became a trainee tax officer – and, briefly, Pete – who went to art college – played in a trad(itional) jazz outfit, Pete Wilson's Confederates, on trumpet (and, less frequently, French horn) and banjo respectively.

Exhibitionists – usually university students – would don boaters or top hats, and a variety of hacked–about formal wear, drink heavily of cider, and launch into vigorous steps that blended a type of skip–jiving with the Charleston in a curious galumphing motion, to the plinking and puffing of an outfit trading in trad. This during a post–skiffle craze bracketed roughly by international best–seller, 'Petite Fleur' in 1959 – attributed to Chris Barber and his Jazz Band but, essentially, a clarinet solo – and the same London–based combo framing the ebullient singing of Ottilie Patterson, Barber's then–wife, over the closing credits of 1962's *It's Trad Dad* movie.

Yet it was not London but Bristol, home of clarinettist Bernard 'Acker' Bilk, from where the pestilence of trad had ravaged Britain, to the detriment of rock 'n' roll and fast–fading skiffle. It had spread beyond the earnest obsession of the collegiate intellectual fringe and 'Ban The Bomb' marches to a proletariat where 'ACKER' was studded on the backs of leather jackets where 'ELVIS' once was, and girls fainted to the blowing of Bilk, Barber, Humphrey Lyttelton, Kenny Ball and Monty Sunshine. After Acker almost touched Number One with 'Stranger On The Shore', a Manchester disciple wrote to ask him if it was about Jesus. [3]

It was pop by any other name – as were Top Ten strikes by The Temperance Seven, jazz only marginally but still booked for television programmes like the BBC's opportunist *Trad Tavern*, and at genre strongholds such as Ken Colyer's Studio 51 in the middle of London, Uncle Bonnie's Chinese Jazz Club (!) in Brighton, and Liverpool's celebrated Cavern.

By 1962, however, most such venues were putting what remained of their jazz dignity into booking trad combos to warm up for what were sounding dangerously like rock 'n' roll groups – like The Aristocrats who copied The Shadows, and in which Entwistle and Townshend had adopted more familiar instruments – bass and lead guitars. During this period too, Pete recorded one of his first compositions, 'It Was You', in a studio – a customised garage – between Acton and an adjacent suburb, Wembley.

Meanwhile, Roger Daltrey had married and found employment in a sheet–metal foundry, the occupational hazards of both interfering with his efforts to teach himself guitar and, less promisingly, trombone. Learning that John now possessed an electric bass, Roger cajoled him into a semi–professional group he was trying to form at a Shepherd's Bush boys' club. This was to have more vocals in it than The Confederates or The Aristocrats. Adding Townshend on guitar, they became first The Scorpions and then The Detours [4], seeking work in the social clubs where London bleeds into Middlesex and Surrey with side–trips for a while to a palais on Kent's Isle of Thanet. Without much hope, they mailed a tape of a few numbers to Jimmy Grant, producer of the BBC Light Programme's chief pop showcase, *Saturday Club*, but the months slipped by without a word.

Boiling down eventually to Entwistle, Townshend, Daltrey (now on lead vocals and unencumbered by an instrument) and Douglas Sandom, a drumming bricklayer in his late twenties, The Detours were marking time by modelling themselves on Johnny Kidd and the Pirates who, after the wife of one of the guitarists decided she wanted him home in the evenings. did not seek a replacement, preferring the simpler expedient of continuing with just bass, drums and *one* guitar behind singer Johnny. In doing so, a prototype was patented – because The Big Three, The Who, Dr. Feelgood, Motorhead, The Sex Pistols, The Jam and other diverse entities reliant on an instrumental 'power trio' were all to be traceable to the Pirates.

However, for all Kidd and the Pirates' pre–eminence, the north–east, where nothing used to happen apart from dock strikes, had become suddenly the most romantic corner of the kingdom with the coming of Merseybeat, spearheaded by the Beatles. After an all–Liverpool edition of ITV's *Thank Your Lucky Stars*, market necessity sent all but the dimmest London talent scout up to the Holy City to plunder the musical gold. Accordingly, having been gutted of all its major talents, Liverpool was left to rot as, like pillaging Vikings of old, the contract–waving host next sailed further down the Mersey to Manchester where there were also guitar groups that had mastered 'Twist And Shout', 'Fortune Teller', 'Money' and other numbers that became British beat standards.

When it was deemed that the Manchester scene had 'finished', the London invaders fanned out to other regions now that every one of them had been deemed to have a 'Sound' or a 'Beat' peculiar to itself. Somehow a lot of the groups everywhere sounded just like The Beatles – looked like them too in days when it was incumbent upon musical ensembles of whatever type to have an almost Midwich Cuckoo regularity of dress and hairstyle.

By the middle of 1964, there came a sign that the search was rebounding conveniently to the capital when Dagenham's Brian Poole and the Tremeloes' version of 'Twist And Shout' penetrated the Top Five, and, come the New Year, The Dave Clark Five's 'Glad All Over' dislodged The Beatles from a long reign at Number One. Furthermore, just as black rhythm–and–blues smashes had been automatically covered – and usually diluted – for the white market in the States, so some recording managers saved themselves a trip to Liverpool by getting groups within a closer proximity to London to steal a march on their northern counterparts by taking first grabs at the R&B motherlode – hence Clark and Poole's respective vanquishings of Faron's Flamingos' Liverpool acented 'Do You Love Me', and 'Money' from Bern Elliott and the Fenmen, toast of the Medway Towns, making the Top Twenty simply because, Barrett Strong's template apart, theirs was the first on 45. In Muswell Hill, The Kinks, however, were unable to duplicate this feat with the two Merseybeat–tinged singles that preceded their chart–topping 'You Really Got Me'.

Nevertheless, there'd been a hint of what The Beatles seemed to be becoming when they'd waved a jovial goodbye over the play–out of ventriloquist's dummy Lenny The Lion's BBC television show and appeared on ITV's *Blackpool Night Out*, taking part in comedy spoofs

28

and, also with hosts Mike and Bernie Winters, crooning 'I Do Like To Be Beside The Seaside'. Gerry and the Pacemakers, The Fourmost, The Hollies, Freddie and the Dreamers and others on the crest of Merseybeat's faltering wave succumbed to pantomime, charity football matches and variety. They'd be soft–shoe shuffling before you could blink.

More the meat of The Detours were the belligerently unkempt Rolling Stones and later 'hairy monsters' detested by adults, like the Kinks, Yardbirds and Pretty Things. Plundering Chicago and Mississippi negro ethnicism, these had sprung from the college circuit and cells of blues archivist–performers onto the new BBC chart showcase, *Top Of The Pops*. 'Their scene was strictly teenage rebels,' noted Ringo Starr, The Beatles' drummer, 'but we went from four–year–old kids to ninety–year–old grandmothers. Their scene was violence. We never created violence, even in the start.' [5]

The Detours were hedging their bets with short hair and uniform suits but a repertoire that leant as heavily on 'uncommercial' R&B as classic rock and the occasional tossing in of a current hit like Johnny Kidd's 'I'll Never Get Over You'. Competent beat groups of their ilk could be found in virtually any town in the country. Indeed, when they renamed themselves The Who in February 1964, there was a similar outfit also called The Who, operational in Sheffield.

Then a miracle occurred. Jimmy Grant reached wearily for a package labelled 'The Detours' among a backlog of 'demos' that had accumulated around the in–tray of his desk. Instead of yawning and clicking it off halfway through the first chorus, Grant rubbed his chin and re–ran the tape. It would do no harm, he supposed, to summon them to a Corporation rehearsal room.

Nervous merriment died to virtual silence as the van pulled up outside the BBC's Maida Vale studio complex on 9 April 1964. Reined by nerves, Daltrey, Entwistle, Sandom and Townshend delivered the goods with cautious accuracy. Afterwards, the Great Man grinned cheerfully and waved as the boys commenced a crestfallen drive home.

Grant's rejection had confirmed that The Who were nothing brilliant. However, to a so–so musical brew were added two transforming ingredients: Townshend's – and, to a lesser degree, Entwistle's – flowerings as songwriters, and, long before that, their awareness of another outfit on the same circuit, Clyde Burns and the Beachcombers [6]. Keith Moon, their energetic drummer, replaced Doug Sandom, as mature as he was reliable, the month after the BBC audition.

The Who had also acquired two managers in hardware manufacturer Helmut Gorden – responsible for financial and legal matters – and Pete Meadon, a north London advertising executive with a fast mouth, who also served as press officer for The Pretty Things. Between them, Meadon and Gorden broadened The Who's work spectrum – which would include spots low on the bill to Gerry and the Pacemakers, The Beatles and Dusty Springfield, and a season at The Scene in central London. Crucially, they also projected their charges as 'the first *authentic* Mod group' [7], and negotiated a one–shot single deal – which required a transient rechristening as 'The High Numbers' – with Fontana, a wing of Philips, one of just four major record labels in Britain then.

As soon as the ink had dried on the agreement, the mercurial Meadon put his mind to songwriting, and came up with something of a contemporary nature. Just as Jimmy Duncan, The Pretty Things' man–of–affairs, had knocked together Bo Diddley–esque 'Rosalyn' as the debut A–side for his rough diamonds, so Meadon came up with a ditty for The High Numbers which grafted Modspeak lyrics to a melody lifted from Slim Harpo's 'Got Love If You Want It', a British R&B set–work, along with the likes of Howlin' Wolf's 'Smokestack Lightning', Diddley's 'Road Runner' and Bobby Troup's '(Get Your Kicks On) Route 66'.

However, lumbering 'I'm The Face' – referring to self–appointed Mod leaders who wantonly redesigned the image from tailor to dance floor – wasn't a worthwhile marketing exercise, despite, purportedly, Meadon attempting to manoeuvre it into the hit parade by buying up five hundred copies spread thinly over listed chart–return shops. Unperturbed, the group – still vacillating between calling themselves The Who or by a name that on a poster could be mistaken for a bingo session – were delighted when Meadon hustled a spread in teen magazine, *Fabulous*, that, accepted his assurance that, so readers were informed, 'The High Numbers are up–to–dates with a difference! They're even ahead of themselves!!' [7]

Certainly, they were turning into a credible, even notorious, stage attraction. With a wardrobe bespoken by Carnaby Street, the group were giving Meadon's sales pitch a veneer of truth by complementing the urban blues mainstays with a copious injection of Motown and

James Brown; hence flashy interpretations of 'I'll Go Crazy', 'Please Please Please', 'Shout', 'Mickey's Monkey', 'Heatwave' and so forth – plus obscurer items like Garnet Mimms' 'Anytime You Want Me' and 'Baby Don't You Do It' by Marvin Gaye – from a more modern strain of R&B that was coming to be known as 'soul music'. Nevertheless, irresistable and danceable concessions to the good, honest trash of mainstream pop plus the first group originals were to put an end to whatever regard was still felt for them by blues purists and the most narrow–minded Mods.

There were no perceptible signs of their alienating such a fan base – or of sly conspiracy – on the July Tuesday in 1964 when Kit Lambert, an entrepreneur then organising the filming of a pop documentary, first encountered the group. Depending on what story you believe, it was either via a mutual acquaintance of himself and Meadon or because he just happened to be driving past and decided to investigate why there was such an enormous queue outside a dingy Wealdstone pub. Drawn inside, privately educated and nicely–spoken Lambert, even older than Doug Sandom, merged into the shadows, torn between the sordid thrill of being out of bounds and a desire to flee the enveloping fug, never to go there again.

One of the reasons he stayed was a homosexual's erotic imaginings about the four louts on the low and rickety stage, but what struck him more immediately was the volume that precluded conversation as they hit all their instruments at once at a staccato 'Right!' and barged into an onslaught of pulsating bass, spluttering guitar, crashing drums and ranted vocals. Over the initial shock, Lambert tuned into the epic vulgarity, and was lost in wonder and half–formed ambition.

Reading Kit like a book – and a mighty avaricious publication it was too – Meadon, allegedly, sent a deputation led by 'Phil the Greek', a compound Hercules on The Pretty Things' payroll, to 'reason' with Lambert and his business partner, Chris Stamp. Nevertheless, after Helmut Gorden was squeezed out via a re–examination of his contract with the group, a fleeting compromise was reached whereby all three of the remaining interested parties controlled The Who's destiny. Soon, however, Meadon was bought out for a few hundred quid, cash in hand [8], and Lambert and, less so, Stamp's names were set thus to become as synonymous with that of The Who as Colonel Parker's with Elvis, and, more to the point, Brian Epstein's with The Beatles.

There remains bitter division about Kit Lambert. Was he a manipulative cynic or merely a bourgeois entrepreneur sucked into a vortex of circumstances he was unable to resist? What is indisputable is that his handling of The Who marked the commercial apogee of Mod.

With his feet on the office desk and yapping into the telephone, he saw himself as a more far–sighted Larry Parnes – the flamboyant 1950s pop svengali and inspired generator of correlated publicity behind personable young men who'd submitted to his master plan. Yet neither he nor Stamp behaved like the stereotypical pop group managers as might be portrayed in a monochrome Ealing film such as 1959's *Idle On Parade* with Anthony Newley as a conscripted rock 'n' roller. Unlike Sid James, Newley's on–screen manager, they did not seem as if all they liked about their clients was the money they could amass, selling them like tins of beans – with no money back if they tasted funny.

Larry Parnes had a homily that ran, 'Take care of the pennies and the lads can take care of themselves'. This attitude was taken more to heart by booking agencies who, without his interest in developing an act's career, saw themselves as no more than their job description stated. Why should they care about sending a loud R&B outfit like lambs to the slaughter to, say, a place where country–and–western sweetcorn was the norm. The commission still got paid, didn't it?

'In those days, there were so many groups that agents just signed up anyone who came along,' sighed Keith Moon, 'We were sent out to the most obscure places, one side of the country one night and the other side the next, and all for twenty quid a night – but it would cost that to get there and back. Most of our pocket money, therefore, had to be borrowed from the agents – and paid back with interest. In fact, you never really earned any money at all. The equipment was paid for by the agency, so was the van that took you to concerts and brought you home, and when the agents got paid for the work we had done, they kept most of it as repayment for loans and paid us a few pounds a week. The agents and the managers and the record companies had everything sewn up, and we were getting further and further into debt.' [9]

Such difficulties were to be brushed aside like matchsticks after Lambert and Stamp took over. Bombastic *parvenus* – moreso than Pete Meadon – rather than being steeped in the lodged behind–the–scenes conventions of British showbiz, they were prone to risk and extravagance in every sense when presenting The Who and later charges to the nation. To whip up publicity for Thunderclap Newman [10] in 1969, Lambert was to mail Radio One disc–jockeys a pill in a small plastic envelope with an attached label reading 'Take this and it will change your life'. It was a powerful laxative.

Overall, The Who, if not Thunderclap Newman, had the management they deserved. When press hounds circled the group, whereas Brian Epstein might have cringed, Stamp and Lambert were all for expletives, frankness about drugs and sex, and a general winding up of adult rage and derision *a la* Rolling Stones and Pretty Things, to ensure that The Who would be worshipped as rabidly by their offspring. Their still–shortish hair apart, The Who satisfied most such qualifications for both the wayward adolescent and his ignored father, disparaging this latest epitome of the fast–encroaching decadence of the age.

With this end in mind, the new regime's first act had been to revert to the group's pre–Fontana name – more impressive graphically – for all time. For a lengthy mid–week residency at the prestigious Marquee in central London [11], posters promising 'maximum R&B' featured Townshend's trademark 'windmill' guitar stance (on permanent loan from Keith Richards of The Rolling Stones). One recital there attracted a glowing report in *Melody Maker* about 'surely one of the trend-setting groups of 1965' with printed reference to 'a most exhilarating drummer and a tireless vocalist'. [12]

However, in the teeth of their growing reputation, the hawking of a Who demo of 'Smokestack Lightning' round record companies had drawn a blank. In September 1964, Decca, for example, reckoned that such material wasn't right for teenagers, 'we know these things, Mr. Lambert'. [13] EMI said more or less the same in October. The same tape was also sent to Mike Vernon, a freelance producer – mainly for Decca – who edited, with his brother, *R and B Monthly*, perhaps the first fanzine of its kind in Britain. To grab Vernon's attention, therefore, was a feather in any aspiring R&B act's cap. His first essay as a producer had been an LP by Texas–born blues pianist Curtis Jones who – like another client, Champion Jack Dupree – had made this sceptr'd isle his home. As well as the bona–fide US article, Mike searched out blues–derived domestic talent. Among his earliest discoveries were The Graham Bond Organisation, The Yardbirds, The Artwoods and The Spencer Davis Group – but not The Who.

Before the year was out, however, it came to the intrigued ears of freelance producer Shel Talmy, who coaxed Decca, against their better judgement, to grant The Who a small initial pressing on its Brunswick subsidiary – with the proviso that he was not to waste too many resources on this latest specimen of the new breed of pop group. All of them are the same, and none of them will last long anyway.

It was decided that fashioning the group after The Kinks, Talmy's main concern, was the way forward for a maiden 45. Thus, Townshend's 'I Can't Explain', based on the salient points of The Kinks' jerky and riff–based smashes that year, was to grace the A–side of 'Bald–Headed Woman', a medley of two royalty–earning items Talmy had dashed off for The Kinks' first long–player.

Of all instrumentalists, drummers were most likely to be ghosted by someone more technically accomplished, because beat groups were inclined to accelerate and slow down *en bloc* to inconsistencies of tempo motivated by the mood of the hour. 'The reasons were purely financial,' explained Clem Cattini of The Tornados, 'You were expected to finish four tracks – two singles – in three hours. A group might take a week to do two titles – not because they were incapable, but because sessions are a different mode of thinking to being on the road. You can't get away with so much. You need more discipline.'

In the early 1960s, among those earning their tea–breaks in this manner were Cattini, ex–Kenny Ball Jazzman Ron Bowden, Jimmy Nicol, and The Vic Lewis Orchestra's Andy White, who – with no slight on Ringo Starr intended – had been hired for The Beatles' first single, 'Love Me Do'. Likewise, Bobby Graham, once of The John Barry Seven, and Phil Lancaster from David Bowie's Lower Third, each claimed to have been engaged by Dave Clark, head to head at the mixing desk with his co–producer, to minister to some of the Five's early sessions.

Yet, if augmented by an additional guitarist, Jimmy Page, and a vocal trio, The Ivy League, on backing harmonies, The Who were all present and correct on 'I Can't Explain'; Keith proving as competent – and inimitable – on disc as he was on the boards.

A more tidy–minded (or lazy) author might represent The Who's consequent clamber to fame like that clichéd movie sequence of dates being ripped off a calendar to a background of clips...a loyal grass-roots following guaranteeing an immediate minor chart entry with the first single...into the Top Twenty with the next...rows of screaming girls...David Jacobs pressing the 'ding!' button on *Juke Box Jury* for the third 45...a Top Ten placing...the limousine gliding to the sold–out theatre...Number One...wild scenes on the boards and off... police cordons...*The Ed Sullivan Show*...the Hollywood Bowl...and a slow dazzle prefacing the heroes' return to *Sunday Night At The London Palladium*!

Success wasn't either like that or quite as instant. Instead, like old millstones, the next chapter in the on–going story of The Who quivered, stirred and groaned reluctantly into its first Tippex–drenched sentence.

In the wake of the release of 'I Can't Explain', they tested again for the BBC – before a panel of seven. Accepted by one vote – despite someone jotting on a pad, 'Overall, not very original and below standard' [14] – they made their first radio broadcast on the lunchtime *Joe Loss Show* on 2 April 1965. Yet, against Decca's policy of expending most of its publicity resources on its more consistently successful acts, it was The Who's visual impact during a televisual debut on ITV's *Ready Steady Go*, aided by pirate radio plugs, that had precipitated the disc's yo–yo progression up the charts.

It had long been Keith Moon's habit to study the charts as a stockbroker might a Dow Jones index. Somehow, he was more elated when 'I Can't Explain' slipped into the Top Fifty at Number Forty–Eight on 18 February 1965 than seven weeks later when it peaked at Number Eight in a Top Ten in which The Seekers – an Australian folk combo – and balladeers Tom Jones, Gene Pitney and Val Doonican sat uneasily amongst The Kinks, Wayne Fontana and the Mindbenders, The Animals and Herman's Hermits. Then 'I Can't Explain' slipped two places before falling to Number Eighteen and then out altogether.

Next up, 'Anyway Anyhow Anywhere' at a high of Number Ten was a lesser hit, but a hit all the same – and its explosive instrumental section ran through the opening credits to *Ready Steady Go* for many weeks before a third Who single, 'My Generation', ended 1965 one position away from Number One. [15] Who could not empathise with the fellows' mortification when only 'The Carnival Is Over' by The Seekers stopped them from lording it on *Top Of The Pops*?

In between TV and radio appearances that eventful year, The Who had scrimmaged round provincial ballrooms and the unsalubrious beat clubs that were littering British towns, doing battle against adverse acoustics – and adverse audiences. Usually, there was little in the way of seating – to encourage dancing – and groups were expected to exude a happy, inoffensive atmosphere as well as action–packed sound to defuse potential unrest amongst over–excited adolescents.

Yet, even in venues where the personality of the group was generally secondary to brawling and the pursuit of romance, The Who were immediately conspicuous, partly because of the novelty of each member presenting a different persona. 'We were a weird mixture,' surmised Roger Daltrey, 'Pete was the angry young man. I was more down to earth. John was always the quiet one – and Moon was our comedy.' [16] Visually, they covered a waterfront from the contradiction of doe–eyed Moon's poly–rhythmic ferocity to Entwistle, stock–still with a face like an Acton winter, attending gravely to the general row.

As it had been when The Rolling Stones had travelled the same route a year earlier, onlookers would keep their distance, and the set might terminate with long seconds of thunderstruck hush until a spatter of clapping crescendoed into a whistling, cheering, stamping tumult. Some caught The Who a second and even third time during this round of engagements. These new fans might have simply jived to the worthy supporting turns on offer, but there'd be a spontaneous rippling stagewards a few dramatic bars into The Who's opening number.

'They now occupy the position the Stones once had,' agreed their malcontented Brian Jones, 'The Who are the only young group doing something new.' [17] One of their strongest assets was Keith's ever more thrashing performance which, though gratuitously busy, still maintained a precise backbeat within the parameters of wavering time–keeping. More exciting still was The Who's expensive if occasional practice (usually when the media were about) of closing the show by smashing up their equipment amid smoke bombs, flashing lights and ear–splitting feedback lament.

In ten months, Keith ruined three drum kits; had broken an average of eight sticks a night, and had cracked a cymbal once a fortnight. Also, amused by the memory, Ray Dorset, later of Mungo Jerry, would recall, 'One of the first times I saw The Who – in Alexis Korner's Ealing club in late 1964 – they were getting thirty pounds for the night, but were still trashing their equipment; Pete Townshend slinging his Marshall cabinets down the stairs.'

Not so thigh–slappingly funny the following October was Keith injuring a girl when he slung a tom–tom into the crowd at the Rhodes Centre in Bishop's Stortford – where about a year earlier he and the rest of Clyde Burns and the Beachcombers had been second–billed to the otherwise unsung Sunspots.

The offending tom–tom was the property of Will Birch of Southend's Flowerpots, who were supporting. He'd been asked by a Who road manager if Keith could use his snare on the understanding that he'd be compensated if any holes were rat–tatted in its skin. Before the night was out, Moon wrecked completely not one, but two of Birch's drums and dented a cymbal during the closing 'Anyway Anyhow Anywhere'. When young Will asked politely for the promised reimbursement, he was asked why he didn't bugger off. [18]

The Who and their entourage had found it easier to deal with ugly situations and cope generally with stardom and its attendant expenses by conducting themselves as if it had been the case from the beginning of their association with Lambert and Stamp. Money seemed to be no object. As well as shrugging off the theft of The Who's overloaded van when it was left outside Battersea Dogs Home (where they had gone, apparently, to discuss buying an alsatian to guard that very vehicle), there was amusement rather than hand–wringing when, during one week shortly before the redeeming 'I Can't Explain' breakthrough, income was less than one fifth of expenditure, mostly on the latest Mod menswear – and, hardly surprisingly, replacement of splintered instruments and amplifiers, and replenishing of spare parts.

A most likely fount of this constant worry for the group's accountants – and the constant running repairs and botch jobs – was Pete's capitalizing on accidental damage to his guitar, sustained on the boards at the Marquee – and Keith endorsing it by laying into his kit likewise for the first of countless times. 'Keith is obviously an aggressive drummer and aggressive personality. Throwing his drums around was the logical thing for him to do,' concurred Townshend, 'In England, the audience wanted aggressive music like the Stones.' [19]

Pete also bandied about the doctrines of 'auto–destruction', originated by Anglo–German artist Gustav Metzger – and the geberal insinuation of 'Art' into pop music – particularly in Britain where The Move were to impinge upon the kingdom's consciousness with a refinement of The Who's take on auto–destruction, and, earlier in 1966,

The Creation closed their show by splashing onto a canvas backdrop a painting that owed less to Jackson Pollock than Tony Hancock's character in the 1960 film vehicle, *The Rebel*. [20]

The earliest attempt at simulating The Who's extreme stage tactics on vinyl was 'Anyway Anyhow Anywhere' – which, overlooking the tinkling piano triplets, has not lost its power after subsequent decades of sonic avant–gardening [21] – and less so in anthemic 'My Generation', title track of a maiden LP. During 1965's Christmas sell–in, this left a tide–mark at Number Five in the album list, signifying that sales of the 45s were but a surface manifestation of the respect accorded the group for their natural vitality and rough–hewn musicianship by sixth–formers, undergraduates and the like who bought LPs as their younger siblings did singles.

While *My Generation* was conceived technologically on basic single–track – regarded now as primitive – a more complicated approach would have emasculated its raw thrust. However, its content *per se* exemplified a new attitude towards a product that had not been regarded previously as a rounded entity but a cynically throwaway patchwork of tracks hinged on an already best–selling single. Testaments to commercial pragmatism rather than quality, these were targeted – especially in the USA – at fans so beglamoured by an artiste's looks and personality so as to be uncritical of frankly sub–standard, haphazardly–programmed output, excused as an exhibition of 'versatility' but of no true cultural value.

The Who album was padded with a hit, true enough, but other tracks were the equal of A–sides in terms of effort and imagination. Even though an exploratory promotional copy was reviewed by *Beat Instrumental* in July 1965, on the LP that reached the shops, most of the US soul xeroxes had been thrust aside in deference to Townshend's snowballing confidence as a tunesmith, not to mention his instrumental collaboration, 'The Ox', with Entwistle, Moon and session pianist Nicky Hopkins. There may have been suspicions that the covers didn't do justice to the black originals, but a mood persisted too that the group's increasingly more idiosyncratic style was no longer compatible to the expectations of Decca.

Townshend's stockpile of songs could fulfil the group's contractual commitments many times over. Into the bargain, his offerings were advantaged by his belief in the disposable nature of pop: 'It should be like the TV: something you can turn on and off and shouldn't disturb the mind.' [22] Yet, with The Pretty Things' *SF Sorrow* lighting the way, Pete was to first dip a toe and then plunge head first into the 'rock opera' medium.

It was almost a matter of course, therefore, that the media latched onto Pete as a quotably 'articulate' pop spokesman, though many found him tiresome and patronising in his efforts to come across as a regular guy like any other boring 'good bloke' from Perth to Penzance. Yet tolerance for Townshend was to border on deep admiration in pockets of punk rock. Among vinyl acknowledgements of this was a frantic 'Substitute' by Pete's drinking partners at the Speakeasy, The Sex Pistols.

Townshend had always been as seemingly devotional himself, whether in his membership of The Creation fan club or, in a later capacity as a publishing executive at Faber & Faber, a proud familiarity with poet Stephen Spender. Recommending copying The Rolling Stones as a recipe for any new group's success, Townshend with Moon and Daltrey had knocked out a hurried single of 'The Last Time' and 'Under My Thumb' as The Who's contribution to Mick Jagger and Keith Richards' costs during their feted drugs trial in 1967. Pete also applauded Keith Moon's visibility along Fleet Street among two hundred protesters against the 'guilty' verdicts – with Mrs. Moon hoisting a placard bearing the possibly ambiguous legend, *FREE KEITH!*. Less public was Townshend's private musical eulogy – entitled 'A Normal Day' – to the drowned Brian Jones two years later.

With no qualms about admitting their corporate preferences, The Who were to slip a 'Pretty Vacant' – arguably The Sex Pistols' most enduring opus – into a latter–day set list – and, long before that, encore with Free's 'All Right Now' signature tune in 1970, complete with the cunning bass harmonics.

These held no fears for John Entwistle who, if one of the most lauded bass guitarists in rock, was, in comparison to his old school chum, merely The Who's second–string composer in the eyes of the world – and if you can't be first, be peculiar. Nonetheless, a minority of listeners found his macabre, cynical creations the most agreeable aspect of The Who. Though John himself preferred Pete's paeon to self–gratification, 'Pictures Of Lily', the discerning Jimi Hendrix's favourite Who track was to be Entwistle's 'Boris The Spider', squashed against the wall it was climbing in *A Quick One* – in which the hallucinating alcoholic of John's 'Whiskey Man' was incarcerated too.

Other subject matters might not have been everyone's bag, but you cannot dismiss lightly a man who also penned pop songs concerning miserliness ('Silas Stingy'), insurance swindles ('I Found Out'), mistaking a woman for a prostitute ('I Was Just Being Friendly'), a deserted husband threatening suicide ('Thinkin' It Over') and other unorthodox topics. That the chap deserved attention was emphasised further by his invention of a challenge to the Twist in 'Do The Dangle' – from the neck after you've kicked away the chair 'and you're dancing on air'. This was to be a highlight of the first LP by John's Rigor Mortis – with a gatefold sleeve monopolised by a grave's headstone 'in loving memory of rock 'n' roll'.

His taciturn stage presence belied a love of performing expressed later in his leadership of at least one more Who splinter group as well as his bellowing of 'Twist And Shout' on a Channel Four pop series in 1983.

John's lead vocal excursions – generally, one per concert – provoked no green–eyed monsters to whisper to Daltrey, glad to take a break. In common with Keith, Roger was as much a fan of The Who as anyone in the crowd. As such, he could be counted on to see to the most oner-ous offices on the group's behalf – as instanced by his courageous self–immersion into a bath of cold baked beans for the sleeve of 1967's *The Who Sell Out*. Yet, though he co–wrote 'Anyway Anyhow Anywhere', he was the least prominent composer in the group. Nonetheless, his later activities thrived more than those of the others – at least by showbusiness standards. These included chartbusters in his own right – beginning with 1973's 'Giving It All Away' – starring roles in large budget movies and, an accolade to his increased versatility as a singer, a try at light opera: not bad going for a Mod from Shepherd's Bush.

As far as Average Joe was concerned, Daltrey was, no matter what truly went on in the confines of recording studio and dressing room, The Who's still, small voice of reason, talking calm sense when Townshend and, especially, Moon were running around like headless chickens. Yet no matter what any of them got up to elsewhere, there lingered a collective pride in a group that, back in 1965, was prov-ing itself proportionally as sound an investment for Brunswick as The Beatles had for EMI's Parlophone.

However, unlike John, George, Paul and Ringo, John, Keith, Pete and Roger were not rewarded with significantly more studio time nor the freedom to requisition all manner of auxiliary instrumentation. There wasn't, therefore, evidence of too much experiment on *My Generation*, but disarming acoustic guitars surfaced on the next singles chart strike, 'Substitute', in spring 1966, by which time they'd played their first headlining show – over The Graham Bond Organisation, The Fortunes, The Merseys and old Middlesex friends, Screaming Lord Sutch and the Savages, at Finsbury Park Astoria – and Lambert and Stamp had transferred the band to Robert Stigwood's independent record company, Reaction.

Amid the legal wrangles that followed, Brunswick hurled at the public any *My Generation* track that took its fancy as a single, and Lambert rather than an aggrieved Shel Talmy, came to occupy the central chair behind the console – but not before a song entitled 'Circles', taped during this apocryphal period, had been pressed on two separate labels. First of all, it was a cancelled A–side by Brunswick, then as Reaction's flip–side to 'Substitute', initially renamed 'Instant Party'. Finally, it was thought prudent to wipe the slate clean by engaging The Graham Bond Organisation – as 'The Who Orchestra' – to provide an instrumental, 'Waltz For A Pig', as Reaction's coupling for the 'Substitute' that battled into the Top Five as the blizzards of writs settled into complicated but fixed financial channels whereby its assorted and incoming royalties could be divided and sent to the sometimes disgruntled parties.

Now Reaction recording artists, The Who's rougher edges were tempered by studio sessions not governed by the clock – and greater scope for artistic exploration. Like unrestrained children in a toy shop, they fiddled about with whatever weird–and–wonderful implement was either lying about their favoured IPC complex, one of the most modern and well–equipped in central London, or staring at them from one of its storeroom shelves.

This would lead, for instance, to unusual percussion effects on 'Disguises' for the *Ready Steady Who* EP; Keith plucking a zither to add texture to Townshend's nine–minute 'mini–opera', 'A Quick One While He's Away' – and more of Entwistle's mastery of the brass family. Instead of the expected bass guitar, the lower register of a French horn trumped throughout a verse of the 1966 single, 'I'm A Boy', prompting elderly Light Programme presenter 'Cheerful' Charlie Chester' to compliment The Who on their *marvellous* driving beat.

Much of The Who's early recorded output was realised during intervals in the remorseless schedule of motoring, motoring, motoring to strange towns, strange venues and strange hotels. The most garrulous participant in the small–talk that crept in when everyone was too fatigued for more profound dialogue, Moon preferred not to seize the opportunity to doze off with the road roaring in his ears. Passers–by would peer incuriously as he wound down the side–windows and shouted disobliging or funny–ha–ha remarks, or thumped a beat on the roof, his face alight with hilarity. Hot–eyed with sleeplessness, he paid the price by blacking–out when all breathable oxygen was rendered stale in one particularly rank venue.

When pressed by loved ones about what such–and–such a town had been like, Keith was damned if he could even find it on a map – for, as The Who zig–zagged across the country, they saw little of Folkestone, Glasgow, Plymouth, you name it, beyond what was glimpsed as they strode across a twilit pavement from van to stage–door.

After they rose to travel, they'd be recognised in corner shops and wayside petrol stations and exposed to either dull watchfulness from adults or being nearly killed with kindness when mobbed by libidinous female fans not much younger than themselves. Watching such frenzies sourly, the road crew needed all their wits about them to cope with the tactical problems of moving the operation from A to B. Once at B, they would buttonhole promoters, organise security, shoo unwanted company from changing rooms and see to the group's food, sleep and overall health requirements both before and after the group bounced onto the boards to face the stinging decibels that greeted even the compere's attempts to keep order.

Even as their luck held while other groups came and went, The Who – well, most of them – still expected it to run out too. To Keith, however, it had happened with the spooky deliberation of a dream, and there were ever–lengthening periods when the eighteen–year–old was so dazzled as to think that pop stars, contrary to definition, were immortal and that he'd never have to consider again a daily grind like the one he'd endured at an electronics firm on leaving school – though Townshend, in benign mood, would reckon that Moon would have been a star even if he was selling matches in the street.

Keith Moon, Keith Moon, Moon, Moon, Keith, Keith...like a Hare Krishna mantra, it was his name that cropped up most in press critiques such as that of 'the most remarkable performance in the second half' [23] of 1966's *NME* Pollwinners Concert when The Who had had the irksome task of preceding The Rolling Stones: 'Keith Moon was going wild...'; 'Moon steadied himself, ready for the attack'; 'Keith smashed into his drums again, again, again...' [23]

However much as their remaining true–Mod afficianados might have refuted the suggestion, The Who were now as much part of the national pop furniture as Cliff Richard, Herman's Hermits, Dusty Springfield, Dave Dee–Dozy–Beaky–Mick–and–Tich, The Beatles, the Stones and everyone else at Wembley Empire Pool for the afternoon extravaganza that encapsulated the beat boom during its hysterical high summer. Though subsiding to mere cheers for Dusty, tidal waves of screams hurled rampaging girls towards crash barriers where they'd be flung back by flushed bouncers, shirt–sleeved in the heat, and aggravatingly nearer to John, Paul, George, Ringo, Cliff, Herman, Dave, Dozy, Beaky, Mick, Tich, Charlie, Bill, Brian, Roger, John, Pete, Keith, you name 'em, than those who'd sell their souls to be. In the boiling *melée* further back, unluckier ticket–holders burst into tears, rocked foetally, flapped programmes and scarves, tore at their hair, wet themselves and fainted with the thrill of it all.

The first excursions overseas by The Who had been, if anything, more uproarious. In Denmark, they were required to play one Sunday evening in two venues sixty miles apart. At the one thousand–capacity *Hallen* in Aarhus – only the fifth Who performance outside Britain – the fans went as crazy as only fans can go, deaf to warnings about rushing the stage from Authority, who stopped the show within minutes as public–address (PA) system speaker columns toppled and the petrified musicians bolted pell–mell to a waiting car in a back alley.

The damage inflicted within the auditorium was but a fraction of the final assessment after the mob spilled into the streets where, armed with bits of broken chairs and the shambles of the equipment left on stage, hundreds of teenagers let off steam in a two–hour orgy of brawling and vandalism. When news of this – and the resulting arrests – reached the ears of town councillors, The Who were barred from defiling the *Hallen* for five years, and were denounced in a front page editorial in the local newspaper – though the next show that night in Aalborg had passed without incident, provoking just a sole negative comment – 'the guitars sounded distorted' – in one subsequent review.

Elsewhere too, they went down well, and the hits kept coming (albeit by now on Lambert and Stamp's own Track Records), but the impetus had slackened slightly. Masking his disappointment, Keith was most notably defensive in interview about the group's fall from ten in 1966 to fourteen in 1967 in the British Vocal Group section of the *NME* readers poll – while in Germany, the influential *Bravo* magazine's 'Golden Otto' award had been won in 1966 by Dave Dee, Dozy, Beaky, Mick and Tich with the Beatles as mere runners–up, and The Who eleven places lower, between The Spencer Davis Group and the native Rattles.

A national breakthough in the United States was a long time coming, despite networked television showings of promotional film shorts, full–page advertisements in the *Billboard* music trade journal, and, in March 1967, a slot on *Music In The Fifth Dimension*, a nine day package show, five performances a day, in a New York theatre with bumptious – but then–supreme – disc–jockey, Murray the K presiding.

Until then, headway had been modest. A couple of Who singles had been regional chartbusters already; 'My Generation' inched to Number 74 in the Hot 100, and a lunatic fringe among their North American devotees started donating expensive guitars for Pete to ritually destroy. However, a lot of hard work and concession [24] reaped dividends in an unarguable major smash during 1967's Summer of Love with 'Happy Jack'. This coincided with a coast–to–coast tour with Herman's Hermits, withering carriers of the 'Hermania' that had filtered across the sub–continent like bubonic plague during the tail–end of the 'British Invasion'.

In flower–power garb, the Middlesex lads had also represented fair Albion at the Monterey International Pop Music Festival a few miles down the coast from San Francisco, then as vital a pop Mecca as Liverpool had been. Though 'Pictures Of Lily' was a relative non–starter, The Who notched up their biggest–selling US single, 'I Can See For Miles' at Number Nine just before Christmas.

Throughout the next episode of their saga, they took the Union for every cent they could get, finishing up in the highest league of the 'adult–orientated rock' hierarchy with its commitment to albums – to the chagrin of Roger Daltrey, who was to wail, 'the loss of the three–minute single is a rock 'n' roll tragedy of unparalleled proportions.' [16] Nonetheless, thanks in part to the remorseless prodding of cultural nerves by what were now 'bands' – not 'groups' anymore – such as his Who, 'rock' – not 'pop' – performers were writing 'musician' on passport application forms less sheepishly, and were endeavouring to operate ambiguously with 'artistic' fancies on long–players, and keeping a weather eye on the hit parade with spin–off 45s.

With *Sgt. Pepper's Lonely Hearts Club Band*'s expensive and syncretic precedent, record companies found themselves underwriting further such 'concept' albums (e.g. *Their Satanic Majesties Request* from The Rolling Stones, John Mayall's *Bare Wires*), rock operas (such as The Pretty Things' *SF Sorrow*, *Arthur* by The Kinks and The Who's first US million–seller, *Tommy* – and all, technically, song–cycles) and other *magnum opi* (The Small Faces' *Ogden's Nut Gone Flake* in its circular sleeve).

Pop – sorry, 'rock' – was now 'relevant,' a viable means of artistic expression rather than an ephemeral tangent to more egghead activity. Three of The Pink Floyd had met during a degree course at Regent Street Polytechnic from which they had emerged as darlings of London psychedelic clubs like the Spontaneous Underground [25] and The Night Tripper (later The UFO), where the likes of Soft Machine, AMM, Hapshash–and–the–Coloured–Coat and Sam Gopal Dream's appeal to a tranced hippy clientele, either cross–legged or 'idiot dancing', also depended less on good looks and tight trousers than the dazzling atmosphere that thickened during incessant extrapolation of tracks from both a latest album and the unfamiliar successor being 'laid down' during a studio block–booking of weeks and months.

These days, members of The Who could attend hippy 'happenings' without fan fuss obliging a hasty departure. Bawling 'It's Keith Moon!' if he sidled past you wasn't 'cool' in the capital nowadays. Almost unnoticed, he'd absorbed the UFO's flickering strobes, ectoplasmic *son et lumière* projections on the walls, and some band playing on and on and on and on.

All the same, he left early because the place wasn't licensed. He also recognized that the Summer of Love was no more the dawning–of–the–age–of–Aquarius than the trad jazz fad had been. Come 1968, and rock 'n' roll revival was in the air, and, after The Move had invested their 'Fire Brigade' with an antique Duane Eddy twang, The Who

45

were being accused of regression as well as bandwagon–jumping for re–inserting into the stage repertoire 'Shakin' All Over', 'Summertime Blues', 'Fortune Teller' and further showstoppers that had got both The Detours and Clyde Burns and the Beachcombers through rough nights in suburban dance halls only five years earlier. These would go down a storm even as The Who, on 17 August 1969, entertained the half–million rain–drenched Americans at Woodstock, viewed from a distance of decades as the climax of hippy culture – and two weeks later at the second Isle of Wight festival where a game Moon went the distance with a broken foot and pumped with pain–killer.

This injury had mended itself by the following February when, after ambitious *Tommy*, a rough–and–ready in–concert album made sense as a holding operation until the next big push. *Live At Leeds* was taken from The Who's two hours on stage at the northern university. There is often much false bonhomie during such tapings, but the audience in the students union hall lend an inspirational framework for The Who to power through a set nurtured over weeks of a lately–completed North American tour. As well as most of *Tommy* – stripped instrumentally to the guitar–bass–drums bones – they could also select from its 'A Quick One' water–test plus a handful of hits and non–original stage stand–bys – and John Entwistle's *omnes fortissimo* 'Heaven And Hell'.

Yet, against the artistic and market triumph of this 'live' bash, 1970 was also a vintage year for a petrification of British pop that was traceable to the Marine Offences Act that killed off the competitive pirate radio stations. On top of Radio Luxembourg turntables still being governed by leftovers from the 1950s Light Programme clique, the cautious programming by the BBC's two national pop outlets had rendered *Top Of The Pops* shallower and less subversive in content.

It had brushed a nadir one schmaltzy 1968 week when the only group presented was The Tremeloes – now *sans* Brian Poole – who were, with Marmalade and Love Affair, a prong of a beaming triumvirate that were doubtful pretenders to The Beatles' throne during this silver age of British beat, constipated as it was with their retinue of dispensable and harmless purveyors of popular song – The Casuals, Cupid's Inspiration, Picketywitch, Arrival and all the rest of them – who faltered after maybe two chart entries.

46

Yet, while Top Twenty penetrations could be taken for granted no longer by The Who, The Kinks and other old stagers who had suffered their first serious domestic Top Twenty misses, there was more than sufficient substratum of encouragement beneath pop's capricious quickstage to assure them that there were more fortunes to be made, more box–office records to be broken, louder PA systems to be assembled, than had ever been known in the history of recorded sound, definitely more than any accumulated in the era when, say, 'Pictures Of Lily' jumped straight in at Number Sixteen in Britain within the first week of release.

Let someone else have a turn as the teenagers' fave rave. Mere awareness of worth was reward enough. Like Sinatra, you could excuse flop 45s as 'too good for the charts' – though Pete Townshend rather spoiled this argument by pleading, 'We're The Who. We can put out crap singles if we want to' [16] when 1972's 'Relay', to which you could only dance if you were desperate, struggled to Number Twenty–One at home, Thirty–Nine in the States, where Keith Moon dwelt almost permanently – mostly in California – throughout the mid–1970s.

He and the rest would answer cursory enquiries about 'Relay' or whatever current record a journalist might or might not have heard. See, the gentlefolk of the press had no inhibitions about concentrating solely on the dear, dead days of op–art ties, *Ready Steady Go* and Monterey now that pop's history as much as its present was being pounced upon as a avenue for exploitation. As the millenium turned, it would make even more sense for over–ripe artistes – supported by saturation television advertising – to plug 'greatest hits' collections of recordings over forty years old as heavily as an all–new one – such as a 2005 Who album by its surviving original members plus various helpers.

The broken–up pulse of 'Relay' would still be heard in concerts by the twenty–first century line–up. Nevertheless, as its comparatively poor sales in 1972 against The New Seekers' hit medley that revived two excerpts from *Tommy* a few months later, and a UK Top Twenty return for a repromoted 'Substitute' in 1976 indicated, most Who consumers, old and new, preferred either the actual sounds of yesteryear or something that struck a similar chord.

Every signpost seemed to point towards reliving the Swinging Sixties. 1973's *Quadrophenia*, The Who's most lucrative non–compilation album – a double too – was an 'opera' about Mods and Rockers, symbols of an age that seemed almost as bygone as that bracketed by Hitler's suicide and 'Rock Around The Clock' to some for whom 'I Can't Explain' antedated conception. The same applied to 'Who Are You', the last new single before Keith Moon's death, riding as it did on the back of a half–baked resurgence of Mod.

'Who Are You' began its journey to the middle of Top Forties on both sides of the Atlantic shortly after Moon's farewell to those who'd never ceased to adore him. It took place on Thursday 25 May 1978 before an invited audience on a soundstage within Shepperton Studios – which The Who had bought the previous August for diverse artistic ventures – to tie up loose ends for a film documentary. *The Kids Are Alright*. Following the 'Won't Get Fooled Again' finale, Keith grinned, waved and vanished into the wings forever.

There was hearsay later about whether Moon fell before he was pushed. Had one of the other three already drawn the short straw to marshall his words and dare the speech that everyone knew had to be made – an ultimatum disguised as a gentle suggestion? Enforcers of their own order, bandleaders as disparate as Cliff Bennett, John Mayall, Frank Zappa and avant–garde jazzer Annette Peacock would not tolerate excessive boozing by their employees either – and God help you if they caught you with drugs. Though by no means such kil-ljoys, Traffic had cashiered drummer Jim Gordon and bass player Rick Grech for related problems in 1971. Now was it Roger, John and Pete's wish for the now–chronically alcoholic Keith to take a sabbatical until such time as his hands were no more a–tremble and his nose no longer empurpled?

In 1989 – eleven years after Keith's passing, and thirteen before the Grim Reaper came for John Entwistle too – it would be rumoured too that Ringo Starr was to drum for The Who on a twenty–fifth anniver-sary tour. With no new LP in the shops, they were milking nostalgia quite openly by fixing unashamedly on their back catalogue. Suddenly, their *aficionados* could not easily deny the notion that The Who were in the same bag as other huge but stagnant headliners like The Beach Boys and a reconstituted Monkees.

The future for The Who, therefore, appeared to be the past all over again – and again and again and again – until Roger and Pete have gone too – or maybe not. Why shouldn't The Who go on forever as an archetypal unit of its own, spanning with differing emphases every familiar trackway of its earliest manifestation and its inter–related embrace of songs embedded in the common unconscious by so much availability and airplay that most of it is heard no more than a sailor hears the sea? Unless the performers make a total pig's ear of them, will anyone be able to say anything constructive beyond 'That's The Who doing "Anyway Anyhow Anywhere", "Boris The Spider', "Pinball Wizard", "Shakin' All Over", "Won't Get Fooled Again"...' Like street lamps or milk bottles, they'll simply be there.

Just as all a typical visitor to the Louvre wants to see is the *Mona Lisa*, sparing only perfunctory glances at what might be essentially finer paintings along the corridors leading to it, the present–day Who performing a new Townshend composition in concert is regarded as a self–indulgence, an obligatory lull requiring a more subdued reaction than that for when 'My Generation' or 'Substitute' makes everything all right again – though nobody could pretend that that's what it must have been like at the Marquee, *circa* 1965.

Notes

1. Master of ceremonies Jeff Dexter's announcement before The Who's performance at 1970's Isle Of Wight festival
2. *NME Rock 'N' Roll Years* ed. J. Tobler (BCA, 1992)
3. *Acker Bilk* by G. Williams (Mayfair, 1962)
4. Who may have named themselves after 'Detour', B–side to Bo Diddley's 'Bo Diddley', issued in Britain in 1963
5. *Melody Maker*, 8 September 1971
6. Nothing to do with Birmingham's Pat Wayne and the Beachcombers, who recorded ten singles – three by Wayne alone, two by just The Beachcombers – for EMI between 1963 and 1966. Clyde Burns was the stage alias of Tony Marsh, later pianist with Screaming Lord Sutch and the Horde Of Savages
7. *Fabulous*, November 1964
8. And learned later that Lambert and Stamp would have gone to ten times that amount. Next, Meadon managed Jimmy James and the Vagabonds, a soul outfit popular in metropolitan clubland, who were to enjoy a Top Ten hit, 'Now Is The Time', in 1976.
9. *All You Need Is Love* by T. Palmer (Chappell, 1976)

10. A group built around middle–aged multi–instrumentalist Andy Newman, who Townshend knew as a mature student at Ealing College of Art

11. 'Playing the Marquee was the biggest thing ever for The Who, when we started,' estimated Keith Moon (*London Live* by T. Bacon (Balafon, 1999).

12. *Melody Maker*, 29 December 1964

13. Decca also turned down The Spencer Davis Group that same week.

14. *In Session Tonight* by K. Garner (BBC Books, 1993)

15. It featured a remarkable solo by Entwistle, who ran up a debt by buying for the purpose an imported Hofner bass for £60. When he broke the strings, there were no spares, obliging him to purchase another £60 instrument. When the strings snapped yet again, a third bass had to be procured to complete the recording.

16. *Inside Classic Rock Tracks* by R. Rooksby (Backbeat, 2001)

17. *New Musical Express,* 17 July 1964

18. *The Day Before Yesterday – Rock, Rhythm and Jazz In The Bishp Stortford Area 1957 – 1969* by Steve Ingless (Scila Publications 1999)

19. *Rolling Stone*, 20 January 1968

20. US title: *Call Me Genius*

21. Most immediately when the lengthy screech–out of 1966's 'European Son' by The Velvet Underground took 'Anyway Anyhow Anywhere' a stage further

22. *Maximum Who* (Italian fanzine, May 1987)

23. *New Musical Express*, 6 May 1966

24. Such as the censorship of 'Substitute' by their US investors on the nebulous grounds of racism, causing the offending line, 'I look all white but my dad was black' to be re–recorded as 'I try walking forward but my feet walk back' (almost a direct quote from 'Circles'/ 'Instant Party')

25. Held every Sunday in the Marquee from February 1966

Stuart Booth remembers Keith Moon *(former university undergrad-uate and student union committee member City University, London):*
'That The Who was made of disparate characters was always appar-ent from their on–stage scraps in the earliest days, and whilst each of the quartet had their own highly individual eccentricities, there was evidence of a split into two camps.

This I witnessed in my final term at the City University, London, when I was on the students union entertainments committee. On Friday 24th May 1968, The Who had been booked to appear for a cost outside budget.

No confirmation was ever received from The Who, their management or their booking agent, despite extensive advertising, and tension rose. About four in the afternoon, however, there was a collective sigh of relief when the gear turned up and roadies set up in the Great Hall – though there was still no word from the group itself until a call at around 5.30 in the union office from Roger Daltrey himself to ask where the gig was, exactly.

Well into the evening, the hall was holding approximately 1,100 eager punters and the support band, Oscar Bicycle, were prevailed upon to play a second set to keep the folks happy, though a feeling of frustra-tion was openly building up.

Down by the front entrance, nail–biting, tense, fearful of big trouble for a non–show and mindful of the true 700 capacity limit decreed by the fire insurance etc., we lurched from back–slapping self–reassur-ance to outright panic, knowing that where we were, we could see the band arrive (if they were ever going to) or scarper when the angry dancers and liggers boiled over into open riot.

Then, by ordinary taxi, a totally together but genuinely anxious Daltrey turned up, saying that he'd passed on the directions to, the other three after the 'phone call, but only by message to the Who office. Gulp! He was escorted to the dressing room, and we waited, even more distressed. Next to arrive was Pete Townshend, equally OK, but worried he was so late and obviously on edge that only Roger was there.

Oscar Bicycle were persuaded to do a third set. The natives were turning ugly. I ran down to the entrance lobby in a state of near ter-ror. As I reached the door, a large black limo pulled up with two like-ly–looking figures in the back seat. However, they showed no signs of disembarking, and a driver appeared, asking if it was OK for the lads to have a few drinks from the limo's bar before coming in.

'No way!' was the unananimous cry, and someone had the sense to get Townshend, who dashed out, yanked open the door and dragged the clearly out–of–it Moon and Entwistle up the steps and pushed them, staggering, along the corridor to the dressing room.

Though I feared the worst, I rushed up the stairs to tell the poor MC – who was trying to keep a near–erupting crowd from goimng ballistic – that we were saved. He did the usual 'what–you've–all–been–waiting–for..' and so forth, and I saw the still stumbling figure of Moon following the other three on stage from the rear.

Within seconds of the announcement, they went straight into the most amazing and totally together–sounding version of 'My Generation', and played a set that was a blinder from beginning to end: not a fluffed guitar riff or drum break! Even Townshend smashing up his instrument at the finish was spot–on! I was gobsmacked and totally impressed. From the time that Messrs. Entwistle and Moon had made their very inauspicious and unsteady arrival to the opening thunderous chords of 'My Generation', I realised that a mere five minutes had elapsed, despite it seeming ages.

There are many types of professionalism, but that night showed me one I had not hitherto experienced – or, rather, it showed me two. Going along the corridor in hope of seeing the gods wind down, a very smooth gentleman in a belted white raincoat came in behind me and asked for the Entertainments Secretary by name.

The latter was actually close behind me. He greeted Kit Lambert and – I saw this with my own eyes – handed over £450 in cash! No paperwork, no contracts, no receipts: cash – and that was it!

Just over a year later, The Who played Woodstock as total world stars – and were paid with considerably more cash than the City University could have afforded.'

'I'm A Boy': Moon's Middlesex Roots

'My musicians weren't restricted. The madder they went, the madder I'd go. Everyone would play harder, and it made a more exciting gig'
- Screaming Lord Sutch

It's hardly the Schleswig–Holstein question, the most complex matter ever to trouble European politics. Nevertheless, few writers have ever got to the bottom of the 'Swinging Sixties'. Some, who had seemed to endure rather than enjoy that turbulent decade, argued that its pop music was an audial symptom of the godlessness of the times. Inwardly, however, they might have been eating their hearts out at being disenfranchised from it – though they needn't have been. Between and after the wars, entertainment – and sport – were legitimate means whereby someone from the humblest background could wash up on an unexpectedly verdant island on the stagnant river to dull and decent old age.

The craze for British beat groups was to create an eventual new squirarchy that adopted recreations and – sometimes sardonic – la-di–da mannerisms that had been peculiar to old money reared into privilege. Once merely locally–produced alternatives to assembly–line chart ballast, they came to epitomise, in however non–doctrinal – even nihilistic – a manner, a V–sign at the post–war apogee of the British people's deep–rooted sense of respectability, thus intensifying the 'us' and 'them' divide between youth and the old and square. It was also a blurted–out affront to the quiet dignity of a true gentleman's name appearing in a newspaper only on the occasions of his birth, his baptism, his marriage and when he shuffled off this mortal coil.

Without a hint of the fuss that was to inform an adolescence extended by adulation, Keith John Moon was prised into the world on 23 August 1946, an extremely hot, windless and very sunny Friday in the midst of a summer drought, and a month after bread rationing was introduced. The family home, where he was still living when he married in 1965, was shared with father Alf, mother Kit and two younger sisters.

It stood in the residential hinterland of Wembley where the Thames bisects what is as much Middlesex as London. Although Mr. and Mrs. Moon's offspring caught and held a vaguely sub–Cockney accent from the cradle, theirs was not a *cor blimey* environment of pubs, back streets, hello–hello–hello policemen and sub–criminal adult dialogue revolving around the boozer, dog racing and dodges for making easy money – as portrayed in *The Blue Lamp*, *A Kid For Two Farthings*, *Passport To Pimlico* and like monochrome movies from behind the seven–foot high metal gate of nearby Ealing Studios Ltd.

Chronicled as 'Wemba Lea' in the Dark Ages, Wembley had been largely woodlands and meadow until lacerated in 1837 by the clattering railway connection to Birmingham and the consequent construction of a station, Wembley Central, which was also to be a stop on the Metropolitan tube line, convenient for daily commutations to and from the inner city and, after the completion in 1923 of a multi–purpose sports and leisure complex open to the sky, visits by up to one hundred thousand spectators at once for hockey, rugby, speedway, the British Empire Exhibition in 1925, the 1948 Olympic Games and, with the erection of the adjacent Empire Pool in 1933, all manner of expositions, trade fairs and indoor entertainments. Wembley Stadium, however, will be remembered principally as the shrine of English soccer.

Yet a gazer from the opposite window of a train shunting through Wembley would register tangles of shopping precincts, light industry and overspill estates of red–raw brick; clerking offices clotted where grimy Victorian monstrosities were giving way to a ruthlessly functional aesthetic; waste–piped backs of crumbling town houses; clusters of advertising hoardings; patches of green that were not farmland, but country parks, recreation grounds and football pitches, and parking lots formed from bombsites created by the Luftwaffe in a connurbation no different to transient outsiders from any other becoming lost in an urban sprawl creeping from the western loop of the increasingly congested North Circular Road and its tributaries.

Like everywhere else too, Wembley was a realm of queues as the country paid for the downfall of Hitler with 'Utility' goods and rationing that lasted well into the 1950s. Some items were so scarce that you could only get them with weeks of saved–up coupons. A meal with chicken – before the grim advent of battery farms – was, for example, a rare treat.

Less inviting were the third–pint bottles of lukewarm milk provided during morning playtime at school, courtesy of the Welfare State which also encouraged a massive advertising campaign – centred on

Norman Wisdom, the peaked–capped 'little man' of British film comedy – to get folk to drink more of the stuff for its calcium and vitamins.
One of the most loathed desserts of many a late 1940s childhood, milk
pudding was very much part of each week's menu.

Yet it is arguable that post–*bellum* Wembley and its environs
– Sudbury, Harrow, Alperton, Ealing, Hanwell, Pinner, Willesden,
Shepherd's Bush, Acton *et al* – on the *diddley–dum–clickety–clack* rail
network that fanned out from London, was comparable to Gauguin's
South Sea island or Byron's Italy in its potential to inspire greatness
or at least accommodate it – though that depends on what you mean
by 'greatness'. Certainly, some famous drummers came from that part
of Middlesex, among them Honey Langtree of The Honeycombs and
The Jeff Beck Group's Mickey Waller. More to the point, with Charlie
Watts, raised in nearby Kingsbury, Keith John Moon was to be a contender as the second most famous drummer in the world.

The first, of course, was Ringo Starr – and like The Beatles' most
junior partner, Keith Moon was to be sucked into a vortex of events that
hadn't belonged even to speculation when, short–trousered and gaber-
dine raincoated, he began his formal education at Barham Primary
School in September 1951. Mid–morning passers–by would catch mul-
tiplication tables chanted mechanically *en masse* by the older forms,
perhaps to the rap of a bamboo cane on a teacher's inkwelled desk.
Music too was taught as a branch of mathematics whereby a dotted
crotchet, say, was expressed diagramatically by 'three of the little milk
bottles you have at school' [1]

As the only member of what was to become The Who not to have
'passed' the Eleven–Plus examination and thereby gained a place at
grammar school – as much a social as an academic coup for ambitious
parents – he finished up in 1957's dry autumn amongst the 'failures'
at Alperton Secondary Modern For Boys, and with a built–in intellectual inferiority complex. Few careers advisors, official or otherwise,
ever intimated that, unless compelled by the Government to fight wars
overseas, Keith and his cronies wouldn't dwell until the grave in and
around the lugubrious district where he'd been born.

An unimaginative and often frightening regime prevalent then in
most state schools was a breeding ground for resentment and revolt.
In class, this was commonly articulated in tiny, covert doodlings in
exercise–books, prior to a graduation to red–herring tactics and dumb

insolence, copied homework and, boldest of all, truancy with its sub–texts of petty shop–lifting; saying 'bloody', 'bum' and ruder words unreproached, and sharing smutty stories over a communal cigarette. Indeed, a legacy of these delinquent days was the smoking that, if not excessive, Keith would never have the will to stop. Perhaps to beef up a self–image as a pubescent rebel, revelling in his wickedness, he would insist later that he was expelled a term before the ordained leaving age of fifteen, and imply that the more faint–hearted teachers thus purchased respite from his incessant 'giving cheek', 'answering back', 'playing the fool' and 'showing off'.

Yet, initially, he'd settled down almost eagerly to class work, and, while wearying of the draconian affectations and futile rigmarole, remained in the top stream for most of his four years at Alperton. If not eligible to sit GCE 'O' levels, he gained lesser but still vocationally–usable qualifications in science and English. Yet, if not the lost cause he'd make himself out to be academically, his extra–curricular activities had had only the most shadowy links with what he was supposed to be learning at Alperton.

His understanding of what books were worth reading and what were not was gleaned chiefly from comics. Furthermore, as well as Barkis remarking that Mrs. Peggotty 'sure knows her cookin' in a US cartoon–strip edition of *David Copperfield*, almost as incredible were the films from the same land mass that Keith and a million or two other children absorbed during Saturday morning cinema sessions. He was certain that no–one in Middlesex, even in the whole of England, ever talked thataway. Neither would a barmaid not bat an eyelid if some hombre was plugged full of daylight in the saloon bar of any of the local pubs. As well as the Wild West, there was much to delight Moon too in this escapist epoch of Martians, robots and outer space 'Things', swashbuckling 'historical' epics, Walt Disney and, when he'd outgrown U–certificate flicks, lonesome film–noir anti–heroes like Marlon Brando and James Dean, narcissistic and defeatist in rain–sodden nights lit by neon.

Sucking on a Woodbine, with Brando, Dean or Norman Wisdom before him on the fleapit screen, Keith might have declared – had he bothered with Wordsworth – that 'to be young was very heaven'. Apart from cigarettes, the only other stimulant available to Keith was alcohol, but he could take it or leave it then. Both whiskey and gin tasted like nasty medicine. Anyway, with all but miniatures beyond individual pockets, spirits were not so much in evidence as Newcastle Brown and Devon 'cyder' in living rooms transformed into dens of iniquity, usually when someone's parents were away for the weekend.

Young for his age, neither did Keith show much interest in girls when table lamps were dimmed with headscarves and armchairs pushed back to create an arena for smooching as a prelude to snogging and attempted completion of sexual pilgrimages.

The soundtrack to these activities effused from plastic 'forty–fives' scattered round the Dansette in the corner. They had started to supercede brittle 78 r.p.m. discs in 1955 – a streamlining that was an apt herald of the 'teenager,' a word now coined to donate all those 'twixt twelve and twenty who were deciding whether or not they wished to grow up.

Nevertheless, it was just after his ninth birthday that the slow pageant of the rock 'n' roll sunrise started to unfold for Keith. On 6 September 1955, a story was syndicated in the *Harrow And Wembley Observer* that a metroplitan magistrate, anticipating the coining of phrases like 'noise pollution' and 'environmental health', had imposed a fine of three pounds and ten shillings on a 'Teddy Boy' named Sidney Adam Turner for spinning 'Shake Rattle And Roll' by Bill Haley and the Comets at full volume for nearly three hours on a gramophone with a tinny, tooth–loosening timbre that had, so its manufacturer bragged, 'a ten–watt punch – as loud as a man can sing!'.

Leader of a big band omnipresent on BBC Radio's Light Programme as Billy Cotton's, Ted Heath didn't 'think rock 'n' roll will come to Britain. You see, it is primarily for the coloured population'[2], but, impinging upon the BBC and its ITV rival's snug little kingdoms as 1955 mutated into 1956, 'Shake Rattle And Roll' had made adult blood run cold at its metronomic clamour. Incited by the national press, girls were to jive in gingham and flat ballet shoes while secretive penknives slit cinema seats when *Rock Around The Clock*, a movie vehicle for Haley – 'the old backstage plot spiced with the new music,' quoth *Picturegoer* [3] – reached these islands.

Haley, paunchy and married with children, would tender apologies at press conferences for his Comets' knockabout stage routines but, what with this 'rock' nonsense going so well, it'd have been bad business not to have played up to it, wouldn't it? Anyway, one of the band had served under respected jazz clarinettist Benny Goodman.

Even with five concurrent entries in in the *New Musical Express* 'hit parade', Bill turned out to be harmless. However, even as hula–hooping and the cha–cha–cha were proffered as the next short–lived fad, rock 'n' roll put forward a more suitable champion in a Mr. E.A. Presley, a Tennessean who dressed as a hybrid of amusement arcade hoodlum and nancy–boy. Drummerless, but with an electric guitarist shifting from simple fills to full–blooded clangorous solo, Presley's first single had been a jumped–up treatment of a negro blues. From then on, his embroidered shout–singing and sulky balladeering had become both revered and detested throughout the free world.

Reports of Presley's unhinged go–man–go sorcery in concert caused Methodist preacher (and jazz enthusiast) Dr. Donald Soper to wonder 'how intelligent people can derive satisfaction from something which is emotionally embarrassing and intellectually ridiculous' [4] Of the latest sensation's debut UK release, 'Heartbreak Hotel,' the staid NME wrote 'if you appreciate good singing, I don't suppose you'll manage to hear this disc all through' [5]. What more did Elvis need to be the rage of teenage Britain?

Though Tin Pan Alley's nose was put out of joint at the proportionally meagre sheet music sales, when it transpired that sixty per cent of the RCA record company's pressings for 1956 were by Elvis, the hunt was up for like fortune–making morons. Needless to say, these sprouted thickest in the States where too many talent scouts thought that all that was required was a lop–sided smirk and gravity–defying cockade. Many saw Jerry Lee Lewis as just an Elvis who substituted piano for guitar and hollered arrogance for hot–potato–in–the–mouth mumbling. While Capitol was lumbered with a pig–in–a–poke in crippled, unco–operative Gene Vincent – 'The Screaming End' – Acuff–Rose would snare two–for–the–price–of–one in the Everly Brothers. There were black Presleys in Chuck Berry and Little Richard; female ones like Wanda Jackson and Janis Martin; mute ones in guitarists Link Wray and Duane Eddy. After Carl Perkins – an unsexy one – came bespectacled Buddy Holly and, unsexy *and* bespectacled, Roy Orbison with his eldritch cry and misgivings about the up–tempo rockers he was made to record by Sam Phillips, owner of Sun, the Memphis studio where Elvis had first smouldered onto tape.

As uncomfortable an Elvis was Tommy Steele, his innocuous English 'answer', whose 'Singing The Blues' was, apparently, the first single Keith Moon ever bought. Before he abdicated in favour of Cliff Richard, Tommy had had his effigy waxed for Madame Tussaud's and was 'sent up' by Peter Sellers – of BBC radio's *Goon Show* – as 'Mr. Iron' who 'doesn't want to bite the fretboard that fed me' and, as Steele actually did, desires to enter 'legitimate' showbusiness, as exemplified by Tommy's prime–time televisual duet with Royal Command Performance veteran Max Bygraves, prefaced by scripted ad–libbing between cheeky young shaver and jovial voice–of–experience.

Despite finding rock 'n' roll objectionable, powers at the BBC had been more obliged to cater for Presley, Steele, Richard and their sort's disciples when the continental station Radio Luxembourg began broadcasting pop showcases in English, and ITV broke the tacit 'toddler's truce' on Saturdays by filling what was previously a blank screen between six and seven p.m. The Corporation countered with *Six Five Special* designed to keep teenagers out of trouble between the football results and *Dixon Of Dock Green* (a spin–off from *The Blue Lamp*) while their parents put younger siblings to bed.

Dr. Soper might have watched it 'as a penance' [4], but *Six Five Special* sought to preserve a little decorum by employing such upstanding interlocutors as disc–jockey Pete Murray – who abhorred Elvis – and former boxing champion Freddie Mills. Comedy sketches, string quartets and features on sport and hobbies were inserted between the pop which, as well as 'rock 'n' roll' by such as trombonist Don Lang and his 'Frantic' Five, also embraced crooner Dickie Valentine, jogalong Joe 'Mr. Piano' Henderson plus traditional jazz and its by–product, skiffle – which was ruled by singing guitarist Lonnie Donegan, an ex–serviceman who reviled rock 'n' roll as 'a gimmick. Like all gimmicks, it is sure to die the death. Let's hope it will happen soon. Nothing makes me madder than to be bracketed with those rock 'n' roll boys'. [3]

Before such cultural reprobates weaved themselves into the then threadbare tapestry of British pop, Keith Moon's upbringing had been as orthodox and free from major calamities as that of any seemingly ordinary bloke just below middle height from his not–too–pointed winkle–pickers to slicked–back, shortish dark hair, glistening with brilliantine. The way to self–advancement seemed to be evening classes at Harrow Technical College pertaining to his employment on the assembly line at Ultra Electronics which, like Hammersmith's Osram light–bulb factory and EMI's disc pressing and packing plant in Hayes, dominated Park Royal, between Alperton and North Acton, as surely as a castle sinister would have done a mediaeval village, cowering in its shadow.

Stopping the service lift between floors for a quiet smoke, Keith took stock, and decided not to sack himself from the drudgery of the inflexible hours at the engineering firm. With the spirit–crushing list-lessness of the totally bored, he put up with it because the wages cov-ered his records, his lung–corroding cigarettes, his tube fares to the West End, his only suit – and, crucially, hire–purchase payments for the second–hand drum kit that enabled him to join Lee Stuart and his Escorts, who modelled themselves on Cliff Richard and the Shadows, a backing group nearly as famous as Cliff himself, especially after their 'Apache' was voted 'Top Record of 1960' in the *NME* Readers' Poll.

'Musical evenings' of any description were not a frequent occur-rence – if at all – in the Moon household, even before television became an indispensable domestic fixture, and pop music started to predomi-nate his life shortly after skiffle had been and gone. Yet,, the fancy that he'd like to make a living as a drummer had entered Keith's index of possibilities after it occurred to him that 'musician' no longer meant sitting in the fourth row of violins and cranking out Beethoven all your life, or, indeed, conforming to any Alperton Secondary Modern dictates about what was and wasn't 'decent' music. You didn't even have to be born into showbusiness. Nor was pop seen necessarily as a preliminary for a life as an 'all–round entertainer' anymore. Since the advent of rock 'n' roll, it could be perceived as less a starting point than the entire purpose, however transient, of an entertainer's career. There needn't be any higher plateau where standing with a teenage audience had no substance.

Theoretically, Keith was well–placed to pursue this goal as the British music business was focussed, then as now, on central London. Nevertheless, despite the ease with which you could travel there, the distance from the city's north–west frontier might as well have been measured in years rather than miles. You could day–dream about sudden rags–to–riches elevation to topping the bill at the London Palladium as much as you liked, but the reality was either contenting yourself or glowering with frustrated ambition when helping the likes of Lee Stuart and the Escorts, The Javelins, Paul Raven and the Rebels, The Art Wood Combo, the appositely–costumed Geronimo and the Apaches, Dougie Dee and his Strangers, The Tomcats [6], The Pete Newman Four or The Detours, pride of Shepherd's Bush, vend entertainment in Church halls, welfare institutes, school dances, sports pavilions and pub functions rooms – exemplified by that within Southall's White Hart, which became Club Tempo once a week. Lower down on the scale, there was providing an alternative to the record–player in some desperate youth club, where soft drinks, a with–it vicar, a solitary light bulb as *son–et–lumiere*, and a wholesome, self–improving reek were the norm, and rough boys got themselves barred for letting slip a 'bloody' or brandishing a cigarette.

How did you get up to the next level? Impossible visions flickered before Keith Moon, even as *Six Five Special's* less pious successors – *Oh Boy!, Drumbeat, Boy Meets Girl, Wham!* and the short–lived *Dig This!* – produced a worthier strain of British rock 'n' roller. You wonder how some might have evolved had they not acquiesced to their handlers' suggestions to follow the Tommy Steele path. As well as Cliff Richard's film musicals of cheerful unreality, Vince Eager (as 'Simple Simon') would dip his toe into pantomime in Southport Floral Hall's *Mother Goose* in 1960 while Marty Wilde – who was giving Cliff more cause for apprehension – announced his wish to 'do the real class stuff like Sinatra.' [7]

Even Willesden's Johnny Kidd, creator of the climactic 'Shakin' All Over' – the equal of anything from the annals of US classic rock – which knocked Cliff Richard and the Shadows' 'Please Don't Tease' from Number One in August 1960, discovered that pop obeys no law of natural justice. Within a year, he and his backing Pirates were to be becalmed outside the Top 50 and supporting acts over which they'd once headlined. They were also softening towards country–and–western, and wondering about the cabaret circuit.

Others, however, remained hostage to the beat. With his Horde of Savages, another local lad, Screaming Lord Sutch was prevented by his image from going smooth. Nevertheless, he – like Johnny Kidd – had demonstrated to Keith Moon and other young admirers of would–be exhibitionist bent that it was possible to escape the orbit of both tedious day jobs and parochial engagements such as Wembley Town Hall where Keith attended what was not so much a Sutch performance as an experience. Into the bargain, one of the Savages was also a Alperton Secondary Modern Old Boy. Guitarist Bernie Watson [8] was recalled by Keith as a quiet and nervous type, but now he was beggaring recognition by entering into the spirit of the eye–stretching proceedings.

Because Moon in later life appeared to have learned much from its criterion of outrage, the career of David, Screaming Lord Sutch is worth chronicling at length. His apparent suicide in 1999 put a tragic full–stop to what was, on its own terms, the triumphant professional career of a sorely–missed British institution. His rise from nowhere was traceable to a fifteen–year–old entering the world of work as an apprentice garage mechanic – or, as he put it, 'a "spanner boy". I used to sing during the tea and dinner breaks, knocking out a rhythm with spanners on the benches.'

One evening in 1959, however, he screwed himself up to mount the stage of the Rising Sun in Sudbury to entertain drinkers with an inspired parody of a pop singer. Amused cheers were still ringing in his ears when the nineteen–year–old chose to become the antithesis of the Elvis lookalikes competing for the attention of Paul 'Dr. Death' Lincoln, a former wrestler, who ran the 2I's, the Soho coffee bar that was the oratorium of British pop in the late 1950s: 'I covered my motorbike crash–helmet with leopard skin, and stuck huge bull horns into it. I also borrowed my auntie's leopard skin coat. As I had long hair for the time too, I came across as a Wild Man of Borneo, screaming out from the crowd when I was announced. I went mad, jumping onto the piano and attacking the crowd. The following Thursday, I was invited back. Soon, I was doing gigs seven nights a week, beginning at places like the Black Bull pub in Barnet with Pete Newman's group – Pete was with Johnny Kidd too – and back at the Rising Sun.'

So it was that David Sutch found the courage to down tools at the garage and become a self–employed window–cleaner so that he could burn the candle at both ends more conveniently.

Screaming Lord Sutch and his Horde of Savages' first extravaganzas both in Middlesex and when re–booked regularly at the 2I's had brought instant national notoriety after Sunday newspapers and a BBC documentary team homed in on this alarming young man, remarking on the pre–Rolling Stones long hair – briefly dyed green – before mentioning the leopard skin loin cloth, the woad, the bull horns, the monster feet, the collapsible cage, the caveman's club, the inevitable coffin and whatever else he'd laid his hands on in an endless effort to elicit publicity for a stage presentation that balanced the slickness of a Broadway musical with the thrilling impression that everything could fall to bits at any second.

The music was almost an afterthought. 1963's 'Jack The Ripper' – 'nauseating trash' sneered *Melody Maker* – brought Sutch closest to a hit – and it was, indeed, a turntable smash throughout Europe, aided as it was by an innovative promotional film seen on the short–lived *Scorpitone* video juke–box. In it, David in full regalia, ghoul make–up and long–bladed dagger stalked Victorian tearsheets. As a schoolboy, I was present in Macari's cafe in Aldershot when two 'bus conductors spent their entire lunch hour and half a satchell of silver watching 'Jack The Ripper' repeatedly, their faces alight with the vacant ecstasy once reserved for public hangings.

While the point was frequently lost without the attendant visuals, the commercial progress of most Sutch A–sides was also hindered by restricted airplay, outright bans – and many venues limiting entrance to his shows to the over–twenties. As these filled to overflowing, cases of fainting and hysteria were not unknown. On top of nights in police cells for sundry breaches of the peace, the retinue was barred from the Granada leisure corporation circuit after its chief show–off plummeted through a house pipe organ during a rash jump from footlights to orchestra pit.

Criss–crossing Europe in draughty, overloaded vans, Sutch was accompanied by many nascent stars. Furthermore, as it was with John Mayall, the number of musicians who can also claim a stint, however brief, on the stage or in the studio with Sutch runs into three figures. Among such helpmates were guitar heroes Jeff Beck and, both from Heston, Jimmy Page and Ritchie Blackmore, and drummers like Viv Prince of The Pretty Things, Led Zeppelin's John Bonham – and Keith Moon – while the diverse worlds of music, drama and literature have been represented by keyboard players Nicky Hopkins, Paul Nicholas – and, yes, Alan Clayson.

I was twelve in 1963 when Sutch inaugurated his political career as a parliamentary candidate for the National Teenage Party in the Stratford–on–Avon by–election caused by the resignation of the unhappy Cabinet Minister who lent his name to the Profumo Scandal.

Gradually, politics came to have as great a bearing on David's life as pop. Often he combined the two via singles like 'Rock The Election' and 1991's double A–side, 'Number 10 Or Bust'/'Loony Rock'. Mostly, he played it for laughs as originator of the Monster Raving Loony Party, its Robespierre, its Danton, its Bonaparte. Detractors might scoff – but he remains the country's longest serving political leader.

As well as the political activism, he ran a pirate radio ship; he engineered a momentous encounter with Elvis Presley that almost resulted in the King's only British performance, and he cavorted with unclothed females outside 10 Downing Street to advertise the 1972 Rock 'N' Roll Festival at Wembley Stadium where he appeared alongside comparable US wild men such as Jerry Lee Lewis and Little Richard. At Brand's Hatch, a dim view was taken of his Lordship pretending to black–out at the steering wheel in the middle of a celebrity race (with the old wooden overcoat rushed out to collect the 'corpse').

The burial of this most famous English–pop–singer–who–never–had–a–hit, at Pinner New Cemetary, brought together representatives from every trackway of his artistic life. On its third anniversary, Savages' drummer Carlo Little organised 'an evening of remembrance' beginning with 'quiet reflection' at the graveside. This was followed by a show at the Ace Cafe, the old biker hang–out on the North Circular, by a bill which included The Downliners Sect and Art Wood, both from the old days, and the sources of endless anecdotes about what Keith Moon said to Speedy Keen at the Union Hall in Watford, and how Carlo could have been a multi–millionaire now if he hadn't given the job with the Stones away by biroing Charlie's name and 'phone number on an empty cigarette packet, and handing it to Brian Jones.

Three days earlier, however, Little had been reminiscing with Watts and his fellow Stones in the VIP enclosure at Wembley during the European leg of their record–breaking world tour. The previous evening, Carlo had been operating a hot–dog trailer outside. As the onions were being fried in readiness for the surge afterwards, what was he thinking as Pavlov's Dog explosions of acclamation punctuated every segment of muffled megawatt noise measured out by the beat of the drummer who'd gone the distance with the Stones instead? Yet, when recovering – as Charlie Watts did – from cancer, he was attractive in his phlegmatic candour, reflecting without regrets that 'a bloke

I taught to play, Keith Moon, who became a megastar, is now dead, killed by booze and drugs'.

Eight years older than his former student, Carlo had bashed a snare–drum and hi–hat in Sudbury's Derek Addison's Rhythm Katz before the Home Office, worried about the situation in Suez, sent for him. During these two years of National Service, a sojourn in the Royal Fusilier Corps of Drums was to have a lasting beneficial effect. Demobbed in 1960, Little was introduced to David Sutch at the Cannibal Pot in Harrow Road, Sudbury, and, on purchasing a full kit, surfaced as drummer and 'musical director' of the Horde of Savages. He left that summer when prospects looked rosier in Dougie Dee and his Strangers, returned to Sutch the following April, and also teamed up – as The All–Stars – with members of Cliff Bennett and the Rebel Rousers (including sixteen–year–old *wunderkind* Nicky Hopkins on piano) to be under the metaphorical baton of a singing mouth–organist called Cyril Davies, who cut a familiar figure in metropolitan recording studios when not attending to his panel–beating business in South Harrow.

With Alexis Korner, another former sideman with Chris Barber's New Orleans Jazz Band, portly, baggy–trousered Cyril had formed the kingdom's first all–blues outfit. Since March 1962, Blues Incorporated – not so much a blues group as a blues revivalist group – had presided at the G Club in a basement along Ealing Broadway. It had been patronised immediately by zealots from London, Middlesex and further, all as devoted to blues as other cliques were to yachting, numismatics and Freemasonry.

In more earnest a manner than Lord Sutch, Blues Incorporated's impact rippled across decades of pop, given those in the watching – and participating – throng who were awaiting consequently inspired destinies as Rolling Stones, Manfred Menn, Kinks, Pretty Things, Yardbirds and Small Faces, while, hedging their bets, Geronimo and the Apaches were to co–exist as The Downliners Sect, a rugged R&B combo, light years away from war paint and feathered bonnets. By autumn, however, the G Club honeymoon was over. 'We reckoned Alexis Korner's band was fantastic the first week,' summarised Dick Taylor, a founder of both the Stones and The Pretty Things, 'quite good the second, but by the third week, we thought it was really a bit off.' Into the bargain, Cyril Davies, mithering about his preference for a narrower interpretation of the music, was to establish a more purist club in Harrow–on–the–Hill. He fronted his All–Stars too at the Railway in Ruislip where Art Wood took his music–mad little brother, Ronnie, a world–renowned Rolling Stone in an unimaginable future.

Charlie Watts had quit Blues Incorporated too, and, like his friend Carlo Little, was drumming non–committally with other groups – including The Rolling Stones, sometimes as far afield as Epsom School of Art and The Boy Blue Club in Woking's Atlanta Ballroom. One night, the Stones shared a bill in a Harrow community hall with The Graham Bond Trio, a tighter, jazzier take on Blues Incorporated. In order to speed up the equipment changeover between sets, Watts agreed to use their Peter 'Ginger' Baker's home–made kit of perspex plus *bona–fide* African drums of thick, shaved animal skins – 'but I couldn't play it. Nothing would happen. I broke three pairs of sticks. He had them set up so that the angle was all wrong for me.' (9)

Though as steeped in jazz as Baker, Charlie pledged himself to the Stones in February 1963. 'I was a bit used to rock 'n' roll,' he elucidated, 'I knew most of the rock 'n' roll guys, people like Screaming Lord Sutch and Nicky Hopkins. I was quite used to Chuck Berry and that.' [10] Conversely, the hands and feet of Carlo Little, a rock 'n' roller from way back, had been on auto–pilot to countless twelve–bar blues shuffles until his overwhelming Sutch duties necessitated his replacement in Cyril Davies' All Stars with a Bill Eyden.

For the rest of the 1960s, Little also served Long John Baldry, Buddy Britten and his Regents, The Echoes, The Circles and, most lucratively, Neil Christian and the Crusaders, another parochial combo, for whom long absences in Germany might explain lack of success at home beyond a solitary chart entry, 1966's 'That's Nice'. While he concentrated on the possible in the Fatherland, with and without his Crusaders, Christian wouldn't have been out of place alongside such as Danny Street and Russ Sainty, xeroxing the hits of others on the Light Programme's *Workers' Playtime*, owing to competence allied with a deficit of vocal individuality. Nevertheless, like Sutch's Savages and Blues Incorporated, Christian's Crusaders served as an incubation shed for many illustrious musicians from Middlesex, among them the ubiquitous Jimmy Page and Ritchie Blackmore.

Just before the onslaught of Merseybeat, many vicinities appeared to have their own Neil Christian and the Crusaders. Cliff Bennett and the Rebel Rousers, for instance held the territory within the drone of Heathrow airport. Off–stage, Bennett enlivened the streets of nearby West Drayton by performing dangerous 100 mph stunts in an MG Sprite. Commanding terrified admiration as a bandleader too, he was also one of few white vocalists able to take on black rhythm–and–blues without losing the overriding passion.

Beyond Middlesex, Dave Curtiss and the Tremors ruled Clacton as Brian Poole and the Tremeloes did Dagenham. If less conveniently placed to strike at the heart of the country's pop industry, Shane Fenton and the Fentones and tambourine–rattling Wayne Fontana and the Jets were the respective toasts of Mansfield and Oldham, where the last chip shops closed at 10.30 p.m. Likewise, Rory Storm and the Hurricanes were – or used to be – the boss group in Liverpool.

There was also a growing preponderance of outfits – like, say, The Javelins – slaying 'em at Cranford's St. Dunstan's Youth Club [11] – or, about to rechristen themselves The Who, The Detours – who, with no demarcated 'leader' were amassing substantial grassroots followings.

Though some local pretty boy might be invited onstage to be Cliff, Neil or Shane for a while, he was not regarded as an integral part of the group *per se*. Most broke up within months of formation but the concept that an acephalous outfit could be a credible means of both instrumental *and* vocal expression was to become the norm from the board rooms of multi–national entertainment conglomerates to the small change of life in households in which, with increasing frequency, grandmothers pleaded for calm amid blazing rows between parents and once–tractable children. Chief among the issues were haircuts, clothes, sex before marriage – and untamed sounds issuing from transistor radio, Dansette record player and black–and–white television. The fog of repression that had followed the Second World War was clearing, even if the Sixties wouldn't really start Swinging for Keith John Moon until they were almost half over.

Notes

1. *The Oxford School Music Book* (OUP, 1951)
2. *The History Of Rock*, volume one, number five (Orbis, 1982)
3. *Picturegoer*, 1 September 1956
4. *Melody Maker*, 29 March 1958
5. *New Musical Express*, 24 February 1956
6. Featuring Acton Grammar schoolboy John 'Speedy' Keen, later of Thunderclap Newman, the motley crew responsible for the anthemic 'Something In The Air', a post–flower power call–to–arms. Produced by Keen's classmate, Pete Townshend, it topped the British charts in 1969.
7. *New Musical Express*, 12 December 1959
8. Who was to precede Eric Clapton in John Mayall's Bluesbreakers
9. *The Big Beat* by M. Weinberg (Billboard, 1991)
10. *Rolling Stones In Their Own Words* ed. D. Dalton and M. Farren (Omnibus, 1980)
11. The Javelins might have vanished from the pages of cultural history had not their 1962 line–up included Ian Gillan, later of Deep Purple.

Dave Berry remembers Keith Moon: *'Towards the end of 1964, I was in something called* Fab 64: The Big Beat Show *at Kelvin Hall in Glasgow. The High Numbers were low on the bill. They'd changed back to being The Who when I next appeared with them at an all-nighter at Tottenham's Club Noreik early in the New Year. We were thrown together on several other occasions in the mid–1960s, but I remember nothing particularly remarkable about Keith beyond the usual chit–chat along backstage corridors and back in the hotel bar. He seemed a very mild–mannered lad back then, whatever may have gone on later.'*

Tony Dangerfield *remembers Keith Moon* (Savages, Rupert's People): 'Early in 1964 the Savages had two days off and Tony Marsh – the keyboard player then – and I decided to do some posing along Wembley's high street. We looked very rock 'n' roll in Levis, leather jackets and peroxided hair. When we came out of a Wimpy coffee bar, Tony glanced over his shoulder, and muttered, "Walk quicker!"

'The reason was that this really up–front and hyper bloke, like a human tornado, was rushing up to us. "I'm in a group!, " he spluttered, "We're called The High Numbers!"

"Who was that?" I asked after he'd cleared off. "That was a twit called Keith who was in my backing group, The Beachcombers, when I was Clyde Burns. He thinks he can play the drums."

The following year, Lord Sutch and the Savages were on the bill at a music industry trade fayre in Lyons with The Who. When we were on stage, Keith shoved the drum podium towards Tony, pinning him to his piano. Then he sprayed him with a hosepipe.

We got our own back when The Who were on by putting the bass drum case over Keith's head,` and pulling him backwards. Chris Stamp told us off for doing that – which was a bit rich, considering what Keith had done during our set.

Later, when I was in an outfit called Rupert's People – who were quite big in France – I was living in a flat in Kilburn with other tenants that included a pirate radio presenter's then–girlfriend, who knew Keith and his wife, Kim. One day, Kim asked her to baby–sit, and I was persuaded to come along too. Keith – and John Entwistle – arrived to pick us up in a Bentley – and Keith was at the wheel!

At a pedestrian crossing along Kilburn High Road, Keith braked sharply, and a Mini ran into the back of us, concertina–ing itself. It was more or less unrepairable – and, technically, the driver's fault – while the Bentley was virtually undamaged. Keith got out to look. The other fellow – some young executive type – was wringing his hands and lamenting about how his new car was a write–off now. "Jesus, man, look at what you've done to your Mini!" gasps Keith before climbing back into the Bentley and shooting off at high speed.'

'Drumming Is My Madness' [1]

'He was among the most talented drummers in contemporary music' [2]

Association with a non–melodic instrument to the rear of the stage prejudices the acceptance of pop drummers as serious composers – and even serious musicians – by those who imagine that any fool can bash drums. An off–the–cuff case is that of Yardbird Jim McCarty who, despite co–writing his group's most enduring songs and his subsequent formation of Renaissance and lesser known but equally adventurous outfits, suffered from years of categorization as an incorrigible rhythm–and–blues swatter before recognition in the 1980s as a colossus of 'new age' music with pieces as innovative in their way as any in the Yardbirds–Renaissance canon. Other talents from behind the kit who were up against similar undervaluation include Thunderclap Newman's Speedy Keen, David Essex, comedian Russ Abbott – and Keith Moon, raconteur, clown, singer by default and sometime actor, whose attempts at songwriting were intermittent at most, but who, as the world came to realise, had an intangible something else.

There would be anti–Moons such as Kiss's Peter Criss and Jerry Nolan of The New York Dolls, but, while the older Clem Cattini – perhaps the first dyed–in–the–wool rock 'n' roller to emerge as a familiar figure on the London session scene – wouldn't let a gatecrashing and plastered Keith at his kit one evening in a Manchester club, he rated Moon highly enough. As for other drummers whose opinions Clem would heed, while they could hear what was technically awry, none could deny Moon's compulsively exquisite crowd–pleasing when in concert with The Who. 'He was totally appropriate for them in the same way as Ringo Starr was for The Beatles', pontificated Alan Barwise, 'Could you imagine Ringo, Charlie Watts or Dave Clark in The Who?'

Unlike these more orthodox beat boom contemporaries, Moon's arms were a–blur in a barrage of perpetual motion on stage. It wasn't always precisely in time, but sometimes this was deliberate – because his embellishments seemed to be off–set by an unbothered maintenance of a backbeat that was firmly and defiantly hesitant by the slightest fraction to both invest material with sharper definition and increase

71

tension – as audaciously as Philly Jo Jones did when dragging the beat behind Miles Davis in the sphere of jazz.

On disc, every one of Moon's individual strokes is discernable, though, as it was on the boards, an endless inventiveness was generally more fiery than serene, more instinctive than erudite, as a master of dynamics explored the most extreme ranges of the kit. Not so much the Hendrix of the drums as the Jerry Lee Lewis, he splattered patterns, accents and even perceivable *glissando* across bar–lines, and created true hand–biting excitement and a sweaty exhilaration experienced only rarely in pop drumming before the arrival of The Who.

Later, Keith would extend his percussive skills with bongo–tapping, timpani–pounding, gong–clashing and conga–thudding at selected points on record – though if such subtleties were implemented in Uncle Sam's baseball parks and concrete colosseums, and the bigger stadiums elsewhere, they were lost on audiences who'd bought tickets for a tribal gathering rather than a cultural recital. Yet, whether or not this attitude degraded The Who's musicianship for the benefit of the spectacle, Keith looked – most of the time – as if he loved every minute, exuding a joyous and involving onstage aura as well as an action–packed methodology nurtured from earliest adolescence.

Perhaps the most singular road–to–Damascus moment was when a thirteen–year–old, bolt–upright in a cinema seat, watched *Drum Crazy* [3], that, if centred on a fall from grace after a drugs conviction, was, essentially, a romanticised bio–pic of Gene Krupa, the handsome and extrovert leader of a wartime swing band, whose daredevilry reinvented the drum kit as a lead instrument. At the top table in the Valhalla of North American jazz percussion, he became a hero – and role model – to a schoolboy half a world away. [4]

Simultaneously forceful and witty amid ensemble passagework and often relentless riffing, Krupa shifted gear with the aplomb of a Formula One racer. Without missing a beat, he'd twiddle his sticks, fling them up in the air and catch them during an era before mainstream jazz was absorbed in a knowing, nodding kind of way, laced with pitying superiority towards those who enjoyed it for the 'wrong' reasons, i.e. that it was fun and that you could sometimes catch fast flashes of knicker when girls jitterbugged to it.

'He was one of the best,' reckoned Charlie Watts, qualifying this with 'Everything he did was was exaggerated. Every move was a big deal.' [5] The New Yorker became such a yardstick by which the most unassuming drummer could judge himself that, after Sandy Nelson had had the audacity to refashion Krupa's 'Big Noise From Winnekta' as a 1959 A–side, it became a set–work for countless beat groups, allowing sticksmen to command the stage under their own voodoo spells for minutes on end – as a reluctant Ringo Starr did when in Rory Storm and the Hurricanes in the early 1960s. He had to admit that 'the audience love it. If there's a drum solo, they go mad.' [6]

Like Starr (and Charlie Watts), Moon appreciated rather than liked Buddy Rich [7] – every smart alec's notion of percussive splendour – and other exhibitors of unaccompanied virtuosity such as Joe Morello from The Dave Brubeck Quartet and The Duke Ellington Orchestra's Louis Bellson – though Keith would be mildly disillusioned to learn that his rapid–fire bass drumming was achieved by simply pumping two of them with both legs. Then there was Elvin Jones, the Terry–Thomas to Buddy Rich's David Niven, who was to leave a more profound mark on those British drummers who fused a rock beat with a businesslike jazz sensibility – or *vice–versa* in the cases of Red Reece in Georgie Fame's Blue Flames' anticipation of 'jazz–rock' by a decade, and Ginger Baker, who was from the same part of London as both Moon and Charlie Watts.

If he resembled a young Old Steptoe, Baker had drummed for Acker Bilk, and was rated as 'bloody good' by Watts, who'd discovered him in 'one of the best – well, the most exciting, if not the best – jazz groups in London,' [8] The Johnny Burch Octet. Both Ginger and Charlie, and, to a lesser degree, Keith, had been captivated by Phil Seaman, 'the greatest drummer in England,' reckoned Watts, 'he used to play timpani style – very unusual in those days – but he played with his fingers like a real timpanist. In those days, he was the nearest thing we had to Philly Joe Jones or somebody like that. I learnt to play by watching Phil Seaman play a bass drum or Red Reece play a backbeat'. [9]

If seven years older – almost to the day – than Moon, when Baker formed the Cream 'supergroup' in 1966, he'd be viewed as a rival to Keith in the later 1960s as Britain's most palpable star drummer. Principal among others causing Moon some nervous backwards glances in the later 1960s would be two fellows his own age: Aynsley Dunbar after he quit John Mayall's Bluesbreakers to lead his own Aynsley Dunbar Retaliation, and, especially, John 'Mitch' Mitchell, whose free–spirited but intrinsically controlled approach likewise stood comparison with that of Moon.

Mitchell also cultivated a similar cheeky–chappie persona. Furthermore, though Moon was present in the Wembley studio where it was filmed in 1968, it was the trendier Mitchell who was chosen to be part of an *ad hoc* 'supergroup' with John Lennon, Eric Clapton, Keith Richards (on bass) and Yoko Ono in *Rock 'N' Roll Circus*, a television spectacular, hosted by The Rolling Stones.

As a child actor, Mitchell had landed a bit–part in the television series *Emergency Ward 10*, forerunner of *Casualty*. He was as precocious as a drummer. Known to Keith Moon even before turning professional, he'd been in a post–'Shakin' All Over' Johnny Kidd and the Pirates. Next, as one of The Riot Squad, Mitch played on several flop singles, and toured with The Kinks. There followed a short spell with The Pretty Things before he succeeded Jimmy Nicol in Georgie Fame and the Blue Flames. As Fame was on the verge of disbanding the group, Mitch was looking for another opening when he was persuaded to try out for what became The Jimi Hendrix Experience.

Mitchell would surface as a foil to Hendrix's risky extemporisations as Keith was to the carryings–on of Pete Townshend – and as Elvin Jones had been to John Coltrane's saxophone–dominated and dissonant strain of hard bop. Partly through the likes of Mitchell and Ginger Baker confessing his influence, Elvin's became a name to be dropped by hip pop consumers when outlines dissolved between jazz and rock in the early 1970s – as instanced by a heavily publicised 'drum battle' between himself and Baker at London's Lyceum ballroom.

Not particularly enamoured with such pageants, Keith Moon had come to understand swiftly that, rather than displaying their skills under the main spotlight, drummers were more satifactorily employed when integrated with the aesthetic intent of a given number. While it was, say, a singer or guitarist who gave it its outward shape and direction, it was frequently the drummer that made the most fundamental difference – and that the finest of them did not make a band sound as if its musical legs had taken root in the stage floorboards, but lifted it off the ground, allowing it to glide easily on the wildest musical winds.

With this perception, Keith was torn between the general notion that a listener should not notice any flamboyance in the drumming on a good record, and his own viewpoint that one should concentrate less on whoever was at the forefront of a piece of music than the fellow ministering to overall effect behind them. Sometimes, however, drums would burst from the melody without any mean display as the disc's principal focus. A minor hit in 1958, 'Topsy Part Two' was an example, based on a pre–war song, 'Uncle Tom's Cabin', and focussed on a solo by Cozy Cole, late of Louis Armstrong's band.

Cole stood on the sidelines of a Top Thirty in which other be–bop swing band percussionists – among them Earl Palmer – were twirling sticks gratuitously on discs that sounded suspiciously like rock 'n' roll – in which crafty cross–rhythms and dotted 'bebop' crochets on the ride cymbal ('*ching–a–ching–ching*') had no place. After breathing the air round Shelly Manne, younger fellow Californian Sandy Nelson mined a lucrative seam of pop as the percussion equivalent of Duane Eddy in that the hits both before and after his 'Big Noise From Winnekta' – like 'Teenbeat' and a revival of The Bob Crosby Orchestra's 'Let There Be Drums' of 1940 – were pared down to monotonous beat against menacing guitar *ostinato*.

Britain struck back with Tony Meehan from Cliff Richard's accompanying quartet, The Drifters – later, The Shadows – who tore pages from Nelson's book with LP tracks like 'See You In My Drums', underlined with bass pulsation. A protege of Rory Blackwell – a Londoner who had, reputedly, broken the world record for non–stop drumming – Jimmy Nicol was waved in to solo too when backing Wee Willie Harris and then Vince Eager. He was to be sent on tour by Eager's manager, the feted Larry Parnes, with his own New Orleans Rockers who planted feet in both the 'trad' and rock 'n' roll camps.

While Nicol's path would interweave briefly with that of The Beatles in 1964 – when he deputised for Ringo Starr for dates in Europe, Hong Kong and Australia – a less shooting–star destiny awaited Burnley's Bobby Elliott who drummed for a local jazz orchestra. Though modern jazz was 'all I ever listened to and all I ever watched' [10], he capitulated to the rock 'n' roll and higher engagement fees of the town's Jerry Storm and the Falcons.

From the audience at the Royal Festival Hall, Johnny Dankworth, a dean of British jazz, voiced his dismay through cupped hands when Lionel Hampton, a Krupa soundalike, jumped onto the bandwagon too. Lapsed UK jazz drummers such as Blackwell and Tony Crombie were also socking a primitive but powerful off–beat less like that of Bill

Haley and the Comets – whose 'Rock Around The Clock' rim–shots were actually quite tricky – than those of Louis Jordan, Bill Doggett, Big Joe Turner and other late 1940s R&B executants – possibly so that their opportunism could be justified because of the blues content in jazz – and *vice–versa*.

With no such pretentions, The Dave Clark Five were to amass a fire regulation–threatening crowd at Tottenham's Royal Ballroom with a repertoire drawn principally from the Top Twenty and classic rock a few years after Clark saw Eric Delaney, a sort of British Buddy Rich, who was given to extravagant gesture and, noticed Dave, 'had timpani with the pedals on them, and he did his thing. It was very jazzy, but I thought, "God, he looks good!" – and it was very simple.' [11] On the rebound from this revelation, Dave bought a kit and began taking lessons from Laurie Jay, who'd been a transient Shadow before working up a couple of small instrumental chart flurries with Nero and the Gladiators.

Delaney's ornate affectations appealed to Keith Moon too, who decided also to put action over daydreaming. Other boys might have gone no further than smiting the furniture to music from the radio, but Keith began exploring avenues with wider implications than inadvertently annoying his parents. Apart from rattling about on biscuit tins (with Cadbury's Roses the most authentic snare drum sound), the cheapest option was a Viceroy 'tapbox', advertised in the *New Musical Express*. With miniature drum, washboard, cowbell and hooter, and costing 39s 11d – roughly the equivalent of three weeks' paper round wages – it was 'ideal for parties and playing with radio or gramophone.' There was also a Broadway 'Kat' snare–and–cymbal set costing £10 4s.

Impressed by neither, Keith's nose would be glued to the windows of the musical equipment shops around Denmark Street, displaying Premier, Carlton and other exclusively British kits, owing to protective government embargos ensuring that retailers could not import foreign makes then.

As his only son's consequent and intensifying rhythmic experiments in his bedroom didn't disturb the rest of the household, Mr. Moon didn't object to Keith's hobby. Indeed, Alf was the guarantor when Keith, a minor, put down his first hire–purchase installment for a second–hand kit. [12] Surprisingly, the neighbours were tolerant when he attacked his new purchase with gusto, showing no signs of ever stopping.

For all Keith's natural sense of syncopation, life was too short to tolerate carping tutorials and practicing for hours daily to be like Gene Krupa. Finally admitting to himself that he was an unadulterated rock 'n' roller – and, therefore, subject to a more stilted discipline than jazz – he listened as hard to D.J. Fontana, who backed Elvis Presley, as Krupa, and initial trial and error brought forth sound hand–and–foot co–ordination, so–so time–keeping, a ragged roll faster than *moderato*, and the beginnings of a naive if impactive personal style.

There were instructional manuals available, but Moon would speak with quiet pride of getting by without ever being able to read a note of standard music script, let alone a drum stave. Moreover, flesh–and–blood tutors were few and far between in his part of Middlesex – so all he could do was continue playing along to records, and watch other drummers either on television or at the local palais where, in stiff evening dress, the bands helped shut off the staider verities of newly–wed couples having to start married life in one of their in–laws' homes, and front doors slammed on the pervading stench of soiled nappies and over–cooked cabbage.

During the night's Veletas, Cha–Cha–Chas and nods to short–lived fads like the Jitterbug and the Creep, there was always some young dingbat these days requesting a Haley or Presley chartbuster from parochial attractions such as The Kirchin Band, whose drummer–leader daubed his sticks with flourescent paint, and had issued a single in 1956 entitled 'Rocking And Rolling Thru' The Darktown Strutters' Ball' after being 'discovered' two years earlier by an EMI recording manager.

For teenagers in Middlesex and the London suburbs, The Kirchins didn't really measure up, but Terry Kennedy's Rock 'N' Rollers came close, especially after their tea–chest skiffle bass was replaced by a conventional instrument. Following a water–testing booking one Sunday lunch time, the outfit gained a lucrative residency at Peckham's Adam and Eve pub. After embarking on a round–Britain trek, supporting comedian Max Wall, they mutated into Terry Dene and the Dene Aces during that unstable teenage idol's 1958 prime. 'He wasn't tempermental in that primadonna way,' estimated Clem Cattini, then the Aces' drummer, 'Terry was just a terribly mixed–up kid. I remember him once chasing round the streets of Edinburgh in just his underwear.'

1959 finished with Clem in The Beat Boys, all–purpose accompanists to Billy Fury, Johnny Gentle, Dave Sampson, Dickie Pride and similar entertainers under the aegis of either or both manager Larry Parnes and producer Jack Good. The group was also on hand for auditions by newcomers like Lance Fortune, Georgie Fame – on whose 'Ballad Of Bonnie And Clyde' Cattini would drum almost ten years later – and Joe Brown.

Joe was to contribute, along with Clem, to 1960's ten–inch *The Sound Of Fury* LP, and be on the bill when Billy headlined a six–month 'Rock And Trad' package tour which amalgamated salient points of Good's pioneering TV pop shows and a Mardi Gras celebration.

If a scintillating presentation, the day–to–day running of this extravaganza was characterized by excessive thrift and geographically–illogical schedules: 'stupid journeys from Edinburgh to the Isle of Wight by coach,' recalls Clem, 'Vomit boxes, we used to call them'. A particularly vexing discussion about wages caused him to storm out of Parnes' Oxford Street office. Calming down in licenced premises adjacent to the renowned 2Is coffee bar, he learned that Johnny Kidd and the Pirates were looking for a drummer.

However, in 1961, the crew abandoned the apparently sinking ship but kept their stage costumes to be The Cabin Boys behind Tommy Steele's brother, Colin Hicks, who was big in Italy if nowhere else. He proved a difficult employer, and Cattini flew home to fall on his feet as mainstay of The Tornados, house band at Joe Meek's Holloway studio, albeit with the proprietor's attendant law–unto–himselfishness. After Cattini gave too frank an assessment about a particular recording, 'all hell broke loose, and Joe threw a stool at me. It missed and hit the spool–holder of this brand–new Ampex four–track. I fled, and he hurled a tape–recorder down the stairs after me. Joe wouldn't listen or take advice from anybody else. What he did was right and that was the end of it.'

Yet thanks to Meek, The Tornados enjoyed a global smash with its second A–side. The first choice for this had been a revival of Caterina Valente's 1955 vocal adaptation of 'The Breeze And I' until it came to the ears of Cattini and, via him, Meek, that Shane Fenton's accompanying Fentones were to issue a rival version. Within a week, Joe had composed and taped a demo of the otherworldly 'Telstar', which, recorded by The Tornados, was the quintessential 1960s instrumental that anticipated many of the electronic ventures of a subsequent and less innocent pop generation.

Cattini's career trajectory demonstrated that venues frequented by Keith Moon could be useful shop–windows for a talented musician. At Wembley Town Hall on 25 June 1962, Moon had been quite openly enthralled by Carlo Little's drumming with Screaming Lord Sutch and the Savages. As it is with many so–called show–offs, Keith was quite a shy, self–effacing person – at least, he was then – and he found himself wanting but not being able to bellow his applause to the ceiling during particularly *bravura* round–the–kit fills and drum–led transitions from chorus to middle–eight.

'Looking at the audience,' reminisced Carlo, 'I could pick out the committed musicians there. They were the ones with their mouths open, the ones who weren't smiling. Keith was noticeable because he paid most attention to me.'

Afterwards, Moon summoned the nerve to worm his way backstage to ask Little point–blank to teach him all he knew. Amused by the lad's persistence, hesitation and final agreement chased across twenty–six–year–old Carlo's face, and for ten shillings – an eighth of Keith's weekly take–home pay from Ultra Electronics – per session, he passed on his hard–won knowledge every Wednesday at seven in his Harrow semi–detached. [13]

The lasting and beneficial effectiveness of these lessons registered with Britain at large when, in front of television cameras, Moon was not the usual nondescript who, delayed by a descent from the drum riser, took a disregarded bow with his group's guitarists and singer just as the applause was dying. Instead, Keith was as prominent as the lead vocalist.

There had been only the most borderline antecedents in the beat boom. Bearing a passing resemblance to *Coronation Street* lothario Mike Baldwin, Bernard Dwyer of Freddie and the Dreamers threw himself heart and soul into the comedy routines that were the stylistic straitjacket worn by this outfit from Manchester, 'entertainment capital of the North'. [14]

Dave Clark had a tighter grip on his Five than Freddie did on the Dreamers. As well as managing them, he ensured that drumming was the chief selling point of 1963's 'Do You Love Me', chart–topping

'Glad All Over' and its 'Bits And Pieces' follow–up, which hinged on a quasi–military hook–line of foot–stomps and snare–drum rataplan.

Four–in–the–bar stamping was also to the fore in 'Have I The Right' by The Honeycombs, which was at Number One in August 1964. Much was made of their Honey Langtree, even if she wasn't the first girl drummer in an otherwise all–male ensemble; The Ravens, signed to Oriele Records, beat them to that one, but both pre–empted The Velvet Underground with their Maureen Tucker by over two years.

Viv Prince was borrowed from The Pretty Things to man the kit when Langtree took a lead vocal during The Honeycombs slot on ITV's *Sunday Night At The London Palladium* in August 1965. He was also short–listed when Keith was poleaxed with whooping cough – rare among adults – for most of The Who's scheduled bookings that December. When this was diagnosed, the three functioning members and their managers gathered to try to resolve the quandary. Entwistle was all for cancellation. Nevertheless, he was persuaded that their only choice was a substitute. Who? Tony Meehan? Clem Cattini? Tony Newman from Sounds Incorporated? What was Doug Sandom doing these days?

Someone mentioned that Viv Prince had just been fired from The Pretty Things for behaviour not unalike that of the indisposed Moon. [15] Someone else added that in the early days, Keith had learned much from studying Viv – but which Viv? Three successive drummers – all called Viv – had passed through the ranks of the Things, but Prince was the most distinguished, his father being the leader of The Harry Prince Five, omnipresent in the dance halls of pre–war Loughborough. After Harry had taught him the essentials of drumming, Viv had evolved an oddly familiar technique that was too swift for the eye to follow.

'I always remember Keith standing in front of the drums,' recalled Dick Taylor, the Things lead guitarist, 'later he would admit that he idolized Viv. Before that, playing drums was quite sedentary, even boring – and through Viv, you'd suddenly realize you could be a drummer and also an extrovert. You could be a star, and play your drums too. I think Keith realised he could be Keith, and didn't have to switch instruments. He could still play drums and let out all his lunacy through the drum kit – because Viv was amazing. He'd hit anything: mic stands, fire buckets, the floor, the guitar you had in your hand...'

Therefore, as the cold stethoscope touched Moon's chest on that strange day, Prince was stirred from an after–lunch nap by a call from Kit Lambert requesting him to prepare for a series of one–nighters with The Who.

Rather than remain huddled under his bedclothes for as long as possible, Keith, not wishing to inconvenience anyone more than necessary – or miss any of what was still great fun – rejoined the others after the minimum time recommended by the doctor. He was still a little pale and wan for the New Year's Eve edition of *Ready Steady Go*, but that didn't prevent him either from missing the gone–midnight celebrations afterwards at the Scotch of St. James.

One of Keith's familiars among the Swinging London ravers was the subject of 1966's 'Minuet For Ringo', B–side of 'Light Of The Charge Brigade', the only solo single by Viv Prince. This dedication was an indication of how well–known rather than how skilful a drummer Ringo Starr had become.

Though Starr, like a vicar shy of sermons, favoured only the most essential adornments beyond a plain beat, Moon preferred him to Buddy Rich and Elvin Jones – though elsewhere within professional circles, Ringo was deemed a lesser drummer than lapsed jazzmen like Bobby Elliott, Charlie Watts – even more outstanding for the frugality of his playing than Starr – The Animals' John Steel, Kenny Slade of Dave Berry's Cruisers – a man of Viv Prince's kidney, who 'used to go round the tables up and down the club, and never miss a beat' [16] – and The Spencer Davis Group's Pete York, who, in 1966 too, started penning a regular column in *Midland Beat* regional pop gazette, full of valuable tips from his own strict practice rota plus learned critiques of the latest kit accessories. While esteeming Keith Moon as 'the Elvin Jones of the pop world' [17], York twitted Dave Clark – as most of the industry's intelligentsia did, partly because there were claims that he did not play on his own records.

Clark also inflicted injury on home trade by using a Trixon kit from Germany after his Rogers drums were raffled for charity – but this was not as untold as that of the more famous Ringo with his Ludwig – from the USA – with Swiss–made Paiste cymbals. Now every other stick–wielder from school children to chart–riders like Chris Curtis of The Searchers and then The Fourmost's Dave Lovelady started beating a Ludwig too. Indeed, because it travelled with the Beatles, the

Ludwig became the standard group drum set for most of the 1960s. Nevertheless, Keith Moon was to remain loyal to Britain's own Premier with whom he inked a sponsorship deal in September 1965. 'He was Premier's Number One,' smiled Who road manager Mick Double, 'And they were very good to us.' [18]

The chief advantage to the company of Keith's endorsement was a high profile that was the antithesis of the customary dogsbody posing no limelight–grabbing challenge to the front line. This was the lot of Mick Avory and Jim McCarty, the respective drummers with The Kinks and The Yardbirds, The Who's rivals as the most adventurous working British pop outfits of the Swinging Sixties.

On the Kinks' first hits, the much put–upon Avory looked on as a hired hand, quicker off the mark, replaced him. He then learned each number off the record for regurgitation on the boards where his playing would be in any case drowned by screams. Apart from hurt pride, it didn't matter. No–one would be any the wiser. OK, Mick?

A session drummer was present too when The Yardbirds were in decline in the months before they threw in the towel in the inauspicious setting of Luton Technical College on a drizzling Sunday evening in 1968. For Jim McCarty, it had ended almost as it had begun when the entity that was to mutate into The Yardbirds, The Country Gentlemen, consisting of himself and other sixth–formers at Hampton Grammar School, had taped a 1960 demo under the supervision of EMI recording manager, John Schroeder. 'It didn't work,' remembered Jim, 'because of the drumming. Schroeder reckoned that Tony Meehan would have made a much better job.'

As well as casting aside adolescent follies like pop groups, McCarty's post as a trainee financial analyst in the City was a typical vocational option for a grammar school boy from the London end of Surrey just as a lowly position at Ultra Electronics was for a secondary modern boy from Middlesex. However, like Keith Moon, Jim's evenings were not being spent relaxing over a post–dinner crossword but playing in a semi–professional edition of what would connect genealogically with a famous pop group. Arriving at the same crossroads as Moon, McCarty too would find the courage to chuck in a soul–lacerating daytime job.

As a Yardbird, McCarty was trusted by their producers to execute the neo–symphonic tempo changes and other intricacies that marked the group's breathtaking style during its two year golden age after Jeff

Beck superceded Eric Clapton on lead guitar. Jim was even required sometimes to either proffer guidance or actually drum on recordings by other artists.

As comparatively mature about personnel undertaking individual projects, The Roulettes, a guitars–and–drums quartet from Hertfordshire, accompanied Adam Faith when, seeing the group boom coming, he'd switched without a pause from lightweight ballads with pizzicato strings to ersatz Merseybeat. Their drummer, Robert Henrit would be called in to help pep up another county outfit, Unit Four Plus Two's third single, 'Concrete And Clay', from a slow, semi–acoustic *lied* to a snappy, uptempo 1965 chart–topper.

Keith Moon admired Henrit at least as much as he did Viv Prince. Try listening to, say, Faith's first 'beat boom' single, 1963's 'The First Time', and imagining that it's Moon instead of Henrit. To me, the two are almost interchangeable. Nevertheless, two years later, The Roulettes, with or without Adam, were a spent force, and few of those who were now aspiring to emulate Moon were aware of his debt to Henrit. Among these were latter–day Searcher John Blunt, Chris Townson of John's Children – who was to deputise for a hospitalised Keith on two British dates in 1967 – and The Mojos' Aynsley Dunbar – later of John Mayall's Bluesbreakers and Frank Zappa's Mothers Of Invention – who, like Mitch Mitchell, metamorphosed into a more sophisticated edition of Moon.

Just as studio engineers were directed to reproduce the corrupted snare sound on David Bowie's *Low* in the late 1970s, so session drummers in the mid–1960s were told to 'play like Keith Moon'. 'Wanted' ads for 'Keith Moon–type' drummers were appearing in *Melody Maker* as regularly as rocks in the stream, and once unobtrusive group percussionists were being stampeded into doing more than just banging out a straight off– beat on the snare. To this end, the exasperated manager of Dulwich's A Wild Uncertainty engineered a visit by Moon to sit in during a Saturday afternoon rehearsal. 'He certainly kicked the band up the arse,' gasped organist Eddie Hardin, 'and, after he left, we didn't speak to our own drummer for hours.' [19]

Because The Who were slow to gain ground in the USA, 'Keith Moon–types' were few and far between during the 'British Invasion' when Ringo and Dave Clark ruled. There were no incumbents who could match the former's homely wit or that smile of Clark's that just about slew me when I was a teenage fan of his Five.

On a far distant horizon, Chad Smith's 1999 audition with Los Angeles outragers, The Red Hot Chilli Peppers, was to begin with him screaming obscenities and thrashing his kit with uncompromising self–confidence, but the US drummers built to last in the 1960s tended to value dogged steadiness and understated images. Off–the–cuff examples are Hal Blaine – who, after serving Phil Spector, was to be heard on as many US hits as Clem Cattini was on British ones – Levon Helm of Bob Dylan's backing Hawks (later, The Band), and Jim Keltner from an Oklahoman family of percussionists, who was in Gary Lewis and the Playboys, the proudly American exception during that 1965 week when the US Top Ten was otherwise all British.

A more erudite specimen is Jimmy Carl Black of Frank Zappa's Mothers Of Invention. He had a a fast friendship with Keith on the set of Frank's 1971 film, *200 Motels,* during hours of hanging around during retakes, camera repositionings *et al.* A Texan who could boast at least two armfuls of Cherokee blood, his musical career began like Keith's with a blowing instrument – the trumpet – before he turned to the drums, becoming so adept that he would remind blues afficianado Zappa 'of the guy with the great backbeat on the old Jimmy Reed records. Frank's music was a challenge, but I loved it. He very patiently taught me how to play all those rhythms and time signatures. I'd never even played three–four before, but he knew I could do it.' [20]

His pal Keith, however, was as good as he was ever going to get around the time of 1971's *Who's Next*, thought by many Who devotees to be their most accomplished album. Nonetheless, Moon continued to shimmer across successive generations of pop as surely as a harvest moon over the story–book meadows and woodlands that his native Wembley had once been.

He had already imposed himself, both stylistically and socially, on Led Zeppelin's John Bonham, with whom he shared a relatively untutored background on his chosen instrument as well as self–immolatory inclinations. Bonham cut a truculent figure in the Moon–esque frenzy of rhythms within rhythms and ringing silverware in 'Moby Dick', the number that would frame a drum solo on 1970's Led Zeppelin II – and one that could last up to twenty minutes on the boards. In spite of his philosophical objections to such displays – and that Bonham's group was a principal rival to The Who in the North American market – Keith joined John on stage to duet on 'Moby Dick' on at least one occasion in a US stadium, both of them beating on a kit of comparably vast expanse to that that Keith used in The Who.

Later in the 1970s too, Moon and Bonham crept up – perhaps unknowingly – upon Sparks, one of the more quirky glam–rock hitmakers, through the reined clamour of the late Norman 'Dinky' Diamond, recruited from Aldershot's boss group, The Sound Of Time, a hybrid of The Small Faces and a more subdued Who.

When punk came in, Rat Scabies of The Damned – in private life, a pleasant young man from Croydon named Chris Miller – was its Moon, not only in the manner of his drumming, but also via artifices like the talcum powder he sprinkled on his skins to shroud himself in musty clouds, and setting fire to a drum kit, liberally doused in petrol beforehand, over the closing credits of *The Trouble With The Seventies*, a British mid–1990s televisual romp on which The Damned appeared with other living relics of the decade that taste forgot.

Making a far more agreeable noise than Take That, Westlife, East 17 and any in–one–ear–and–out–the–other boy band on *Top Of The Pops* then, The Walnut Dash, a trio from Essex, contained drummer Malcolm Moore, whose principal income came as a hireling for Westlife's tweely choreographed stage shows. Letting off steam in his spare time, he kept thrillingly slapdash and Moon–esque pace with the Dash as a verification of the faded ideal of musicians performing a song as opposed to producing a production.

It was also a V–sign at such as the Japanese invention of a drum machine that, within the strictures of exact time–keeping, would make a deliberate flesh–and–blood–like mistake – perhaps fluffing a floor–tom paradiddle – every twentieth bar in order to preserve at least a vestige of humanity within the gutless exactitude that has removed from the very bedrock of pop much of the do–it–yourself rough–and–readiness, endearing imperfections, spur–of–the–moment dynamism and thrilling margin of error made manifest, if not entirely originated, by The Who's lost drummer.

Notes

1. The title of a Nilsson composition for Ringo Starr's 1981 album, *Stop And Smell The Roses*, which would not have been out of place on 1975's *Both Sides Of The Moon*, Keith solo album, in the ambulant, blaring broadness of the instrumentation behind the nonchalant and vaguely camp vocal.
2. Times obituary, 10 September 1978
3. US title: *The Gene Krupa Story*
4. And another closer to home in anti–Moon Jerry Nolan of The New York Dolls, who, perhaps surprisingly, used to follow Krupa from engagement to engagement in New York.
5. *The Big Beat* by M. Weinberg (Billboard, 1991)
6. *New York Times*, 21 June 1989
7. Legend has it that, when The Who appeared on the same bill as his Orchestra in Chicago in 1969, Rich told Keith Moon, 'You can't drum, but you sure put on a great show.'
8. *Best Of Guitar Player*, November 1994
9. *Rhythm*, June 2001
10. *New Gandy Dancer*, undated (*circa* 1984)
11. World–wide Dave Clark Fan Club newsletter, No. 58, December 1984
12. The set–up used by jazz and the first rock 'n' roll drummers was a standard dance band kit which, by the mid–1950s, was bass drum and pedal (right foot), small tom–tom (mounted on bass drum), snare drum for the off–beat (right hand). two cymbals ('crash' – for sudden accentuation – and 'ride' – for continuous playing) on stands. To the left, the hi–hats (two cymbals facing each other) are brought together with a snap by a foot pedal to provide eight–to–the–bar stresses or a 'matching' but more unobtrusive off–beat to the snare. Later, the hi–hat stand was heightened to be within easy reach of the stick. The drum shells were usually of wood.
13. Mitch Mitchell was among Little's successors as Lord Sutch's drummer.
14. Though their two–year run of UK chart strikes – from 1963's 'If You Gotta Make A Fool Of Somebody' to 'Thou Shalt Not Steal' – embraced no A–side designed specifically to be funny.

15. Describing Prince's enlistment in The Pretty Things, singer Phil May said, 'We were sort of novice lunatics, but then suddenly they hand us, like, the High Priest of Lunacy.'

16. *Not Like A Proper Job: The Story Of Popular Music In Sheffield, 1955–1975* by J. Firminger and M. Lilleker (Juma, 2001)

17. *Midland Beat*, May 1966

18. *Rhythm*, November 2002

19. *Ain't Life A Bastard* by E. Hardin (Sarsen, 2004)

20. Among Black's ventures after the completion of *200 Motels* was a building–and–decorating business with Arthur Brown after the God of Hellfire had relocated to Texas.

Robert Henrit remembers Keith Moon (*drummer with the Roulettes,
Unit 4+2, Argent and the latter day Kinks) Keith Moon was the most
natural drummer I have ever seen, and completely unique. He was
unschooled, and because of his technique (or lack of it), The Who
played in a certain way. He simply didn't worry about which hand he
should be hitting the cymbal with. If the left hand was available, he'd
happily use that one.*

*Once, he turned up at the flat I was living in at three in the morning
– after the Speakeasy – and said, "Dear boy, I want to tell you something. Can I come in for a cup of tea?" I let him in, and he told me
how I'd always been his favourite drummer, and how he'd learned
everything from me.*

*I have a letter that Pete Townshend sent after Moonie's death, telling
me too how I'd always been Moonie's favourite drummer.*

*In other respects, I always looked on Moonie as being a flawed gen-
ius – because he'd work hard at preparation. If he threw a TV out of
a window, it would be working all the way down to the ground because he'd attached it to a long aerial and mains lead.*

*One night in Rotterdam, I wandered into his dressing room, and he
was sitting there with a crate of twelve bottles of Remy Martin brandy and a DRB Special Gretsch snare drum – a collector's item. He
had a drink in his hand, and invited me to have one. "Dear boy," he
said as he handed me a bottle, "This one's for you. The rest are for
me." The snare drum was for me too, but I was too embarrassed to
take it. I certainly regret it now.*

*To be frank, I don't know whether Moonie was an alcoholic. I never
really gave it a thought. He would turn up in his Bentley at lunchtime
outside my drum shop in Wardour Street, and start drinking, expecting me to join him. All I know is, his doctor advised him that drinking
brandy would be better for him than drinking Scotch.*

Dave Munden remembers Keith Moon (drummer with The Tremeloes): 'The year must have been 1966; the place, the Carousel Club, Copenhagen. The Tremeloes were playing there on the same night that The Who were on at another city venue, the Tivoli Hit House.

We had just played our first set, and were downstairs relaxing at a very long table, along with some of our friends and fans, when in walks Keith Moon and John Entwistle, who we invited to sit with us and have a drink. Whilst talking together, Keith asked me if John and himself could join us on stage for the next set. Of course, we agreed, but I told Keith that if he destroyed my kit, I'd punch him on the nose. He played my drums very carefully, and we finished the show with no accidents happening.

Going back to our table in the club – which, by then, must have had forty people sitting at and around it, Keith pulled a huge wad of Kronor from his pocket, exclaiming that he'd just received some roy-alties for Danish sales of The Who's records. Then he said that the drinks were on him for the rest of the night until the money ran out. Keith was very nice and very generous, a bit eccentric, but a really great bloke.'

'A Fool's Paradise': The Shane Fenton Audition

'Keith and I played too busy. Bobby kept a nice solid beat' – Lloyd Ryan

Around the time his school career slipped into its final decline, Keith, his adolescent hormones raging, began looking for an opening in a pop group, and was to join Kingsbury's Lee Stuart and the Escorts in 1962. While religiously attending rehearsals, Keith came to realise that the other personnel weren't going to be that dismayed if the outfit fell apart. They saw it it as a vocational blind alley, a folly to be cast aside on departure to the world of work or the marriage bed. Indeed, the ceiling of Lee Stuart and his Escorts' ambition appeared to be not so much plebian and non–sectarian 'youth clubs', but 'young people's clubs', attached to Churches like the Sacred Heart in Mill Hill.

The powers–that–be at these places thought that sport, purposeful hobbies and the open–air were just the ticket to take adolescent minds off nature's baser urges and any other distractions from loftier ideals. When not out canoeing, hiking or booting a soaking–wet piece of leather about, you could be watching a slide–show or engaging in a 'Brains Trust' on topical or ecclesiastical issues. As well as book–learning eloquence during such discussions, a sports jacket, 'sensible' shoes, cavalry twills and short–back–and–sides might mark you as an eligible young bachelor for a tweedily earnest maiden who looked as if she couldn't wait for a game of chess or ping–pong, followed by a chat about life–after–death over an orange squash.

All this was anathema to Keith, who didn't go in for books, was an incorrigible shoplifter, and scandalised the more bigoted of Wembley's heterosexual chauvinsts by wearing a gold lamé suit, bought on the drip, in the street. He was not a 'young person', but a less respectable 'youth' who liked to watch the fun when seedy–flash louts of more powerful build than he barged *en bloc,* without paying, into dances, purely to make trouble and snarl with laughter as the with–it vicar pleaded ineffectually. Now and then, fists swung harder than Lee and his Escorts as their music soundtracked beatings–up. Usually, however, their music was a background noise to the pursuit of chaste romance: boys weighing–up whether or not to risk an exploratory, tongueless kiss on a dancing partner's lips during one of the 'smoochers' in a repertoire focussed on approximations of classic rock and current hits.

While he never missed an engagement, Keith tired of the trivial round of recurring parochial dates, and had no conscience about playing non–committally with other groups whose calendar might prove more attractive. His talent for self–promotion was such that many were convinced that he was always *about* to soar to the very summit of pop. He could do just that whenever he felt like it, but why should he? He was the greatest already.

Nevertheless, disturbed that the fish weren't biting for him, he was immediately interested when an opportunity to break loose of the suburban orbit manifested itself in a boxed advertisement in *Melody Maker*'s 'Musicians Wanted' column in November 1962, concerning a vacancy in Shane Fenton and the Fentones. Keith knew all about them. From somewhere in the Midlands, they'd managed a quantum jump to a regular spot on *Saturday Club*, the Light Programme's principal pop showcase – and a stack of entries that had hovered around the middle of the hit parade after the combo had been signed to Parlophone, an EMI subsidiary.

Their opposite numbers at Decca were Brian Poole and his Tremeloes from Essex, who, within months, were to score a Number One with 'Do You Love Me', a xerox of a year–old US smash, that would vanquish a simultaneous cover by up–and–coming fellow Londoners, The Dave Clark Five.

Fenton and his boys, however, were struggling as the watershed year of 1963 loomed. Their last single 'Too Young For Sad Memories', had flopped, and, with Parlophone's patience snapping, there was a lot riding on its follow–up, 'Hey Miss Ruby'. Yet, in their own right, The Fentones had just notched up a second strike in the lower reaches of the Top Fifty. In identical pink suits and matching white Fenders, the three guitarists iced 'The Breeze And I' with intricate synchronized footwork – just like The Shadows – during their spot in the proceedings when Fenton, in the wings, composed himself for the big finish. Then they'd pile into Ray Charles's 'What I'd Say', wherein Shane could take it down easy, work up audience participation, build the tension to raving panic and, finally, sweep back into the wings, leaving 'em wanting more.

Even without the rose–tinted spectacles, The Fentones, with Shane as their Cliff Richard, were, therefore, well–placed to develop into at least semi–serious challengers to the suzerainty of The Shadows – and, arguably, The Tornados – as the kingdom's top instrumental unit. Thus there was a sense of marking time on the understanding that, sooner or later, another hit would come the way of The Fentones with or without Fenton. In any case, everyone was still earning twenty pounds a week – not a bad deal in the early 1960s when half that amount was considered an adequate wage for a young business executive.

This income was derived chiefly from a full itinerary of zig–zagging one–nighters and back–to–back package tours. Saturday night attendance figures would rise if there'd been a *Saturday Club* session that morning. There was also a promise of a chance to mime 'Hey Miss Ruby' on ITV's scream–rent *Thank Your Lucky Stars*. Even if that particular trail went cold, Shane Fenton and the Fentones intended to conduct themselves as if this was still a possibility – and the fans would too. .

As the late medieval period of British pop gave way to its High Renaissance, it wasn't yet certain whether a swing towards acephalous beat groups with an overwhelming emphasis on vocals was in any way permanent – or that it would render *passe* both Shadows–type choreography – or Shadows–type anything – and solo singers like Shane. Yet, perhaps sniffing the wind, The Fentones' drummer, Tony Hinchcliffe, tendered his resignation and uprooted to South Africa.

His former colleagues wasted no time in booking a basement rehearsal studio in north London for open auditions to find a replacement. Armed only with a pair of sticks, Keith was one of the half–dozen or so hopefuls sitting on a wooden chair, awaiting a turn to beat the common kit set up for each to use. Was it so unreasonable for a self–confident sixteen–year–old amateur to hold in his heart the exciting hope that he'd be the chosen one – the pop equivalent of the chorus girl thrust into a sudden starring role.

After all, even further from the core of UK pop than Middlesex, a unknown teenager from Blackpool, Derek Fell, had passed through the ranks of The Shadows. Of the same age, Jimmy Nicol, merely a drum repairer in a London branch of Boosey and Hawkes, had achieved a more qualified stardom when enlisted into David Ede and the Rabin Rock whose upbeat muzak was forever on the Light Programme. This was an apt prelude to Nicol's next post – under the baton of light orchestra conductor Cyril Stapleton. He was also hired for a session with Cleo Laine, *grande dame* of British jazz.

In Birmingham, the studio band of *Lunch Box* contained nineteen–year–old Pete York, awaiting his destiny with The Spencer Davis Group. He was drumming gladly on this, the lightest of ITV's light entertainments, for the money he could not earn in various local jazz outfits. Pete Morgan, likewise, forsook Oxford's Climax Jazz Band for what became The Fourbeats 'after much heart–seaching arithmetic'. [1] Other jazz drummers who also yielded to such temptation included Newcastle's John Steel, who 'drifted into working men's clubs and any sort of stuff like that I could get – and then eventually I got into supper–club work in a resident trio with bow–ties, playing "Fly Me To The Moon"'. Back in Middlesex, Mickey Waller had thrown in his lot with a British 'answer' to The Champs [2], The Flee–Rekkers – who'd enjoyed a 1960 Top Thirty placement with a rocked–up arrangement of 'Greensleeves'.

Though he was still holding down a 'proper' job, Mickey was far ahead of Charlie Watts, whose first public engagements were with an unremarkable semi–professional unit whose principal stock–in–trade was Jewish wedding receptions. 'I never knew what the hell was going on,' confessed Charlie, 'as I'm not Jewish. What you really need on those jobs is a good piano player. If the piano player's daft, you've got no chance. I don't care if you're Max Roach, you'll only last half–an–hour.' [3]

While Watts and John Steel tapped out across–the–board favourites in parochial obscurity, and the likes of Jimmy Nicol opted for grey facelessness outside the main spotlight, Keith Moon pondered. He'd reached something of a crossroad. It wasn't too late for him to make a proper go of Ultra Electronics, instead of just waiting for clocking–off time to roll around – but such a noxious resolve could be held at arm's length as long as there remained even the remotest possibility of a more glamorous alternative.

He found himself staring round at the other candidates for the Fenton job. Far too young to be losing his hair, Bobby Elliott, as a Lancashire schoolboy, had kept scrapbooks of US jazz drummers. With cymbals positioned carefully horizontal like Buddy Rich's, he'd splattered patterns and accents across bar–lines in a trio with a weekly residency at a parochial jazz club which also accommodated distinguished visitors from London like Johnny Dankworth, Harold McNair – and Don Rendell, who offered Elliott a job as his full–time drummer, but 'maybe even then I knew jazz was a minority sport. You'd get eighty people on a good night. Then I'd play a Saturday afternoon rock session down the Nelson Imperial Ballroom, and there'd be seven hundred and all these girls, and I'd think, "Hang on. I'm no fool." You'd hear Earl Palmer on the early Little Richard stuff. Well, that's drumming for me.' [4]

While Bobby had undertaken a nigh–on two–hundred mile journey from the north, Lloyd Ryan hadn't had to come much further than Keith for his try–out. Equidistant from the Thames were Ultra Electronics and the Merton Park film complex where Ryan had been a general runaround before becoming a professional drummer, a career move that, so he considered, 'saved me from a life of crime'. Though only a couple of years older than Keith, Lloyd had already served in the all–purpose bands in a summer season variety show headlined by television ventriloquist Ray Allen; a pantomime with Mike Berry – a chart contender on a par with Shane Fenton – and *What A Crazy World!*, a long–running London musical that was to be turned into a film. He was fresh from a tour *sur le continent* with Gene Vincent when he introduced himself to Elliott, Moon and the other drummers in the afternoon queue. These included George Roda – a Canadian who'd backed Lance Fortune, a vocalist who'd had his fifteen minutes in 1960 – and a certain 'Mick Fleet', a beanpole of a lad, who'd hacked off the final syllable from his surname for the occasion.

A squeak of feedback launched Shane Fenton's search for a new Fentone – though it was lead guitarist Jerry Wilcock who took charge as each of the testees showed how they could cope with mutually familiar rock 'n' roll standards. No–one was an obvious no–hoper, but it boiled down to a toss–up between Roda and Elliott. There was nothing to suggest that the former wasn't the *beau ideal*, but it was Bobby who a sharp–eyed Lloyd Ryan spotted when the group performed on a televised pop concert in mid–1963.

In the meantime, Lloyd had applied for the post of drummer in Chris Farlowe and the Thunderbirds, who had just returned from a stint in Germany, but, after this went to Carl Palmer – destined to be the 'P' in pomp–rock trio, ELP as Mick Fleetwood was the 'Fleetwood' in Fleetwood Mac – the gifted Ryan forged a fulfilling career of master

classes, tutorials and studio work as a 'drummer's drummer', appreciated for his boundless versatility, exacting standards and easy–going
professionalism.

As for Shane Fenton and the Fentones, their next single, 'A Fool's
Paradise', suffered the same depressing tumble into the bargain bin
as 'Hey Miss Ruby' – as did a Fenton solo effort, 'Don't Do That'.
Confronted with the rearing monster of the Big Beat, the two factions
separated officially after a poignant showdown on *Saturday Club* in
July 1964. The Fentones soldiered on, taping a cancelled vocal A–side,
'Money Honey', with Ginger Baker on drums – while Shane made a
calculated withdrawal from the pop mainstream as a song–and–dance
act with his wife. He also speculated in the administrative side of
the music industry. Among those he aided in this capacity were The
Hollies, who were to absorb Bobby Elliott into their number in time
for 1963's 'Searchin'', the first of a long run of smashes for the most
distinguished Merseyside group after The Beatles.

Yet The Hollies were on the wane ten years later when Fenton was
in the ascendant as glam–rock luminary, 'Alvin Stardust' – and The
Who endured a troubled US tour, notable for a drug–addled Keith
Moon being half–led, half–carried semi–conscious from the stage to
the dressing room by the road crew during a recital at San Francisco's
vast Cow Palace – which had filled all of its seats more or less by
word–of–mouth four hours after the box–office opened three weeks
earlier.

After their drummer's collapse that evening, a volunteer from the
audience climbed up to rattle the traps for the rest of the show. When
the news reached the rest of the world, people wondered what was the
matter with Keith Moon. No question: he was in a bad way.

This is probably a senseless hypothetical exercise, but, for a few
minutes, let's transfer to a parallel dimension in which Moon has become a Fentone after all. After the quartet's sundering in 1964, he
clung on in showbusiness, drifting from pillar to post, from group to
unsatisfactory group. The last straw was a booking in an auditorium
above a pub in High Wycombe with The Diddley Daddies, who'd once
made the finals in a *Ready Steady Go* battle–of–the–bands contest.
Keith joined during the rapid turnover of personnel that had followed
the drummer's defection to Geoff B's Looners early in 1966.

After the usual harrowing soundcheck, Keith showed the others what a hell of a fellow he was by holding down three whiskey–and–cokes and six pints of ale while the support group valiantly over–ran. As the promoter jabbed at his watch, the Daddies stopped trying to sober Moon up, and, emitting a palpable aura of self–loathing, slouched on stage before an audience of nine. Small too was the agreed percentage of the gate. There was also a freak cold spell with heavy rain all day as well as something good on television and a strike by the local newspaper, this precluding advertising.

Glazed listlessness had set in before the opening number's coda. Keith continued to experience fatigue without stimulation as he reacted instinctively to, say, the prelusive 'weeeeeell' from the vocalist that pitched everyone into another twelve–bar rocker and that changeless four–four: a backbeat not even a half–wit could lose. To Moon, the Daddies' stretch on the boards went by as a complete blur like some run–of–the–mill job he'd done for years. Everything sounded the same, mere vibrations dangling in the air.

The strangest feeling came over him as the Daddies' launched into Bo Diddley's 'Who Do You Love' with its relentless shave–and–a–haircut–six–pence rhythm. It was as if he was effectuating a premonition or watching himself in a war film during a battle's 'slow moment' of dreadful clarity. Quite deliberately, Keith overturned his kit and, chuckling to himself, booted again and again at the tom–toms rolling across the floor, and drop–kicked the snare into the wings. He raised aloft the bass drum weight–lifter style and chucked it into the blackness beyond the footlights.

The other musicians were cowering in the wings now. Keith hurled a separated hi–hat at them like a discus as he stumbled about aimlessly, and began next to tear at his clothes. However, the promoter, after looking as though he was about to do something, actually did. With appalled dignity, he strode purposefully into the light. He was too late – for, prior to clenching himself into a foetal position, Moon, glistening with deranged glee, knee–dropped to the floor, splayed out his left hand on the boards, and brought the rim of a crash–cymbal down with all his force onto the digits like a butcher cleaving a chop off a pork loin. The sharp edge and the recoil didn't do his other hand much good either.

Jump–cutting to the mid–1990s, he was a fixture in the saloon bar of the Master Robert, a boozer off the Great West Road that divided Middlesex. There, he rambled with groggy and misplaced pride about his meagre achievements as a member of lost and long–disbanded beat groups. To anyone listening, he reasoned in so many words that they had been as much the embodiment of the Swinging Sixties as The Beatles, just as a drop of water was part of the ocean, all–powerful and immortal.

He'd had everything it took. But for his accident and the correlated destruction of his kit, he'd still be in the business now. It wasn't just that either. If only that season in Hamburg hadn't been cancelled because the organist's Jewish mother wouldn't countenance him setting foot on German soil. If only there hadn't been a power cut when Shel Talmy was there. If only the vocalist hadn't had a sore throat at the Marquee. If only the bass player hadn't written off the van the day before that string of one–nighters with The Small Faces. If only we hadn't lost our way...

One maudlin evening, Keith brings in his photo album, turning the cardboard pages with what was left of his fingers – 'me with Carlo Little, Ritchie Blackmore and Lord Sutch', 'me with Shane Fenton – or "Alvin Stardust" as he started calling himself', 'me and Jerry with Bobby Elliott at the Three Coins in Manchester. Bobby was with Wayne Fontana then, you know...' Those regulars kind enough not to look fed–up still found old Moon, his repeated reminiscences and his re–showings of his pictures, mind–stultifyingly boring, but he didn't care about them any more than a chimp in the zoo does about the people peering through the bars.

Notes

1. *Beat Merchants* by A. Clayson (Blandford, 1995)
2. An amalgam of Los Angeles session musicians, remembered chiefly for 1958's horn–freighted 'Tequila' – also the party– piece of the saxophone–playing frog in the 1960s puppet troupe dominated by Pinky and Perky
3. *The Big Beat* by M. Weinberg (Billboard, 1991)
4. *Rhythm*, June 2001

Lloyd Ryan remembers Keith Moon: *'After the Shane Fenton audition, Moonie and I went for a snack in a nearby cafe, but I didn't see him again until two years later when I was playing in support groups on the same national circuit as The Who – places like Eel Pie Island, the Marquee, even the Cavern.*

I was also teaching drums two days a week in a studio at my old tutor, Maurice Placquet's music equipment shop in Churchfield Road, Acton. Phil Collins was a pupil of mine – and Graham Board, who worked with Bill Wyman and Buck's Fizz, though he's best known for the East Enders theme.

One day, John Entwistle came by with Keith Moon, and he and I tried out a few things. I showed him an easy way to do triplets round the kit – which became a bit of a trademark for him in The Who. He came on a few more occasions. I found him a nice guy, very keen to learn and improve himself – and I couldn't understand all this "wild man" nonsense that came up later.

It's difficult to quantify his ability as a drummer. His timing was faulty. He'd speed up and rush the fills, an extremely loose player. He was a tuneful rather than technical drummer – and he was ideal for The Who, an integral part of the band both musically and as a personality – just as Charlie Watts was in the Stones and Ringo in The Beatles.

Keith was a fan of Gene Krupa, not only for his playing, but the way he looked on stage. Like Krupa too, Keith brought the drums to the front of the overall sound, turned them into a lead instrument. Also, thanks to him playing double–bass drums, Premier had a boom time for kits like that. They were doing so well out of him that they let him have as many kits as he liked to smash up – though he used a Ludwig 400 snare.

'If Everybody Had An Ocean Across The North Circular Road ...': Beachcombing In Post–Rural Middlesex

'Jan and Dean never told it like it really was'– Keith Moon [1]

GIs on passes would burst upon the fun palaces of of central London in garb in which only blacks, spivs and the boldest homosexuals would be seen dead – padded shoulders on double–breasted suits with half–belts at the back, 'spear–point' shirt collars, two–tone shoes and broad, hand–painted ties with Red Indians or baseball players on them. Sartorial visions, they would acknowledge bemused or envious stares with waves of fat wands of cigars.

For youngsters of Keith Moon's inclinations and background, the United States seemed the very wellspring of everything glamorous from the Coca–Cola 'Welcoming A Fighting Man Home From The Wars' – so its hoarding ran – to his mother's mention of The Ink Spots whose humming polyphony had enraptured the London Palladium in 1947 when native music aired on the British Broadcasting Corporation's three national radio stations with their Musicians Union–regulated needle–time, meant quasi–operatic Kathleen Ferrier, *The Pirates Of Penzance* and *Melody Time* with the Northern Dance Orchestra.

Yet, even after the 'generation gap' widened and this new 'teenage' breed started being courted as independent consumers, the BBC as a universal aunt with its stranglehold over the nation's electric media still gave the public only that music that it *ought* to want – hence television's *Black And White Minstrel Show*, Victor Sylvester's strict–tempo *Come Dancing, Spot The Tune* with Marion Ryan, and Cy Grant's calypsos during his slot on the topical *Tonight*. BBC TV's executive body's only concessions to teenagers was *Teleclub*, a 'magazine programme for the under–twenty–ones', containing as it did 'acts by young professional entertainers, sport, interest, a personal problem and "your turn"' [2] with music directed by the avuncular Steve Race.

As Keith approached adolescence himself, he might have supposed that the 'square' sounds he picked up on the wireless was because they were emitted from a cheap make, but, from new Braun transistor to cumbersome radiogram, it was the same on all of them, even when you twiddled the dial from the Home Service to the more agreeable Light Programme. Also catering for the over–thirties there were *The*

Billy Cotton Band Show with its connotations of Sunday lunch–times and resulting armchaired languor; depressing *Sing Something Simple* marking the end of the weekend, and programmes monopolised by such as The Beverley Sisters and Donald Peers ('The Cavalier of Song') as well as musical interludes in series for younger listeners, built round the ilk of ventiloquist's dummy Archie Andrews, 'Mr. Pastry,' and Lancastrian 'schoolboy' Jimmy Clitheroe.

There was little middle ground between 'How Much Is That Doggie In The Window' and 'Love And Marriage'. Now and then there'd be lewdnesses like 'Such A Night' by Johnnie Ray ('The Prince of Wails'), and *Radio Rhythm Club* was permitted one 'folk song' per programme. Sometimes too, you'd catch a watered–down blues, sung with a resident vocalist's plummy gentility, on *Services Calling*, an Entertainments National Service Association (ENSA) series, but, these instances apart, you jumped from nursery rhymes to Frank Sinatra as if the intervening years had been spent in a cultural coma.

The search for anything 'teenage' was as fruitless on Independent Television (ITV) when it began in 1956 with weekly spectaculars headlined by North America's Patti Page ('The Singing Rage') and, straight from some palais bandstand in London, Dickie Valentine in stiff evening dress. While *Round About Ten* was a bit racy in its embrace of Humphrey Lyttelton's Jazz Band, the inclusion of 'The Teenagers,' a winsome boy–girl troupe, in Vera Lynn's *Melody Cruise*, was something of a false dawn.

Nevertheless, after rock 'n' roll infiltrated the BBC's sedentary wavelengths, Keith Moon's imagination was captured as surely as Don Quixote's was by the castles of Castile. How could anyone old enough to have borne the brunt of the Depression or fought Hitler have guessed that it would mean more to Keith than anything else. Nothing – women, money, you name it – would come close. His wasn't a scholarly nature, but, almost as if he was embroiled in formal research, he would delve as far as he was able beneath the showbusiness veneer of rock 'n' rollers he admired.

Evening after evening, he'd catalogue and gloat over his growing collection of vinyl treasures. Having invested an amount of cash that was equal to a fortnight's pay for his Saturday delivery round for a local butcher, Keith intended to get his money's worth from every one of these new plastic ten– or twelve–inch 33 1/3 long–players (LPs), spinning them to dust, and finding much to notice, study and compare.

As for singles, while he bought the latest by Elvis Presley, Tommy Steele, Little Richard and other hitmakers, further purchases were quite erudite. His predeliction for escapist horror and space movies in the 1950s was reflected in a liking for gimmicky US singles like 'The Fang' by Nervous Norvus and Billy Lee Riley's 'Flyin' Saucers Rock 'N' Roll'. With the turn of the decade came questions about extra–terrestrial life, courtesy of the Ran–Dells' 'Martian Hop', and Gene Vincent reprimanding his woman for 'messing around with those Martian Men' on 'Spaceship To Mars', showcased in the 1962 movie, *It's Trad Dad.*

Back on Earth, The Hollywood Argyles' 'Short Shorts' had been quoted among topical musical vignettes in 1958's 'The Purple People Eater' by Sheb Wooley [3]. 'The Monster Mash' by Bobby 'Boris' Pickett and the Crypt–Kickers would have a similar effect. Both tangential and capable of full integration into any pop era, this timeless narrative was a US Number One in 1962, but, when first issued, missed the charts completely in Britain. So did the attempts by Nervous Norvus, Billy Lee Riley, The Ran–Dells and The Hollywood Argyles. A million–seller at home, 'Purple People Eater' wasn't an especially big hit In Britain – and neither were many 45s relating to the musical genre that, more than any other, sent Keith Moon into a reverie that no–one else could penetrate.

Among exceptions were two instrumentals, 'Pipeline' by The Chantays and The Surfaris' 'Wipe Out' – hinged on machine–gun–like tom–tomming. When these both reached 1963's Top Twenty, it was a concurrence thought worthy of a general *Record Mirror* feature about a fad that geography prevented from catching on in London and the Home Counties. Its concluding sentence was 'Don't let the fact that you can't stand on a surf board put you off the excellent surfing records'. [4]

A year later, 'I Get Around' by the consequently much–copied Beach Boys climbed as high in the UK charts as 'Pipeline' and 'Wipe Out', but whither the Boys' 'Surfin' USA', 'Fun Fun Fun' and 'Californian Girls' – North American smashes that were to become eventually as well known over here? Jan and Dean's 'Surf City' likewise fought shy of the Top Twenty as did like releases that, loaded with technical jargon, celebrated surfing, its companion sport, hot–rod racing, and other pleasures available to teenagers on the USA's West Coast. Chugging rock 'n' roll accompaniment was overlaid with vastly infectious melodies and soaring chorale, freighted with interweaving harmonies and crowned by a cool cruising falsetto.

In a pre–video age, Keith sat through a particular teen–pic with the customary balloon–headed story–line, just to savour less than thirty seconds of Jan and Dean. Yet, as it had been with classic rock when he was still at school, there were no specific boyhood heroes. Yet Keith worshipped the form *per se* as other lads might footballer Danny Blanchflower or boxer Henry Cooper – the Londoner who, at Wembley Empire Pool on 18 June 1963, floored 'Louisville Lip' Cassius Clay, who was saved by the bell, in the third round.

How do such obsessions start? How about yours? Was it because your first remotely romantic encounter – a chaperoned kiss under the mistletoe – was soundtracked by *Session With The Dave Clark Five*. Perhaps a teacher on whom you had a crush supported Sheffield Wednesday.

Keith Moon never revealed whether any incident or person turned him onto surf music, only that, in so many words, the spiral into dependency become breakneck. As well as listening to what was in the grooves of the discs, Moon became preoccupied with their creators, seeking insights into artistic conduct, clarification of obscurer melodic – and, if relevant, lyrical – by–ways, and generally searching for information about what made the musicians tick. The nearest he could get in the early 1960s was reading what articles, interviews and snippets of news there were in *Record Mirror, New Musical Express* and, when no–one was looking, *Mirabelle, Boyfriend* and further of his sisters' comics.

What began as a hobby becomes a craving, almost a religion. he developed an ability to talk with great authority about his special interest, and was baffled that others didn't find it just as absorbing. In his bedroom, shelves groaned beneath the weight of his surf record collection as he gorged himself with hours of listening over and over again to the same discs that had come not only from the high street record shop, but, via mail–order import, from the most remote independent record companies, and had wended their way across the time zones from the 'Sunshine State'.

Sometimes he'd focus on maybe only the guitar or bass, then just the drums. Furthermore, while he enjoyed the tactile sensation of handling the packagings of, say, Jan and Dean's *Drag City, Little Deuce Coupe* – The Beach Boys' 'car' album – and, less often, the Surfaris LP that cashed in on 'Wipe Out', he also made myriad private observations whilst learning much from sleeve notes, composing credits and listings of personnel. No detail was too minor to be less than fascinating.

Both before and after joining The Who, his investigations led him to the canons of associated artists, some of them very obscure. Horror-surf crossovers, 'Ghost Surfin'' – a 1964 opus from Bobby Rydell's Philadelphian (!) backing outfit – and 'Ghost Hop' by The Surfmen nestled in Keith's record rack, along with 'The Swag', a revival of a Link Wray number, from The Tornados [5], pressed by a fly–by–night record label after taping in a studio complex located in a back–of–beyond Californian desert town under the aegis of none other than twenty–one–year–old Frank Zappa, someone who would loom small – but loom all the same – in Moon's legend

He would discover years later that The Surfmen's guitarist, Ray Hunt, was to pass briefly through the ranks of Zappa's nascent Mothers Of Invention. He had known already that a Fender Stratocaster had sparkled under Hunt's fingers in The Surfmen, but in the wider world, this electric instrument would be forever associated with Dick Dale, the 'King of the Surf Guitar' whose influence has been acknowledged by such as Steve Vai, Stevie Ray Vaughan and, apparently, Jimi Hendrix, as much as Hank B. Marvin of The Shadows' similar metallic picking and copious use of tremelo arm was by Pete Townshend.

Dale's contribution to the soundtrack of *Pulp Fiction* has since assisted him in arising anew as elderly icon of a new generation of fans, transfixed by the driving riffs, *staccato* double–picking and depth of sound – punctuated by trademark shuddering *glissado* descents – from the thick–gauge six–string he dubbed 'The Beast'.

Keith Moon, however, was a 'Dick Head' from way back, and, during his residency in southern California, was genuinely charmed to meet and record with Dale – who, as on–going conversations revealed, also began as a drummer and brass player 'after I'd dented my Mom's cookie cans with cutlery, beating along to big bands on the radio. Then I bought myself a trumpet.' However, it was the youth's ability as a guitarist – 'I played it like a drum kit: different rhythms, the hi–hats, the snare, the turnarounds' – that gained him a three–year residency at the Rendezvous, a coastline ballroom in suburban Los Angeles, where, even with their maiden 45 in the local Top Forty, The Beach Boys were grateful to be booked as Dale's unpaid intermission act. Known admirers, they'd pay respects over the next few years with renditions of 'Let's Go Trippin', 'Misirlou' and further Dale sound–pictures of peacock heroics when shooting the curl.

After topping the city charts, Dale's 'Let's Go Trippin' hovered in *Billboard*'s *Hot 100* for several weeks – and, if follow–ups were less successful, the buzz from California was sufficient to make an LP, *Surfer's Choice*, a worthwhile exercise. Its spin–off 45 was 'Misirlou', which livened up beach parties from Honolulu to Miami. Next, a vocal piece, 'Mr. Peppermint Man' – anticipating Roger Daltrey's 'My G–G–G–Generation' stuttering by two years – preceded a cameo in *Beach Party*, a movie in which, so foyer posters proclaimed, 'the urge meets the surge!'.

Thus this phase of Dick Dale's career peaked. There were to be no more *Hot 100* strikes after 1963's 'The Scavenger' from *Checkered Flag*. Yet hot–rod racing also left its mark on a later LP, *The Eliminator*, for which Beach Boys' associate Gary Usher was reeled in as producer to make it more 'contemporary'. Somehow, his studio exactitudes made Dick sound uncannily like any other surf instrumental exponent. Certainly, the *au naturel* excitement of the Rendezvous bashes never came across on disc. 'That's why I quit recording,' Dick told Keith on first acquaintance, 'Dick Dale was sick of engineers telling him they've been doing it for twenty years, and putting limiters on the guitar so that it sounded tinny.'

More of a kindred spirit to Moon than clean–living teetotaler Dale was Dennis Wilson, The Beach Boys drummer – and a sexual braggart who, on completing a tour with the group, would come home to his wife with gonorrhea, and upset her further with a continued membership of a 'beaver patrol' he called 'the Golden Penetrators'. Wilson's drug addiction and overall unreliability caused him to be suspended from The Beach Boys prior to him drowning in a local marina in 1983, his judgement of the water's temperature and his own fatigue impaired by too much vodka. [6]

So much for the Californian Dream. When ignorant of its underside, Keith had visualised some sort of Eldorado – golden sand, endless summer, two girls for every boy – far beyond the the sphere of the grey–clouded get–up, get–to–work, get–home, get–to–bed groundhog days that passed for a life when he was at Ultra Electronics and then as an office boy at British Gypsum, a plastering firm in central London .

Yet he found respite from Dullsville by insinuating his way, late in 1962, into what, with a little friendly persuasion, could be as close as he could possibly expect any local combo to be to the sound that wafted from California. Middlesex wasn't renowned for the size and formation of its waves, and, despite the name, Clyde Burns and the Beachcombers were, essentially, an across–the–board beat group. However, they were amenable to inserting a couple of surfing classics into a repertoire that was otherwise geared to embrace good–old–good–ones, novelties like The Coasters' 'Little Egypt' – which gave Keith an excuse to dress up – and the passing joys of an increasingly less North American Top Twenty.

Even as Merseybeat spread like a disease across British pop, 1963's charts still included slop–ballads that your grandmother liked by insipidly handsome boys–next–door such as Ronnie Carroll and Mark Wynter, and continuing variations on the Twist – as much the rage world–wide as traditional jazz had been in Britain alone. Classic rock was elbowed aside by the hipper regional outfits for renderings of 'Twist And Shout' (and just plain 'Shout') by The Isley Brothers, Dee Dee Sharp's 'Mashed Potato Time' and, from The Orlons, 'Shimmy Shimmy' and 'The Wah–Watusi.' The subject matter was less directly to do with mobility but the beat essentially the same in such as The Marvelettes' 'Please Mr. Postman,' 'You Really Got A Hold On Me' by The Miracles and The Contours' 'Do You Love Me'.

These would become the common property of countless other groups after the Olympic flame of Merseybeat was carried to every nook and cranny of these islands. As The Beachcombers also familiarised themselves with The Beatles' self–penned hits too, they consolidated rather than developed their surf material. Nevertheless, as long as Keith survived as a professional entertainer, he mined that seam of pop, as exemplified most conspicuously on 1966's *Ready Steady Who* EP with its covers of 'Batman' and the alarming 'Bucket "T"' – both sides of the most recent Jan and Dean single, forever on the fitted record–player in The Who's customised Austin Princess – and a xerox of The Beach Boys' xerox of The Regents' 'Barbara Ann'. Lead vocals on the latter two items were not by Roger Daltrey, but their chief advocate – and the effect of an any–old–how spontaneity over expertise was not unattractive, however uneuphonious Keith's counter–tenor was without electronic assistance. Imagine an excerpt from the soundtrack of an Ealing re–make of *American Graffiti*, and you'll get the idea.

What might have been described in mid–1960s pop journalist parlance as 'blues chasers', these selections were not as much at odds with The Who's – and the beat boom in general's – predominantly rhythm–and–blues determination as you might think. 'Wipe Out' was heard over the opening credits to the first series of *Ready Steady Go*; The Yardbirds' second single would be what drummer Jim McCarty described as a 'surfing' overhaul of Sonny Boy Williamson's 'Good Morning Little Schoolgirl', and 'Help Me Rhonda'–esque *baw–baw–baw*s were to rear up in 'What To Do' on the Stones' *Aftermath* album.

Among more blatant domestic responses were Episode Six's 'Mighty Morris Ten' hot–rod send–up, plus competent versions of 'Pipeline', 'Wipe Out' and Jan and Dean's 'The Little Old Lady From Pasadena' by, respectively, Bristol's boss group The Eagles, The Saints – who evolved into The Peddlers – and The Freshmen, an Irish showband whose crack at The Beach Boys–via–The Rivingtons' 'Papa–Oom–Maw–Maw' in 1967 was plugged on every pop showcase going on Radio–Telefis Eirrann.

Four years earlier, Billy J. Kramer's Dakotas had crept into the UK Top Twenty with a Chantays–styled arrangement of the main title theme to *The Cruel Sea*. Not blessed with hits , but adored in their native Birmingham, Mike Sheridan and his Nightriders absorbed surf to a degree that few other beat groups – notably Dagenham's Tony Rivers and the Castaways – did, while The Surfers – who supported The Who at the Rhodes Centre, Bishop's Stortford one October Saturday in 1965 – and Cardiff's Surfbeats went the whole hog. [7]

Moon may have given such outfits his blessing, and been pleased to note that surf music was still alive in the British–dominated US Top Thirty in 1965 with such as 'New York's A Lonely Town (When You're The Only Surfer Boy)' by The Tradewinds. [8] However, he wasn't so sure about 1966's *Pet Sounds*, the 'Good Vibrations' 'pocket symphony' and other masterworks by a Beach Boys becoming more and more estranged from the surf. If anything, he was more taken with

US acts such as The Turtles, The Association and The Happenings, who had, in their different ways, tapped into what became known as 'sunshine pop' by borrowing from the Boys' (and The Four Seasons') neatly–dovetailed grasp of vocal counterpoint.

Had money been an object, Keith would have started listening in advance to successive Beach Boys discs before it changed hands at the record store. Gradually, he was to no longer treat the mildest disparagement of them as a mortal insult. Yet, when they were headlining hours of pop at something called the 'Garden Party' at Crystal Palace, open to the sky for sixteen thousand rain–drenched customers on a June Saturday in 1972, he'd be observed in the artists' enclosure, chatting with proud familiarity to Dennis, Al, Mike, Bruce, Carl *et al.*

A more legitimate colour than mere ligging had been given to Moon's presence in that he had been appointed the so–called Garden Party's master–of–ceremonies. Taking his responsibilites very seriously, he had brought along several different stage outfits, and was quite prepared to keep the chat going during all the hanging about as road crews collided with each other during endless centuries of equipment changeovers, soundtracked by thuds, amplified mutterings, electronic crackles and the high–pitched *peeeeeeeee!* of feedback. No question, it was a bastard of a day. By mid–afternoon, everything was well behind schedule, but, if no Ken Dodd, Keith – a matchstick figure framed by sky–clawing scafolding – proved an entertaining interlocutor, improvising round verbal themes like a jazzer round a melody, and unfurling quite a polished patter, discernable even through a muffled sound system.

It became clear that he had a soft spot for the main support group, twelve–piece Sha Na Na. Having taken them under his wing, he was now going so far as to pitch in with them on stage. Moreover, they'd been flattered, but, initially, not quite comfortable on the occasions when, following them round Britain during the tour that had preceded the Crystal Palace show, he'd chosen to join in the larks in their coach rather than be chauffeured in a limousine like the star he was. Finally, on Keith's recommendation, Sha Na Na would be John Lennon's choice to open his One–For–One charity concert in New York a year later.

They had emerged from a Columbia University glee club in 1968 with a repertoire derived exclusively from the 1950s and earliest 1960s, and a stage act that embraced a jiving contest for audience participants.

Looking the anachronistic part – gold lamé, brilliantined cockades, drainpiped hosiery *et al* – a fully professional Sha Na Na were rock 'n' roll revival latecomers, but were on a par with Flash Cadillac and the Continental Kids and Cat Mother and his All–Night News Boys as the most prominent representatives of the US wing of the movement, whose examples were an encouragement to archivist–performers such as Darts, Shakin' Stevens and The Stray Cats to further the cause of a seemingly outmoded musical form.

A Surprise Hit at Woodstock on the afternoon before The Who's dawn performance, Sha Na Na blended slick choreography and a harlequinade of costumes with unadulterated olde tyme rock 'n' roll – with lead vocals from a pool of no less than five gyrating singers, backed by instrumentalists with lurid *noms de theatre* like Jocko Marcellino and Screamin' Scott Symon. If the dusty original 78s and 45s had emotional significance, Sha Na Na's vinyl retreads would emit a peculiar afterglow, but a self–composed number 'Bounce In Your Buggy' from 1972's *The Night Is Still Young*, was a near–hit in Britain; the combo's onstage recreations of old sounds were fun, and, when he experienced them, the mind of their most high profile fan may have slipped back to Wembley, *circa* 1962, when the world was young. [9]

It seemed so far away these days: Alperton Secondary Modern, Screaming Lord Sutch at the Town Hall, British Gypsum, Clyde Burns and all the other people and places that had informed the years of struggle and the unbelievable outcome. Keith had stayed in touch with the other former Beachcombers, who had never begrudged him his run of luck. In reciprocation, when switching from whiskey–and–Coke to neat brandy down the Speakeasy, Keith was prone to plunging into orgies of maudlin reminiscences. You could stand him a feed in the Ritz but he'd still be sentimental about when he used to small–talk on the pavement with The Beachcombers, while chomping newspapered fish–and chips.

Back in the sitting room of the studio flat in up–market Primrose Hill where he'd moved with his child–bride and their daughter late in 1966, Keith Moon's hi–fi would pulsate to the kind of music The Beachcombers used to play. He didn't listen to much else.

Notes

1. *Rolling Stone*, November 1972
2. *Radio Times*, 14 July 1956
3. Alias 'Pete Nolan', the Steady Older Man in the television cowboy series, *Rawhide*
4. *Record Mirror*, 24 August 1963
5. Of similar vintage but spelt slightly differently to the makers of 'Telstar'
6. Ringo Starr was amongst the guest drummers that got The Beach Boys through an eponymous 1984 album and existing stage dates, following Wilson's death.
7. At the end of the century, British surf music would still be going strong with Bracknell's Surfin' Lungs and Tyne–and–Wear's Interceptors amongst its brand–leaders.
8. A 'four–strong group from Providence' according to their press release – but actually Vinnie Poncia and Pete Anders, a multi–tracked professional team from a Big Apple songwriting 'factory. After forming a songwriting partnership with Ringo Starr in the early 1970s, Poncia was to enter Moon's social circle in California.
9. By 1974, however, Sha Na Na's nascent vision, once unmotivated by financial reward or personal popularity, had degenerated to a dreary repetition that took its toll in discord and unresolvable internal problems.

Alan Holmes remembers Keith Moon (Sounds Incorporated): Keith liked to have 'Ride The Wild Surf' by Jan and Dean on automatic replay whilst shagging.

I remember us playing with The Who in Leeds at either the Tramshed or at the University. Their first number had Keith on lead vocals. I think it was The Beach Boys' 'I Get Around'.

There's also a story I heard of him and John Lennon glueing a coin to the pavement in Oxford Street, and heckling people who tried to pick it up from Lennon's Rolls, which had blacked–out windows and speakers mounted under the mudguards.'

'Zoot Suit': Moon And Mod

*'The Mod era came along and we changed our name to the In
Betweens. Suddenly, Johnny had a Mod haircut, and Mickey
Marston, the other guitarist, started wearing a Parka and hanging
'round with scooter people. The rest of us hated the Who and all that'
– Dave Hill (Johnny and the Vendors)* [1]

For a lad from Wembley, Soho was quite exotic in the early 1960s
with its bistros, strip clubs and the aroma of percolated coffee and
mega–tar French cigarettes. It also contained the 2 I's, which now had
the tell–tale signs of having known better days with its yellowing photo montage of Tommy Steele, Cliff Richard, Marty Wilde, Adam Faith
and lesser lights who probably hadn't been near the place since gaining their respective recording contracts as would–be English Presleys.
In the ascendant was the open–all–night Flamingo where prototype
Mods, even back in 1959, would recognise each other by their clean,
short–haired pseudo–suavity and whim–conscious dress sense.

It was flattery of a kind that Moon was accepted not as a suburban
stripling barely old enough to quaff a cherryade on the premises, but as
just one of the crowd when first he ventured into a Flamingo all–night-
er. The headlining act was Georgie Fame and the Blue Flames – who
Clyde Burns and the Beachcombers were to support there on several
occasions.

For the most part, the Middlesex group assumed a sharp corporate
persona by garbing themselves in uniform black suede winkle–pickers and starched white hankerchiefs protruding from the top pockets
of bronze suits – though Keith wore his *gold lamé* one also bespoken by Cecil Gee, tailor to the stars. Non–showbiz Mods were clothed
elsewhere along Charing Cross Road and the surrounding streets of
Soho where it was easier to keep apace with the times. Unlike Sloane
Rangers who were to be ruled by seasons, true Mod was open–ended
and in constant flux. It was, so Pete Meadon, The Who's first manager,
would pontificate, 'clean–living under difficult circumstances.' [2]

See, everything had to be just so: all or nothing. The back vents
on double–breasted bumfreezers were precisely five inches one week,
seven the next. At the Flamingo on Saturday, you had to be electric–
blue Italian. Go back the following Thursday, and it'd be US collegiate

Ivy League. How wide are lapels now? I only bought this shirt six days ago, but it's got a *pointed* tab collar, which means I can't ever wear it again.

Essentially, Mods existed only in the capital – at least until London–style boutiques sprang up in other cities and the bigger towns, and individuals like Reg Presley of The Troggs, then unknown outside their native Andover, became the local fashion leader, thanks to visits to his London in–laws via Carnaby Street. After Mod reached the masses – principally via *Ready Steady Go* and pirate radio – around the middle of 1964, you could be merely a few steps behind Swinging London with gear from the nearest high street.

Furthermore, most beat groups, even if olde tyme rock 'n' rollers at heart, projected themselves as at least cursory Mods, some giving themselves *de riguer* abstract non–pluralized names as necessary: The Accent, The End, The Static, The Frame, The Gass, The Cat, The Move, The Buzz, The Carnaby and so forth. With practical approbation from The Animals, Stafford's Hipster Image secured a one–shot 45 with Decca, and an outfit from central Birmingham with the unmitigated audacity to actually call themselves The Mods thumbed noses at a rash of other opportunists by topping a 'Local Group' popularity poll in *Jackie*.

Mod, nonetheless, had become as unstoppable as bubonic plague. Besides, being a Mod was a soft option because your parents were less likely to moan about your turnout. They would even help pay for a motor–scooter as long as you didn't get into fights with rough boys in leather windcheaters or *smoked* those Purple Hearts that you read about in the papers. On the strength of appearance, so–called 'Mods' wouldn't get turned away from the parish dance. They'd even earn praise from the vicar for looking so smart. As Keith discovered at Ultra Electronics – and David Cook, later 1970s film actor and pop star David Essex, in a corresponding works in Ilford, you could have the most menial job in Christendom and still look the part without inviting the sack. At the same time, you could make yourself known to other initiates by signs as conspiratorial as a freemason's handshake. Some Mods identified themselves by simply leaving all coat buttons undone except the top one.

With middle class bohemians generally heading for the G Club in darkest Ealing, the clubs of inner London had worked up a sharper–

dressed, principally male clientele, usually from a lower social caste. With their deepest musical roots in an alien US culture, groups like Clyde Burns and his Beachcombers were tolerated, and were regarded as Mods by bumpkins in Wembley, Uxbridge and Staines where all the excesses in which metropolitan Mods allegedly indulged belonged to speculation while sharing a cigarette behind school bike sheds. I know someone whose sister's friend once *touched* Georgie Fame.

In regions further beyond the pale of London, the 1950s wouldn't end until 1966, and 'Mod' clothes – that no Londoner had been seen dead in for perhaps a year – weren't much more than gang uniforms in which no pretence was made towards dandification or keeping up with the on–the–spot Carnaby Street (and, later, King's Road) front–runners. You *could* be ostensibly 'in' as long as you had Chelsea boots, hipster flairs in Billy Bunter check and a corduroy jacket with faint faecal odour – which were worn to every local hop until you outgrew them. Nevertheless, some would follow Roger Daltrey's early enterprise in customising clothes to ersatz Mod standards on his mother's sewing machine.

Lambrettas with up to half–a–dozen mirrors would phut in Parka–ed cavalcades along country roads – as would the greasier mechanical steeds of Rockers – later demeaningly called 'Greasers' – in their less mutable costumes of real or imitation leather jackets, jeans, motorbike boots and T–shirts. Though forgoing the oiled, duck–tailed cockades, Rocker girls sometimes dressed the same but more frequently it was flared skirts and stilettos.

Their taste in music was the classic rock 'n' roll on the juke–box of ordained hang–outs like the Top Ten cafe in Aldershot, the Rendezvous in nearby Fleet and the North Circular Road's Ace, where interlopers were subjected to gormless hostility. Among leading Rocker outfits were The Nashville Teens from the stockbroker Surrey town of Weybridge, and The Rockin' Berries, whose vocalist, Clive Lea, had defied all comers in an 'Elvis Of The Midlands' talent contest. From Lord Sutch's Savages, bass player Tony Dangerfield was singled out by Joe Meek, who 'visualized me as another Billy Fury. To promote my first 45, I was introduced to Vicki Wickham, producer of *Ready Steady Go*, but she decided that my image – jet–black quiff, mohair suit and so on – was too retrogressive for the show'.

More than Tony's 'I've Seen Such Things', 'Terry', a 'beat–ballad' by Keith Moon's friend, Twinkle caught, if not the mood, then *a* mood of 1964. If a fixture on the juke–box at the Ace, it too suffered a banning on *Ready Steady Go*, not for the death content so much as its non-conformity to the programme's Mod specifications – and the inherent confusion of a London dolly–bird in John Lennon cap, striped jumper and kinky boots – 'I never wear anything except boots' ran one press release – slumming it in the Ton–Up cafe with a leather boy whose idea of a good time was perhaps an evening on the dodgems at some backdated funfair in the sticks. It was like *West Side Story*, wasn't it: a Mod loving a Rocker?

Just as 'Terry' put *Ready Steady Go*'s producer in a quandary, Who singles may not have sounded completely out of place in the Ace, even if the group could always count on *Ready Steady Go* – as vital in its way as *Oh Boy!* had been in the late 1950s – whenever they had a new release to plug. Indeed, as instanced by Moon's unbothered string-pulling to procure an interview on the programme for visiting Beach Boy Bruce Johnson, *Ready Steady Go* belonged more to The Who than The Beatles for reasons summarised by sixteen–year–old David Cook, a *habitue* of the Flamingo, which was now advertising itself as 'the Swinging Club of Swinging London'. He considered that The Beatles' compromising four–song spot on 1963's Royal Variety Show 'meant that they couldn't be any good'. [3]

Cook's malfunctioning scooter came to a halt during a summer drive with Mod mates in 1964 from the East End to Clacton, 'leaving me to run the risk of being pummelled by passing Rockers in sad lay–bys.' [4] On the previous 29 March, a tabloid had run a front page story of holiday-makers cowering as Rockers and Mods fought their first major battle. This instance of scuffles, stonings and deckchair–hurling on the beaches of Clacton by the two principal factions in mid–1960s British youth culture, seems in retrospect as portentious in microcosm as the Anglo–Saxon Chronicle's entry for 789 AD about 'three ships of the Northmen' attacking Weymouth Bay, and precipitating further–reaching Viking ravages that would trouble Britain over the next three centuries.

In truth, emnity between the two tribes was never as virulent as journalists under the editorial lash made out. Usually, provincial Mods and Rockers would simply congregate at opposite ends of a cafe – though there were still ructions at dances, and at the predetermined invasions of seaside resorts during bank holiday weekends. 'It wasn't so much violence as hordes of young people running around and looking for the excitement that others were committing,' expounded John Albon, an eighteen–year–old in Brighton in 1964, 'We were like a huge mobile audience though in fact we were the main act. There were fights but they were kind of hit–and–run. Nevertheless, the tradition of police manning–up for public holidays continued right the way through to the mid–1960s.' [5]

After the stage act aligned with terrific Top Ten singles – 'I Can't Explain', 'Anyway Anyhow Anywhere', 'My Generation', 'Substitute' – had made The Who pin–ups of would–be Mods everywhere, Kit Lambert and Chris Stamp became all too aware of the publicity inherent in booking the group to play Mod strongholds in Margate, Clacton, Hastings and anywhere else where there was likely to be newsworthy shoreline trouble with Rockers, especially when a new record release was pending.

Yet business rivals alighting with nit–picking hope on the remotest indication of The Who's fall had been unable to uncover any evidence of backhanders for so many spins a week of the inaugural 'I Can't Explain' on pirate Radio Caroline, which had commenced operations the previous Easter from a ship anchored off–limits in the North Sea.

Saturation plugging of new discs by this – and Radio Atlanta, Radio London, Scotland's Radio 242, the short–lived Radio Sutch, Radio Invicta and Radio Essex plus other stations broadcasting mostly just beyond the kingdom's territorial waters – pushed many deserving artists (and undeserving ones) into at least the lower rungs of the charts until August 1967 when the Marine Offences Act became law, and listeners would recall exactly where they were, and what they were doing during Radio London's consequent final hour. Caroline, however, soldiered on for another year, its presenters' cheerfulness on air belying the starker realities of creaking cordage, engine room reek, seasickness, mayday messages and the underlying physical and legal insecurity. It was on its last legs when some of the daft pirate jingles were incorporated into *The Who Sell Out*, then the group's work–in–progress.

The Who thus acknowledged its debt to pirate radio, but the US soul music that had filled much of the group's early performaces had been at least as advantaged – because, unlike the BBC, the disc–jockeys tended to spin the originals rather than domestic syndications. This reflected an understanding that, when hardcore Mods were poncing themselves up for a night out, it wouldn't be Fender's Orieles' 'Turn On Your Love Light', 'Seventh Son' by Southampton's Soul Agents and First Gear's 'The In Crowd' warming up the Dansette, but the respective blueprints by Bobby Bland, Mose Allison and Dobie Gray. This didn't mean that the British covers weren't worthy, only that it was cooler to at least *say* you preferred the US versions. Yet, when Mods were grooving to whatever British outfit was playing the Flamingo, just because they weren't eating the same quality of musical food, it didn't mean they were starving.

Anyway, to quote the title of a 1967 single by Ben E. King, what is soul – apart from maybe the most abused expression in music? Is it someone who sings as though he needs to clear his throat? Is it Roger Daltrey's strangulated passion conveying the impression that he's as excited by the notion of imminent sexual congress as James Brown? Is it the West Indian next door lilting a never–ending 'Stand By Me' as he creosotes the toolshed – or the hammy ritualism that most of the Motown and Stax revues exercized in the mid–1960s? Let me hear you say 'yeah'.

One more question: although they specialised in Mod music, were The Who ever *bona fide* Mods? If they were, they belonged surely to the greasiest end of the spectrum. After Mod faded, they felt it was safe to insert Detours crowdpleasers like Eddie Cochran's 'Summertime Blues' and Johnny Kidd's climactic 'Shakin' All Over' into the set. It was also OK for Keith to say he liked esoteric exponents of rock 'n' roll such as Link Wray and Creedence Clearwater Revival. By 1973, this was compounded by his and Townhend's contributions to *That'll Be The Day*, the 1973 film set in the late 1950s. That same year, John Entwistle's Rigor Mortis paid vinyl respects with renditions of Little Richard's 'Lucille', Elvis Presley's 'Hound Dog'. Johnny Cymbal's novel 'Mr. Bass Man' and self–composed 'Gimme That Rock 'N' Roll'.

Even if this apparent *volte–face* had taken place in 1965, it's likely that The Who would have weathered the storm, owing to the fundamentally toothless nature of Mod. Witness the sudden isolation by his peers of the central character in The Who's own celluloid retrospective of the era, *Quadrophenia*. Moreover, when entities with names like The Lambrettas, The Merton Parkas and, gawd help us, The Low Numbers were active during the Mod Revival's 1979 zenith, The Who's concert at the Conference Centre in Brighton – the town that hosted unwillingly many of the old campaigns against the Rockers – was packed with *nouveau* Mods – mostly spottier and punier than the original article – but Pete and Roger's derisive catcalling of the 'We are the Mods' doggerel was unchallenged. Fifteen years earlier, the overall response might have been the same, though Mods to their very souls like *Quadrophenia*'s 'Jimmy Cooper' – staring, humourless creatures anyway – may have felt betrayed.

Notes

1. A Wolverhampton unit connected genealogically to Slade
2. *Sunday Times*, 28 November 2004
3. *Melody Maker*, 2 November 1971
4. *A Charmed Life: The Autobiography Of David Essex* (Orion, 2002)
5. *Beat Merchants* by A. Clayson (Blandford, 1995)

Dick Taylor remembers Keith Moon (The Pretty Things): *It must have been about 1966 when Keith and I were at a party in Surrey hosted by Mike McGear. We found a set of bow and arrows – the real deal, not a toy – and then we spotted Rod Stewart – Rod the Mod, as he was then – preening himself in front of a mirror in another room. The door was ajar, but he didn't notice us.*

We debated whether or not to shoot an arrow at Rod to break the spell of his narcissism. After some procrastination, we took aim, but finally bottled out.

Not long after that, Keith was at my flat in Fulham the night before The Pretty Things had to go to Denmark. He crashed out, and in the morning, I was bent double in excruciating pain with what turned out to be a kidney stone. Nothing would do, but Keith insisted on driving me in his Rolls to the nearby St. Stephens' hospital for emergency treatment.

'I've Been Away:' Moonrise Over Sweden

*'Med Scandtzes basta Keith Moon–imitation och
Lagerberg pa ostyrig feedback–gitarr' – Lennart
Persson's sleeve notes to* The Tages, 1964–68 CD.[1]

Pop is an erratic business. This was especially so in Scandinavia during the mid–1960s. While they couldn't get arrested in Britain, The Renegades, an otherwise unsung outfit from Droitwich, topped the Finnish charts with a cover of The Sorrows' 'Take A Heart'. Another case study could be that of The Moontrekkers who, after their solitary week in the UK Top Fifty – with 1961's 'Night Of The Vampire' – had been and gone, could stroll unrecognised through a supermarket in their home London suburb of Muswell Hill. They had been on the point of disbanding when a 1963 single, 'Moondust', swept into the Swedish Top Twenty.

That, however, was nothing to the triumphs of The Downliners Sect from Twickenham who, if lost among the rhythm–and–blues also–rans they had influenced at home, found themselves suddenly at Number One in Sweden with 'Little Egypt' (by coincidence, Clyde Burns and the Beachcombers' opening number when Keith Moon was with them). Further smashes put the Sect briefly and debatably ahead of The Beatles there – to the degree that an imposter calling himself 'Keith Grant' – after the Sect's singing bass player – based himself in Gothenberg where he demanded and received massive engagement fees as leader of his Sect–like R&B ensemble, Train.

It would be in Sweden too that, of all European territories, The Who gouged the most lurid wound, deluging its Top Ten three or four singles at a time and undertaking quasi–royal treks around the country, starting with a flying visit in October 1965 in which they confounded expectations by *not* breaking a single drum stick, guitar string or, indeed, any of the equipment borrowed from a mightily relieved support outfit. However, drawing a record–breaking audience of eleven thousand in an outdoor stadium in Stockholm the following summer, they delivered the required feedback–ridden, loudspeaker–stabbing, microphone–on–cymbal goods during what was, historically, Keith's first performance with a double–bass drum kit.

The next day in Kungsor's Kungsparken, the *Eskilstuna Kuriren* newspaper reported only a cymbal stand and snare–drum falling over. Like conjurer Tommy Cooper's comic nervous procrastinations prior to a complicated trick, there persisted a 'Will they? Won't they?' suspense wherever the 'My Generation' finale for the remaining four shows on this expedition loomed. Nevertheless, the closest The Who came to wrecking their gear was during the final date at a gala in Orebro, plagued by gremlins, mosquitoes, June humidity and bouncers laying into a crowd drunk on local moonshine.

Despite Townshend swearing that The Who would never work in Sweden again after that, the group were back again in 1966's cold, wet autumn for a punishing seven concerts in five days, memorable for their unprecedented loudness and Moon who, wrote Malmo's *Sydsvenskan* journal, 'looked as if he had come out of a shower after only a few songs.' [2]

Box–office receipts remained astronomical, but The Who were turning into as common a forthcoming attraction in Sweden as they'd been around the west London suburbs in 1964. Like London buses, if you missed a tour, there'd be another one along soon, if you waited. Yet, after 1967, appearances in Sweden were rare, partly because of the breakthrough and necessary concentration on the more lucrative United States. Nonetheless, this or that latest Who single continued to be plugged scrupulously via promo film on *Popside*, a Swedish Broadcasting Corporation television magazine as vital in its way as *Ready Steady Go* and Germany's *Beat Club*.

Furthermore, with the genuine article unavailable, an aptly–titled Who pastiche, 'Guess Who', reared up in the recorded portfolio of The Tages, one of the country's own top groups. There came too the flattery and annoyance of attempted pre–emption by local hopefuls such as The Hi–Balls who copied 'I'm A Boy' note–for–note, and – with a lead vocalist sounding even less like he understood the words – The Lunatics with 'Pictures Off Lily' (*sic*). Misprounced lyrics also marred – or brightened – 'La–La–La Lies' by Lee Kings and 1968's 'Mary Ann With The Shaky Hand' by The Troublemakers. After getting those lush Scouse harmonies off to a stentorian 'T' on Lennon and McCartney's 'Tip Of My Tongue', The Mascots too latched onto The Who with a workmanlike 'So Sad About Us', but, like the efforts by

121

The Lunatics, Lee Kings *et al*, it was riven with the clipped solemnity of someone singing in a language not his own.

No Stockholm Sound or Fjordbeat was to take over the planet, and, even on their own soil, hardly any of these talents checkmated the originals in the charts. Even the covers from British albums were eclipsed when the labels with rights to Who product hurled at the market tracks that weren't considered worthy of issue as singles in Britain. Most germaine to this discussion, the cover of Jan and Dean's 'Bucket T' – with Keith Moon on lead vocal – had been buried on track two, side two of 1966's *Ready Steady Who* EP at home. However, as the A–side of a Swedish 45, it headed the list for a fortnight in a land where Moon thus became, debatably, the most idolised member of The Who for all time.

Notes

1. *The Tages, 1964–68* (EMI, 1992) – a retrospective of one of Sweden's top 1960s beat groups
2. *Sydsvenskan*, 24 October 1966 (translation)

Rick West remembers Keith Moon (Tremeloes): *'We did a tour with The Who in the mid–sixties. One night, Keith brought an air pistol and walked along the backstage corridors, shooting out all the light–bulbs. We all had to change in the dark with glass everywhere. We never knew what he would get up to next.*
Keith was a madman, but a great bloke.'

'Love Ain't For Keeping': Birds And Easy Money

'Everything was taken care of. I never paid for, say, a car home from the Speakeasy – and I don't know who did, but I was still given my pocket money. You never had to put your hand in your pocket. None of us had a fiscal situation to worry about. Questions weren't asked' – Phil May (The Pretty Things)

When first he touched the brittle fabric of fame, eighteen–year–old Keith Moon had no steady girlfriend. Nevertheless, he had sudden access to plenty of unsteady ones for whom his face on editions of *Ready Steady Go* proved a powerful aphrodisiac. The strongest motive for any red–blooded youth, no matter how high–minded, to be in a beat group was that no matter what you looked like, you could still be a hit with young ladies. Look at Ringo and his nose – or, closer to home, Pete Townsend's hooter. Look at Bernard Dwyer, resembling more a used car salesman than a drummer in Freddie and the Dreamers. Look at Freddie himself. Look at Bobby Elliott, who everyone knew was as bald as a coot beneath his wig.

Advantaged by picaresque good looks, Keith got quite used to attempts to grab his attention from 'birds' in suede, leather or fishnet, ringing the stage apron to ogle with unmaidenly eagerness the enigma of untouchable boys–next–door. Now and then, the attire, bone structure and slow–and–easy movements of a dancing Ace Face might be noticed, but, apart from that, a sort of *droit de seigneur* prevailed for those on the bandstand.

Though the one–nighters that were The Who's bread–and–butter for most of 1965 were quite ticklish operations at times, each evening's love–life could be sorted out during the interval with a boyish grin, a flood of libido and an 'All right then. I'll see you later.' Without having to display even perfunctory chivalry, you could just snatch some willing–looking bird by the arm and manoeuvre her into the romantic seclusion of, say, a backstage broom cupboard for a knee–trembler that could be over in seconds or stretched out like toffee, depending on how much it took for your legs to give way – or how much time you thought you had before the second set.

As 'I Can't Explain' teetered on the edge of the charts, Keith's desire wasn't exactly verging on the satyric as, allegedly, Roger's was, but his boasts about his conquests weren't the exaggerations and down-right lies they'd once been, even if a lot of the females he obliged transgressed the unwritten *machismo* code instilled into many men throughout Britain and continental Europe that condoned their own infidelities, but not those of their women. After an emotional goodbye to the organist of one visiting group, a fun–loving town girl would be seen the following night in a clinch with the bass player of the next one to appear at the local palais. When cognisant of the situation, Keith did not spoil such a dalliance by getting jealous and sulky with someone who needed someone who didn't care anymore than she did.

As *omerta* is to the Mafia, a vow of silence concerning illicit sex persists still among bands of roving minstrels. Yet Moon's period of no–strings frivolity seemed to peter out during his wooing of Patsy Kerrigan, a trainee hairdresser, not quite sixteen. Until then, she'd known few who lived much differently from her own people in a gen-teel part of Bournemouth where they'd rooted themselves after her fa-ther's job as a plantation manager had taken them to far–flung corners of what was left of the British Empire. As a post–script, Patsy had been sent to a Roman Catholic boarding school where an awakening to the excitement of pop had coincided with confrontations with her wimpled teachers. This had led to her premature entry into the world of work.

Whatever her way with shampoo, curlers and banal chit–chat, Patsy had never lacked male attention, and was a good advertisement for the salon in that, shedding her puppy fat, she'd blossomed into a pocket Venus with a willowy figure, pert breasts, an avalanche of natural blonde hair and an assured if impersonal poise as she titivated some aged virago's tortured curls. Another customer – the proprietor of a local 'charm school' – asked if Patsy had ever thought of becoming a model.

This hadn't been the first such compliment paid to her, but it was the incentive for Patsy to broaden her horizons beyond blue rinses and conditioner. She had, so she was told, the potential to be in the same mini–skirted league as Twiggy, Pattie Boyd and Jean Shrimpton, the new 'faces' of *Vogue, Seventeen* and the fashion pages of Sunday sup-plements. Rather than Twiggy's severe angularity or the raw drama of Jean's cheekbones–to–die–for, Patsy's glamour was less calculat-ed or complicit. A toothy, lisping Pattie Boyd type, she conformed to Shrimpton's *haute couture* Diaghilev, Mary Quant's observation of how mandatory it had become for Swinging Sixties dolly–birds to 'look childishly young, naively sophisticated – and it takes more sophistication to work out that look than those early would–be sophisticates ever dreamed of'. [1] As such, Patsy could be visualised on the cover of a schoolgirls' annual that balanced pop and fashion with features on pets, badminton, ballet, ponies and making a lampshade: conventionally beautiful and jiving in a not–too–way–out mid–calf dress with a short–haired boy, her eyes not focussed on him.

By the end of 1964, Patsy was responding to her adopted professional forename 'Kim', and a career of catwalks and cloth was beckoning on the night an older friend introduced her to her future husband after The Who's last major sixth had reverberated at a south coast venue as 1964 mutated into 1965. Keith had shivered with delight at her friendly smile, even if it beamed no subliminal signals. He'd wanted to possess her immediately, but, for all her air of fluffy innocence, Patsy–Kim would yield nothing of her dignity and self–respect. Put crudely, she was no 'hole in one'.

Late the following summer, Kim's announcement to Keith that her period was overdue and that she'd been sick that morning indicated that they'd been an 'item' for quite a while. The product of a relatively sheltered childhood, she'd been disconcerted that metropolitan Keith had hardly lived like a monk, even before the onset of The Who's national breakthrough, and that he attached a certain cachet to being as illustrious for his carnal athletics – and drug intake – as his prowess as a drummer. Nonetheless, Kim discovered that a brash outer shell contained surprising gentleness and sensitivity – so sensitive that he'd fly off into crockery–smashing histrionics and assault sometimes if she said so much a civil hello to any bloke not on his mental list of those who he judged to have no erotic interest in her. Yet, while forthrightly capable of sticking up for herself, Kim was content for now to be an adjunct to his self–image as a renowned man about the London clubs, much–travelled, a bit of a card and more than able then to both hold down his drink and stand his round.

City lights would not lose their allure for Moon. Whereas fellow pop millionaires were to flee to mansions in 'Hollywood–on–Thames' – as George Harrison did to olde–worlde Henley, Ringo Starr to Ascot and Jimmy Page of The Yardbirds to Windsor – and a general countryside serenity far removed from whatever terrace or semi–detached they had been raised, Keith ventured only as far as Chertsey in 1971, which, though sunny afternoon idylls were blighted only by the whoosh of an occasional Concorde from faraway Gatwick, was still within the yet–unbuilt London orbital motorway,

Otherwise, he either billeted himself on his parents or installed himself in flats in the inner city where, initially, he was subjected to muffled giggling from fans who'd winkled out his ex–directory telephone number; undertook marathon vigils outside the block, and daubed its environs with Who–related graffiti.

He didn't find the situation entirely unpleasant. Routinely unfaithful to Kim and subsequent women who gripped his arm as proprietorially, he would pick and choose from the perpetually loitering 'skirt' – and those clogging the pavements near the dwellings of other pop stars. In 1973, he gained access to Gary Glitter's Kensington apartment block, theoretically as protected as Howard Hughes' Las Vegas penthouse, by bribing the very security officer paid to keep riff–raff out. Compounding his cheek, he brought with him two tatty Jezebels who'd been hanging around. When Glitter – formerly Paul Russell, the Elvis of Hillingdon Youth Club – answered the door, they topped off the occasion by pushing past and repairing directly to one of the bedrooms for several hours, leaving it acrid with spent passions.

Not wishing to appear less than a liberal–minded host, Glitter fought to control his features as Moon – 'a bit barmy and absolutely out of it all the time' [2] – repeated this performance with different sisters–in–shame on consecutive days. The hammer that Moon had taken to what Gary held as moral verities found its mark when 'the next time Keith called round, he shoved a girl into my bedroom and just pushed me in after her.' [2] Next, the glam–rock overlord of his own volition took advantage of his position, and invited a female fan up – and another and another and another... Eventually, he gave up trying to guess if they were under–age.

In 2001, Glitter would serve a brief jail term for accumulating images of child pornography from the internet, and it's possible that the journey to his ruin began when Keith Moon dropped by: 'I think that's when my outlook on success altered. Keith's attitude to fame was, "Why are you working so hard for it if you're not going to have a bit of fun with it when you get it? Life isn't a dress rehearsal". He introduced me to a circuit of places where having a famous face would get you in and make sure you had a good time, usually with someone else footing the bill. We'd go to clubs, restaurants and every celebrity party on offer, where we'd get very wrecked and generally behave like we thought pop stars should.

'I think the reason he and I got on so well was that there was quite a bit of the Keith Moon spirit in me, just waiting for someone to bring it out – but associating with him also became a liability as he used to sleep less than I did. Some nights, I'd be so exhausted all I wanted to do was stay in bed by myself, but Keith would call about 2 a.m., wanting to hit the town. I'd try to ignore his thumping on the door, but he'd tear up strips of paper and poke them through the letterbox. His plan was to smoke me out. It always got me up too, but on several occasions started a small fire. I had to buy quite a few new front doors.' [2]

With amused exasperation, Gary philosophised that these replacements and worse inconveniences went with the job – and he couldn't crab about perks of the kind that Keith had been enjoying since the mid–1960s. Glitter would learn – or be compelled by the official receiver – to rein his extravagance, but Moon never did on the understanding, however erroneous, that, while pop was a fickle mistress, he was so amply set up by the later 1960s that there was small danger of him having to scratch a living again. Nonetheless, when Keith died, the Inland Revenue's net had been closing in, and he'd set aside nothing consciously to meet a demand amassed over thirteen inflationary years in a high–risk business in which his main source of income was his quarter of a budgetary receptacle for all net takings from concerts by The Who.

Since 1965, rarely had Keith to prove identity to sign a bill, and he became quite unused to actually paying for anything with actual bank notes. Even small change was as unnecessary to him as eyesight to a monkfish – or so he thought. On more than one occasion abroad, blithe ignorance about exchange rates would almost leave him without a bed for a night whose blackness would be his sole shield against the commotion that would accumulate around him like it had the Elephant Man after he drifted through the steam of a train's undercarriage at Liverpool Street Station, fresh from an overseas freak–show.

Typical of many a working–class lad who'd never called hotel room–service from a bedside telephone before, Moon's consumption was more conspicuous than those for whom wealth was second nature.

While he'd have occasional but tenacious bouts of circular and frequently only half–comprehended discussions with an affable Lambert and Stamp about Who finance, Moon was immature about hard cash – not that he had the chance to handle much of it as a pop star. With most group earnings tied up, his wallet held little real capital, obliging him to borrow small amounts from Who menials, usually the road management.

Larger bills were settled through the office. Whenever he wanted more than the regular amount with which his bank account was transfused, he only had to ask – though there were raised eyebrows sometimes. Thus he built up the biggest individual overdraft to harry The Who's company ledgers after a dam burst for a river of wastefulness to carry off gluttonous restaurant lunches, bottle after bottle of costly liquor, peak–hour trunk calls to faraway places, and wanton purchases of trendy caprices to lie swiftly forgotten in a desk drawer. With a stroke of a pen, he could award himself a state–of–the–art stereo, a Bentley, a sudden foreign holiday, a house extension, even a whole house. Affordability was less the issue than the spendaholic's buzz at the moment of transaction, the promise of personal transformation that a costly acquisition could effect.

It was a boom time too for anyone in the vicinity when bounties trickled from his coffers, particularly when he insisted on settling the slate for everyone's drinks over a whole evening in one of few watering holes these days where he wouldn't have to listen with heavy patience to any stranger's starstruck twaddle. 'Keith Moon came into St. George's Hospital to have his hernia repaired,' recalled medical student Sam Hutt [3], 'he'd bashed the drums so hard that he'd given himself a hernia. I got very pally with him. He was a lunatic and a bit dangerous, but a lovely bloke at heart. I'd go down the Speakeasy from time to time with Keith and watch him spill champagne everywhere. The typical thing was: "A bottle of champagne! Blow me, I've knocked it over. Let's have another bottle!".' [4]

If merely peckish in the sort of diner where you were expected to order a full meal, Moon would satiate his appetite with the soup before directing the waitress not to bother with the other courses, just bring the bill for them. More seriously, the purchase of successions of expensive cars was beyond rapture for a fellow who once, after he'd been looked up and down by the salesman, would be conducted out the back of the showroom to look at motors judged to be more his price range.

Since the Sixties started Swinging, however, dealers weren't so sure about smiling archly at seedy–flash little men pacing up and down rows of gleaming Mercedes and Rolls–Royces fitted with walnut fascia, one–way windows and all the latest electrically–operated accessories. Vaguely paralleling the scene where Anzak, the village drunk is elevated to justice of the peace in Brecht's *Caucasian Chalk Circle*, there was much bowing and scraping by one London car vendor when an assistant's scornful remarks about Moon's dishevelled appearance and alcohol–garnished breath led an offended drummer to reconsider buying a brand–new Mercedes. He was pacified, however, by a promise that the adjustment of driving–seat contours to his – not his chauffeur's – buttocks would be fast–tracked, and the vehicle delivered without any of the accustomed delay.

Heedlessly, Keith would consign entire racks of clothes to the dustbin because, when he got them home, they hadn't looked as impressive in front of his mirror as they had in the boutique. His butterfly concentration embraced too all manner of hobbies exhausted almost immediately. Often, he'd lose interest while merely glancing at instructions for setting–up a newly–delivered gadget. If such free spending was mentioned in gossip columns, it was accepted – even lapped up – by readers as the prerogative of glamour.

For both the star and his devotees, little would seem odd by then. Keith would, in any case, be devoid of resistance to the force that had effectively finished off his old life as a limousine delivered him to his parents' normally sleepy street where children would swoop from nowhere to see the smile and wave that was diffused generally as he hurried indoors.

Yet, now that he was of world–renown, the past was never far away – especially when relatives he hadn't realized existed turned up on stage–doors. Keith could not locate where their lineage crossed with his own but, as warlords were entertained at mediaeval banquets by jesters, he let them stay to amuse him as they span again what must have been a very likely tale to have gained them admission to his dressing–room.

Certain journalists were allowed in more readily, but, to even the most favoured of these, Moon, when answering ill–informed and

damned insolent questions about lady friends, either proffered an im-
aginary one or denied that he was keeping up a 'just good friends'
farce with anybody in particular. Partly, it was to protect Kim, what
with the none–too–pleasant stares and even physical threats from girl
fans that had fanfared the Who 'family', opening like an anemone and
swallowing her. Yet, while he cared about Kim, Keith preferred a nosy
world to think that he was still 'available' to women who didn't necessarily go all the way, only if they truly loved you.

In the early days of their spooning, however, there hadn't been any
obvious indication that Keith was ever untrue to Kim. Indeed, three
was a crowd when the two's canoodling went beyond the bounds of acceptable ickiness. However, particularly when The Who's work spectrum broadened to different hemispheres as the decade wore on, he
had no qualms about exchanging body fluids, very publicly on occasions, with women from amongst the hordes aspiring quite openly to
an orgasm at his thrust.

From the audience, some would so give in to nature's baser urges,
that they'd simply point at him whilst jerking a phallic forearm, hoping that he got the message that tonight could be his night. Members
of the road crew were, therefore, not astonished when instructed to
bring the more personable of those who'd caught Keith's roving eye up
to his hotel suites. If in more gregarious a mood, he might be sighted,
holding court in the bar, drink within reach, to a veritable bevy of dolly
little darlings.

It was a trifle unsettling for Kim to imagine that her Keith's waking hours between one show and the next weren't spent innocently
shuffling cards, shaking a dice, or slapping a table–top in time when
Pete or John demonstrated a latest opus on an acoustic guitar. Matters
had come to a head when Kim's pregnancy was confirmed, and, after
weighing the decision carefully, appeared quite agreeable to cohabit-
ing with Keith at the Moon family home in Wembley, handy for West
End nightclubbing until the final weeks before labour.

Kim's own Mum and Dad were appalled. Bearing a child outside
wedlock wasn't what happened to girls like their Patsy, but to 'common' people. The most ruinous of British social disgraces, it was a
stain as indelible as Lady Macbeth's damned spot. In her father's native Ireland, 'fallen women' like Kim could, with the full approval of
parents and Church, be incarcerated and forced into what amounted to

slave labour in Magdelen Asylums, a network of vast laundries run by the so–called Sisters of Mercy, an order of nuns – like the sort who'd run the convent school from which Kim had been removed. [5]

For unmarried fathers, no matter how high the percentage of fault, the repercussions were less onerous – often no more than admonitions along the lines of 'You've had your fun and now you must pay for it' – and that wasn't necessarily the case if the brat was adopted or aborted. To Mrs. Kerrigan at least, either option was preferable to Kim going through with a wedding that would have to be represented as the outcome of a sudden love match between her daughter and the dashing young 'musician' – if that's what you called him.

When separated from her husband by the early 1970s, Kim's mother would warm to Keith, going so far as to become his housekeeper and domestic drinking partner, but neither she nor Mr. Kerrigan had been present at the Surrey registry office ceremony in autumn 1965 where, without their knowledge, Keith and Kim were said to have tied the knot as soon as could be arranged after the doctor's glad tidings. There were, apparently, just two legally–ordained witnesses: Who tour manager Phil Robertson – and Twinkle, a singer the same age as Kim, who'll always be remembered for 'Terry', a 'death disc' concerning a motor–cyclist who, irked by his girl's flightiness, zoomed off to a moonlit end of mangled chrome and blood–splattered kerbstones.

Twinkle's *entree* into the record industry came via her elder sister Dawn whose literary talents had earned her regular features in *Boyfriend, Jackie* and other schoolgirl journals. Nepotic pieces in these – and a television debut on ITV's *Thank Your Lucky Stars* – guided 'Terry' with neo–mathematical precision to Number Four during 1964's Yuletide sell–in.

Graciously, Dawn did not spill the beans about the secret Moon nuptials, though, after the respective in–laws were over their deceived surprise, there'd be a second ceremony on 1966's St. Patrick's Day – a gap between The Who's *Saturday Club* pre–recording and a slot on *Ready Steady Go* to also plug 'Substitute' – followed by a rumbustious reception dominated by the groom's friends and relations. Mrs. Kerrigan was pointedly absent, though Mr. Kerrigan tried to smile as five minutes seemed like that many hours when he was among these folk with whom he had so little in common.

The information that Keith intended to marry the girl had been received with acute irritation by Chris Stamp and Kit Lambert who, for all their 'new broom' effect upon British pop management strategy, had been learning their craft in an era when a male pop star would lose some of his following if he got married. As much the public face of The Who as the lead vocalist, Keith getting hitched was as likely to affect the group's popularity far more than low–profile Charlie Watts's wedding the previous October had that of The Rolling Stones. On the other hand, though broken–hearted females had mobbed London's Caxton Hall that dark day in 1954 when Dickie Valentine and his fiancee signed the register, he'd survived a tougher decade in that respect as a chart contender.

It is tempting to compare the first years of Keith and Kim's espousal with that of lackadaisical but happily in love young Mozart and his young wife as portrayed in the 1984 bio–pic, *Amadeus*. Yet the Moons' was, overall, a difficult marriage, and little explanation could be offered its only issue – a daughter named Amanda – about why Daddy played inexhaustably with other people's children while showing little overt affection towards her after the initial bouts of tickling and pillow–fighting fun when she was an infant. Before she'd left primary school, Keith would be almost permanently away. A man preoccupied with success is apt to be an inattentive husband and father, but the road to a comfortless spring morning in the London Divorce Court nine years later could not be ascribed to one solitary cause.

Sundown usually brought to Keith an onset of high spirits, and it was sad to sink them into a sofa when they cried out to be shared with others a taxi ride away from the guilt–inducing pong of nappies being changed. Therefore, there was no immediate let–up in his frequenting of West End night spots.

He'd long been a nightbird by then: surly, dressing–gowned breakfasts in the late afternoon to line his stomach prior to excursions a few hours later to 'in' clubs like the Ad–Lib near Leicester Square, the Bag O' Nails off Carnaby Street or the cloistered Scotch Of St. James, a bee–line from Buckingham Palace. As Sam Hutt implied, Keith was to retain most hedonistic loyalty to the supercool Speakeasy, a stone's throw from Oxford Circus, but he was often seen in other pop star hangouts, attractive for their strict membership controls, tariffs too highly priced for the Average Joe, flourescent lighting that flattered the most homely icons, and no photographers admitted.

An alternative to cutting a rug at these or newer watering–holes like Tiles or Sybilla's was to breeze down to the Revolution in Mayfair to hear Lee Dorsey or The Ike and Tina Turner Revue. Slumming it, he might troop over to Wardour Street's Flamingo, Marquee or Crazy Elephant to mingle amongst Mods up too late to pester anyone for autographs. Instead, they'd be grooving to Zoot Money's Big Roll Band, Chris Farlowe and his Thunderbirds, The Spencer Davis Group, The Graham Bond Organisation or, less often since his 1964 Number One with 'Yeah Yeah,' Georgie Fame. Sometimes, Keith would need little coaxing to get up and have a blow himself. If touted still as The Swinging Club Of Swinging London [6], the Flamingo wasn't the Harlem Apollo but it was the nearest to it he seemed ever likely to experience unless The Who took off in the USA.

Some of his nights on the town finished in the abodes of various of the Quant–cropped dolly–birds, who outnumbered men five to one in the Scotch and the Ad–Lib. Yet, in his own eyes, Keith was a 'one–gal–guy' in that his casual romantic adventures did not adulterate his emotional allegiance to Kim. Nonetheless, there were too many times when the wretchedness of Kim's own devotion cut keenly. As quizzical as she was upset, Kim implored Keith to help her grasp what all these stories about him and other girls meant. When his dirty deeds were uncovered, so unnerving were Keith's mental self–flagellations that Kim might have preferred him to have shouted back or to have groped for some reasoned excuse for his conduct.

Yet though neither of them were lovestruck teenage Mods anymore, he was not beyond extreme strategies if not to rekindle the flame of their lustful courtship, then remind her of what it had been like. Nevertheless, as they subsided into 'Tara', their leafy acres in Chertsey in the early 1970s, a strange question occurred to Kim: what would remain hers if she and Keith split up more decisively than they had already on several occasions since 1966? If in the midst of even more material comforts now, their partnership – of two old friends who used to be lovers – was not proportionally blissful.

The mist of resigned despair thickened over 'Tara', and incessant circular arguments and cliff–hanging silences were the prelude to an estrangement that would soon find Keith half a world away. Tax laws in Britain had already driven Maurice Gibb of The Bee Gees to the Isle of Man, The Rolling Stones to France and Dave Clark to California. More of a magnet for Moon's migration there too, however, was its scope for playing the field as he had done during previous visits with such as Pamela Miller, one of a mostly female cabal centred in Los Angeles who were notorious for imposing themselves upon favoured rock stars, notably Frank Zappa and his Mothers Of Invention. [7]

However, Moon's extra–marital amours would climax during a visit to London in a liaison with Annette Walter–Lax, a Swedish model nearly ten years his junior. After this took a serious turn, she joined him across the Atlantic where, until Keith put a brake on a life of suit-cases by buying a house in Laurel Canyon, they roamed from hotel to footloose hotel where switchboard or room service would relay complimentary tickets and social invitations offering flattery without friendship, souvenirs without wisdom, and fatigue without stimulation to one whose every work–shy action was worth a half–page in *The Sun* or *Los Angeles Times*. Flying from boredom, if Keith wasn't on an aeroplane with Annette, they'd be in the departure lounge waiting for the next one, jetting from Los Angeles to New York to London and back again with the ease of daily commuters on the 8.28 from Wembley Central to Charing Cross.

As it had been with Kim, Annette explained away Keith's vacilla-tions between merriment and equally wild–eyed uptightness as a com-bination of jet–lag, vocational pressures, the ordeal of conviviality that came with the territory, and the sobering thought that unless he drew back from the abyss of booze and pills, he could be dead within a year. She cultivated too an abstracted tolerance of – or indifference to – his accumulation of eye–stretching bills for costly objects he couldn't see without wanting to possess.

She also feigned aloofness to retain composure, but a frank nature could not allow her to stay silent about the cheery promiscuity that he either continued or resumed once she was his. Yet Annette wasn't so naive to presume that her pop idol of a man didn't enjoy a fling or two while The Who were on tour. Besides, she believed him when he said he loved her in emotion–charged farewells as he left for the airport and another distant stage.

Notes

1. *Quant By Quant* by M. Quant (Cassell, 1966)
2. *Leader* by G. Glitter and L. Bradley (Warner, 1991)
3. Later, country–and–western entertainer Hank Wangford
4. *Days In The Life: Voices From The English Underground* ed. J. Green (Heinemann, 1988)
5. The last Magdalen Asylum closed in 1996. This grim chapter of Irish history was the subject of *The Magdalen Sisters*, an acclaimed 2002 film.
6. *Where To Go In London And Around*, 27 October 1966
7. Some were taken on as domestic staff by the late Zappa who, intrigued, invited them to form a group, Girls Together Outrageously, to record an album, *Permanent Damage*, for his Straight record label. Pamela Miller and other of the Girls also starred in Zappa's *200 Motels* movie.

Derrick Timms remembers Keith Moon (The Moondogs): *At the Speakeasy, he used to piss on people's shoes in the middle of conversations. On the other hand, when Ashley Holt, the singer with Warhorse, expressed admiration for a leather coat he was wearing, Keith took it off immediately and offered it to Ashley.*
Around that time too, I stayed at the Hiatt House on Sunset Strip where my room had just been completely refurbished – because Moon had occupied it the week before.

'Girl's Eyes': The Moon Muse

We must get some spare time to ourselves, and it's not that we are lazy. Look at Pete: he's written about ten originals in the last six weeks' – Keith Moon [1]

Before 'I Can't Explain' had reached the Top Ten, the last thing a teenage Mod, whether in the Marquee, Wembley's Starlite Ballroom or some palais in the sticks, wanted to hear from The Who was a home–made song. If the group attempted anything more than the familiar, it was regarded as an unofficial intermission: a chance to chat to friends, go to the toilet, anything other than dance or listen.

It didn't matter, therefore, that Keith Moon felt he had neither the knack nor the appetite to compose. Where did it get you anyway? With the demarcation line between performer and jobbing tunesmith per-sisting well into the 1960s, it was understood that, if a working out-fit contained individuals with any such aspirations, it wasn't a caste–within–a–caste so much as an eccentricity, a bit of fun. At most, it was a half–serious contingency plan so that, should the group turn sour, it might be possible to get somewhere purely as a writer.

There was, however, fat chance of Frank Sinatra, that jackpot of all pop composers, trying an offering by the likes of Pete Townshend or John Entwistle, The Who's would–be Gershwins, when howls of affectionate derision were all that they might expect from their own kind. Critical prejudices brought forth the same hectoring arguments (like hook–lines from diabolical songs): 'You can't beat the Yanks at that game anymore than you can at anything else. The group doesn't need more than what they play already? If they did, could a twit like you come up with anything of the necessary standard?'

Often, a twit like him would realize that a song was no good as soon as he started coyly chugging its introductory chords, but Townshend especially was handsomely endowed with a capacity to try–try again, and, after a nascent 'I Can't Explain' was taped during the High Numbers era, group originals became an accepted part of the package when Kit Lambert and Chris Stamp began laying their charges on with a trowel around the record companies.

By the time The Who hit their chart–making stride towards the end of 1965, plenty of other outfits were also developing composition to an extent that had been unheard of before 1962. With internal sources of new material and their own publishing companies, a lot of these bloody beat groups were giving the music business a nasty turn. Goddamit, the rules of a 1964 *Ready Steady Go* spin–off, a televised battle–of–the–bands–type tournament named *Ready Steady Win*, insisted on at least one original per entrant. To the further detriment of the worker–ants of Denmark Street – London's Tin Pan Alley – the long–players and demo tapes of The Beatles, The Rolling Stones, The Kinks, The Who, The Hollies, The Small Faces, The Zombies, The Pretty Things, The Moody Blues and Unit Four Plus Two – acts containing individuals or teams that had found their feet, hoevver transiently, as marketable songwriters – were scrutinized for potential smashes.

The Stones' *Aftermath* album, for example, yielded 'Out Of Time', a 1966 Number One for Chris Farlowe; 'Yesterday' from The Beatles' *Help!* remains the most 'covered' track of all time, and Dave Berry found himself the Presley of the Flatlands when, in 1965, his version of 'This Strange Effect' by Ray Davies of The Kinks became Holland's biggest–selling disc ever. As late as 1968, a revival of 'I Love You', a self–penned Zombies B–side, was a surprise US Top Twenty entry for a combo from San Jose called The People, who were then a support act on a Who US tour.

Yet, while his monopoly of The Who's A–sides was a personal triumph, Townshend was never to be as prosperous as a writer for others as Lennon–McCartney, Jagger–Richards, Ray Davies or even Chris 'I Love You' White. Nevertheless, The Merseys – also managed by Stamp and Lambert – were to bubble under the domestic Top Fifty with Pete's 'So Sad About Us', and 'Join My Gang' by Oscar [2] and The Barron–Knights' 'Lazy Fat People' were two significant Townshend creations unrecorded by The Who. He was also the wellspring of much tilting at the charts by The Fleurs de Lys, The Untamed and further also–rans.

There were, however, no takers for 'The Ox', the finale of the *My Generation* LP [3], which was bestowed with an Entwistle–Townshend–Moon–Hopkins [4] credit. An instrumental, it hinged on a twelve–bar blues chord sequence [5] and, from Moon's record collection, 'Waikiki Run', the soundalike UK follow–up to The Surfaris' 'Wipe Out'. Played with an overcast aggression – with drums to the fore – 'The Ox' in its different way was the equal of this sound picture of crashing waves and the seethe of dragging shingle, and also precipitated discussion about a totally instrumental side–project without any involvement from Roger Daltrey (then something of a Who *bete noir* anyway), along the lines of Manfred Mann's contemporaneous *Instrumental Asylum* EP.

If this was ever a serious intention, it progressed no further than a remaindered 'Hall Of The Mountain King' – a robust five–minute 1967 adaptation of the Grieg suite that had been a minor hit in like rocked–up fashion for Nero and the Gladiators six years earlier – and, selected for *A Quick One*, 'Cobwebs And Strange', featuring Keith clashing orchestral cymbals and the others on various blowing in-struments, marching round an omni–directional microphone. More than a little bit daft, it was on a par with Ray Charles's 'Pop Goes The Weasel' from 1965's *Live In Concert* and 'Mother's Lament' on Cream's *Disraeli Gears*: a modern pop album's frivolously iconoclastic conclusion that made Shane Fenton and the Fentones sound like Zappa jamming with Hendrix. Moon's name was to be in brackets next to the title, but Entwistle claimed authorship of the melody of 'Cobwebs And Strange' – which seems to have been derived in any case from 'Eastern Journey' on Tony Crombie's 1959 LP of incidental music to the televi-sion series, *Man From Interpol*. [6]

'Dogs Part Two', the 'Pinball Wizard' coupling, would be just as throwaway as indicated by the presence of canine vocal duo, Jason and Towser, co–residents of the Entwistle family home . Both they and Keith were listed as its composers. 'Waspman', another Moon B–side – of 1973's 'Relay' – was, with its chanting and apposite buzzing nois-es, a hark–back to the 1950s when, as Harry Robinson, leader of *Oh Boy!*'s house band, Lord Rockingham's XI, reminds us, 'You couldn't have a rock 'n' roll instrumental without somebody saying something in it. Don't ask me why, but you had to have some human voice on there.' [7]

Under no commercial pressure to compose, Keith's instrumentals were of less value to The Who than than the percussive power and subtleties he lent to Townshend's – and Entwistle's – patterns of chords and lyrics. Yet when not making a nuisance of himself during some boring mechanical process in the studio or cudgelling up a scarcely–heeded opinion about a play–back only marginally different from the first eighteen takes to which he'd listened, Keith's shadowing of Shel Talmy and then Kit Lambert's methods had rendered him sufficiently schooled in the aural possibilities of the studio to be among those proposed for freelance commissions as producers by Immediate, the country's most successful independent record label of the 1960s – and during the optimistic genesis of The Beatles' Apple Corps, whose disc releases were monitored by EMI.

As well as suggesting theoretical apportion of trackage, shortlisting of devices and effects, and further jargon–ridden console gambits, it's probable that Keith also contributed to Townshend's and Entwistle's compositions after a piecemeal manner by slinging in rhymes, bits of tune and twists to the plot – such as the revelatory notion of setting the 'religious' part of *Tommy* in a holiday camp [8] – when, say, standing over John at the piano or watching Pete – a one–man melody–maker, librettist and arranger – pacing up and down, bedevilled with a instinct that might have manifested itself at some inconvenient moment in perhaps a lift, backstage passage or during lunch in some wayside cafe.

Keith was under no illusions about his own abilities in this field. More discontented a victim of disheartening indifference to his efforts, John may have moaned before resigning himself to be treated as but a tool for Pete's masterworks, but Moon – like Daltrey – did not hold in his heart the hope that the rest might consider something he'd made up superior to a few of the non–originals that'd been in and out of the set since their first hour together on stage [9] or – but, no, that could never be – as one of the sides of a single. Nevertheless, an opportunity presented itself when, by accident or design, Keith and John were the only Who members to materialise at an IPC session in either December 1965 – when Moon was green about the gills from whooping cough – or, more likely, the following August.

With a pound–sign over every fretful quaver, the pair put together 'In The City', the only published Entwistle–Moon song. John insisted that he'd penned the bulk of this ersatz surfing ditty, which finished up as the B–side of 1966's 'I'm A Boy'. As it had been with The Beach Boys' 'Surfin' USA', 'In The City' brought the seashore sport to an unlikely location – in the 'Well, you can surf in the city' line. For good measure, the participants threw a couple of erudite hot–rod references into the cauldron of a light–hearted piece, topped with Keith's falsetto, that focussed principally if indirectly on the 'two girls for every boy' aspect of Jan and Dean's 1963 million–seller, 'Surf City'. Rip–off or send–up, it wouldn't have been out of place in the Californian lads' repertoire – and I must add the raw information that the maiden 45 by known Who admirers, The Jam, in 1977, was also called 'In The City'.

Bearing a more standardised title, the only solidly *bona fide* number attributed to Moon alone that was considered worthy enough for release materialised after Chris Stamp created, via Essex Music, a publishing receptacle – with attached advance against royalties – for compositions by all four of The Who. In the first instance, they'd agreed to donate two tracks each to the forthcoming *A Quick One*. Songs, however, did not come as readily to Moon and Daltrey as they did to the other two – and, for all the steady drip of financial incitement from their investors, Roger managed only one, 'See My Way', and Keith just the dubious 'Cobwebs And Strange' – and 'I Need You', the same title with which Ray Davies had gifted a Kinks B–side the previous year, and George Harrison the item to which he mimed in The Beatles' second movie, *Help!*.

As he didn't play a melodic instrument, the construction of Keith's 'I Need You' had been less impeded by the formal do's and don'ts that otherwise inhibit creative flow when, instead of rampaging round central London one night, he stayed in to give this composing lark a whirl. For hours of unusual quietude, he nagged at the ghost of a hookline, maybe a sketchy opening verse, surrounded by a tape recorder, cigarette butts, smeared coffee cups and sheets of paper full of scribbled lyrics and notation peculiar to himself. Then John or Pete were asked to ascertain its key and underlying chords from his dah–dah–dah–ing of a tune that, if effective, wasn't much more than a support edifice for the words. Nonetheless, Keith's grappling with his muse resulted in a hard–won, but convincing song that was recorded by The Who just before a tour of northern Europe in autumn 1966.

It had been inspired by 'I need you like I need a hole in the head', a catch–phrase that had once been heard all around the clubs as a short cut to instant bonding before being dropped quite inexplicably, never to be uttered again. [10] There was also an in–joking passage in which Keith impersonated various fellow scene–makers – notably John Lennon murmuring about somebody named 'Jingo' – and an appropriation of a couplet, albeit entirely relevant in context, from 'The Price Of Love', which had all but topped the British charts for The Everly Brothers the previous summer. Yet 'I Need You' was quite abstract, introspective even, in its meditations on the fragility of celebrity and its associated sycophancy. It touched too on the contradiction of observed and uptight relaxation with only your equals arguing with you, and hangers–on and liggers on the spot with the promptness of vultures, either serving as unpaid and unrecompensed round–buying minions or dispensing sex almost out of politeness.

Another vision of a world which stardom had restricted to only his immediate environment was 'Girl's Eyes', a Moon number, *circa* 1967, which wasn't to reach the public until sixteen years after his death when, for the fan who has to have everything on which The Who so much as breathed, it was included on a CD box–set, *30 Years Of Maximum R&B*. It addressed not the club–going gold–diggers who had figured in 'I Need You', but expressed clumsy sympathy for the anonymous female, who, devoid of the capital's *sang froid*, gazed in weepy but silent worship from the front row of an otherwise screaming mass as amorphous as frogspawn.

A magazine picture of Keith on a bedroom wall might have greeted her when she first opened her eyes in the pallor of dawn. No fragment of information about him from the pages of *Jackie* or *Fabulous* was too insignificant to be less than completely absorbing. From the stage, he perceived what he was sure was a telepathic message from her. 'I know you and you know me,' it read, 'We understand each other in a secret way.' In 'Girl's Eyes', fan and pop star became as one. 'Dearly beloved audiences,' he smiled at a question about The Who's following from a *Melody Maker* scribe, 'I think we're all fans really.' [11]

That moony 'Girl's Eyes' didn't get past quality control may have drained Keith's confidence as a writer. As Townshend continued to hog this division within the unit structure, Moon, like a travelling salesman with a foot in the door, was obliged to make a pitch with his most enticing wares. Into the bargain, he hadn't the wherewithal to make a convincing demo and, no Scott Walker as a singer, was thus disadvantaged further by having to demonstrate an item *a capella*.

Yet there'd be occasions when, excitedly, he'd sometimes drop everything to develop some flash of musical inspiration. After a while, however, it would become too much like hard work and he'd hope the telephone would ring. If not, his egg–and–chips would be getting cold or something good just starting on television. This songwriting business mucked up the day's fun. Maybe he'd have another go tomorrow. Well, maybe...

Notes

1. *New Musical Express*, 10 December 1965
2. Alias Paul Nicholas, once Lord Sutch's pianist, and a future co–star of 1973's *That'll Be The Day* movie.
3. And the B–side to the 1966 single, 'The Kids Are Alright'
4. Session pianist – and one of Paul Nicholas's predecessors in Lord Sutch's Savages – Nicky Hopkins played on many Who recordings during this period.
5. One the three basic structures that recur in rock 'n' roll. The others are the 'three–chord trick', and the I–IV–minor VI–V 'turnaround'.
6. 'Cobwebs And Strange' was also to underscore the 'Heinz Baked Beans' section of *The Who Sell Out*.
7. *Halfway To Paradise: Britpop, 1955–1962* by S. Leigh and J. Firminger (Finbarr International, 1996)
8. Earning Keith a credit for its 'Tommy Holiday Camp' vignette
9. At Greenford's Oldfield Hotel in May 1964
10. It had also constituted half the chorus of 'That's What I Said', a 1962 B–side by The Dave Clark Five. 'Hole In The Head' was the B– side of a 1965 single by Paul Dean and the Thoughts. In parenthesis, Dean was actually – it's that man again – Paul Nicholas.
11. *Melody Maker*, 31 December 1966

Yeah, like, I'm really sorry, OK?: Precursors, Contemporaries And Descendants

'Though I appreciate Moon's "pyrotechnic" percussive style, I'm kind of more impressed with his off–stage antics – to the extent that one day I intend to drive my Nissan Micra into a saucer of milk, and hang the consequences' – Bruce Brand (drummer with The Masonics)

You reckon Keith Moon was a nutter? On Saturday the 5th of February 2005, Geoff Huish, a twenty–six–year old Welshman, was so convinced that England would retain the upper hand in a televised rug-by match against his national team – who hadn't had a victory against its traditional rival for twelve years – that he told fellow drinkers at his Caerfilly social club, 'If we win, I'll cut my balls off.' They of course thought he was joking. However, when England was beaten, Geoff went home, severed his testicles with a knife, walked back to the club and slapped them on the bar. One of his shocked friends called an am-bulance and Huish was rushed to hospital. Police told local – and then global – newspapers that Huish had a history of mental problems.

Unlike Geoff – and homicidal and suicidal Joe Meek with his sin-gle–barrel rifle and enraged destruction of near–priceless studio equipment – Keith knew when to stop – just – and his private sweet-ness, even introspection, peeped out to family and close friends, even as they counted the emotional cost of devilment inherent in his 'other self'. To outsiders, he seemed lucid enough in interview, and when he'd knocked back more alcohol and swallowed more pills than he should, he remained capable of getting a grip on himself for the most public occasions, aided by measures taken to ensure that as little information as possible leaked out about cry–for–help instances of wrist–slitting, overdoses and threats to jump from ledges many storeys high.

Damage limitation, however, became more difficult towards the end when he transcended mere craziness to teetering on the edge of insan-ity to those who, speaking in low voices and glancing towards him at this music industry shindig or that awards ceremony, insisted they could sense an aura of lunacy effusing from Moon as others might the 'evil' from the late child murderer Myra Hindley's eyes. It was something Keith came to perceive himself, that muttering, then the falling silent, the steady staring and the wondering if he was real.

Was Moon ever truly off his rocker? Did he really warrant a chapter to himself in a book called *The World's Greatest Cranks And Crackpots*? [1] Had he – like Friedrich Nietzche, the German philosopher of irrationalism – lost his mind during an unremitting contemplation of his fame and glory, wallowing in his own screams of laughter – and sorrow. On the 500th edition of *Top Of The Pops*, Cliff Richard was scheduled to mime to a hit – as were The Who. Prostrated, allegedly, by frightening paroxysms of grief after a bust–up with a girlfriend the previous afternoon, Keith recovered sufficiently to go through the motions with the group but, next, led the road crew in an invasion of the wardrobe department in order to shower the Bachelor Boy with assorted wigs in the middle of his number.

Pop stardom at the age of eighteen – and that's all Keith was when 'I Can't Explain' reached the Top Ten – can be too much for an immature youth whose greatest fear was 'having to grow up' [2], and who discovers that a television studio audience and unseen millions beyond are actually paying heed to him. Trying to recapture that buzz as newer sensations came along, and a *Top Of The Pops* appearance by The Who became as commonplace as a write–up of a whist drive in the *Harrow Observer*, he began resorting to that hyperactive behaviour that children do when they sense a drifting away of adult attention.

On the threshold of eminence, Keith had been able to say boo to a goose, but not much more. In his earliest days as a Beachcomber, there'd been times when he'd fought to control his features when the older fellows belched and said rude words, and he strived not to put his foot in it with some inanity. It happened gradually, but such inhibitions flowed out of him and, determined that nothing was going to show him up for the virgin boy he was, his voice got louder, jokes coarser, eyes brighter and face more flushed before, unused to holding down so much ale, he staggered off to vomit. A toilet bowl fogging in and out of focus was the final vision to penetrate Keith's brain as he slumped into the velvet–blue oblivion that was the prelude to the first hangover he'd ever promoted. He'd never been, or ever would be, all that fond of beer anyway.

In the inaugural years of the success that followed, his frank and unashamed retellings of his off–duty skylarkings made him a source of 'good copy' – plain speaking laced with quirkiness. He wasn't as renowned a talker as Pete Townshend, but plenty of his oft–requested explanations of his conduct were jotted down by nicotine–stained fingers. Here are some off–the–cuff examples:

'I get bored, you see. When I get bored, I rebel. I took out my hatchet and chopped the hotel room to bits. It happens all the time.'[3]

'The organisers wanted us to scrub around our fireworks and smoke bombs – but we need a finale. They had a sort of pond there, and the water jets are controlled by special switches – so I just chucked half my drums into the water, switched on and lo! A most novel effect as the drum kit was shot twenty feet into the air on top of giant water jets'.[2]

'If you're sitting around after a show and there's something you don't like on the TV, you just switch it off by throwing a bottle through the screen.'[3]

'I suppose to most people I'm probably seen as an amiable idiot, a genial twit. I'm a victim of my own practical jokes'.[3]

'If we are playing somewhere for the first time, we make sure we give a spectacular performance to win over the audience. Once they have got over the initial shock, we concentrate more on what we are playing. It means we have to play harder at first. Naturally, I have to hit harder than the normal pop drummer, and the equipment breaks sooner'.[4]

'Fun: that's what it's all about – fun. Everybody thinks I'm laughing at them, but I want them to laugh with me.'[2]

The press were delighted with an alarming young man who was to Mod culture what Screaming Lord Sutch had become to British politics. An inevitable result was that Moon felt impelled to not only live up to his frolics, but outdo them and turn the fictionalised ones into re–timed truth, just as Roger Chapman, vocalist with Family, was to exaggerate his nanny–goat vibrato – because, having read about it in reviews, the fans expected it. Likewise, Gene Vincent, radiating depravity wherever he went, began waving a gas–pistol about on stage during one too many weeks of relentless touring, actually firing it and thus emptying Hamburg's Star–Club.

Then there'd be The Doors' rabble–rouser–in–chief, Jim Morrison, exploited as a cross between a modern Dionysus and a pop–singing Marlon Brando, obliged to play up to it with antics that went far beyond merely complaining about police harassment. With microphone in hand and alcohol in nervous system, causing uproar and the correlated interventions of local constabulary amused the former Albuquerque public schoolboy – especially as teenagers were frequently as upset as adults by just his swearing, even if it was to be surpassed a quarter of a century later by the brutish *braggadocio* of rap.

A known stimulant abuser and heavy drinker too, he was impressed by 'ideas about the breaking away or overthrowing of established order. I am interested in anything about revolt, disorder, chaos, especially activity that has no meaning.' [5] He may have been enacting some aspect of this at Miami's Dinner Key Auditorium in 1969 when his ritualized cavortings concluded with his arrest for 'lewd and lavicious behaviour'. According to keyboard player Ray Manzarek, the self–proclaimed 'Lizard King' was sending up his sex symbol status with a routine involving a towel, and may have accidentally exposed himself. He'd escaped with non–custodial sentences for similar offences, but it was predicted that this time he'd be gaoled – and The Doors would finally close.

Initially, only the most sinless of Keith Moon's frolics were brought to general notice by a media that, for all Kit Lambert's best efforts to turn The Who into Rolling Stones–ish bad boys, judged any besmirching of a madcap but intrinsically innocent image – akin to that of one of Just William's Outlaws – as untimely when no–one wanted to know that he was any different from the cute way he'd been when wiping away sham–tears as compere Cathy McGowan bade farewell on the last ever edition of *Ready Steady Go* in December 1966.

Save the scandal for the Stones – or maybe The Pretty Things while they were still hot. See, like a pre–psychedelic Beatle, the winsomely irrepressible Keith of the mid–1960s could not be imagined urinating, passing wind, cursing, breaking the law or masturbating any more than a sexless cartoon character, teddy–bear, Beatle or Herman's Hermit. By contrast, it was hard fact that three Stones were fined in 1965 for relieving themselves against a wall in a petrol station forecourt, and that guitarist Keith Richards had booted a footlight–level heckler in the face during a riotous Stones concert in Blackpool. One of Colchester's Fairies, another bunch of tempermental, long–haired ne'er–do–wells, had caused death by dangerous driving, and a Pretty Things road manager was prosecuted after some unpleasantness with a shotgun after an engagement in Swindon.

In the context of this discussion, a thumb–nail sketch of The Pretty Things' early career is worthwhile for its parallels and bearing on that of Keith Moon and The Who.

The Things' abandoned drive and reprobate image had held instant allure for talent scouts looking for a group to combat the Stones. Before 1964 was out, a first single, 'Rosalyn', peaked on the edge of the Top 30, and the Things notched up their biggest smash with 'Don't Bring Me Down', a stop–start arrangement riven with beatnik slang ('chick', 'man', 'dig', 'rave'). Climbing almost as high, the self–penned 'Honey I Need' follow–up in spring 1965, lived in a careering riff thrashed at speed behind a ranted vocal: punk or what?

They flashed into respectable homes via *Top Of The Pops* cameras; singer Phil May's cascading tresses – the longest male hair in the country – flickering across a complexion on which no hit record could prevent adolescent spots erupting. While the most liberal Mums and Dads were as aghast as they'd be when the comparatively short–maned Who destroyed their equipment on *Ready Steady Go* a few weeks later, the effect was most keenly felt by their short–back–and–sided sons, guiltily transfixed by the Things' androgeny, offset only by lead guitarist Dick Taylor's beard.

'They had everything it took to overtake the Stones,' estimated Screaming Lord Sutch, 'but in those days "all publicity is good publicity" didn't always apply because, though they were years ahead of their time image–wise – the Sex Pistols of their day – it was too much for the general public in the mid–sixties. The Stones just about walked the line; the Pretty Things went way over it. This was a time, remember, when simply getting married could still ruin a pop star's career. The man–in–the–street couldn't imagine any of the Pretty Things ever being married – except to each other.'

Such notoriety increased turnout at bookings, even if curiosity–seekers with only the vaguest notion about the music they had paid to hear, helped fill the often unsalubrious new beat clubs packing the shires where the Things, rather than the Stones, emerged as patron saints of legion also–ran R&B combos who'd ditched Beatle–esque stage suits and big smiles for motley sullenness.

Back in London, it was cool for everyone who was anyone to like The Pretty Things too. On his first UK tour, Bob Dylan asked to be introduced – as he would to The Who – and would namecheck the 'sweet Pretty Things' in 'Tombstone Blues'.

'Judy Garland used to come to our flat a bit,' added Phil May, 'probably because she and our drummer had a mutual interest in the bottle. We used to go to Freddie Mills' Nite Spot, the Starlite Rooms and these other rather strange night clubs that were patronised by a mixture of leftish celebrities and gangsters – and CID flying squad, funnily enough. The Krays tagged onto us – because if they were Public Enemy Number One, we were Number Two.'

An uncertain transition from rhythm–and–blues to self–conciously 'weird' singles and *SF Sorrow*, a rock opera that pre–dated *Tommy,* coincided with one more fat year in the domestic Top Fifty. As Britain's overseas ambassadors, the Things experienced a large–scale re–run of the hysteria at home. An uproarious televized festival in Holland ended with a blackout. TV cameras were, however, on hand to immortalize their inebriated drummer, a certain Vivian St. John Prince, being escorted from a – grounded – Kiwi Airlines 'plane after an altercation with air hostess and pilot. Outstanding Pretty Things dates in Australasia were undertaken with Mitch Mitchell from Georgie Fame's Blue Flames, but New Zealand was sealed off altogether as if the Things were deadly microbes threatening swift epidemic. Elsewhere, they threaded through customs areas resounding with as much jack–in–office nastiness and red tape that bureaucracy could gather.

Too often in a condition of alcoholic or narcotic disrepair, Prince's antics, so the – sometimes erroneous – tales were (and are) told, also included chopping at a hotel's dining tables and water pipes with a fire–axe; hurling a tape–recorder through a door panel; pissing on Sandie Shaw's illustrious feet, and crawling beneath a proscenium, slurping whiskey from a shoe, dousing the stage floorboards with the inflammable spirit and flicking at a cigarette lighter.

Yet for all the pointing fingers at the trouble there was over him, Viv's busy technique had been noted by The Who and other outfits, who hired him to deputise whenever their usual drummers were indisposed. Amused by the memory, Denis D'Ell of The Honeycombs would recall, 'When we appeared on *Sunday Night At The London Palladium* in 1965, we borrowed Viv from the Pretty Things so that Honey Langtree, our usual drummer, could go centre stage to sing a duet with me. Viv had quite a reputation as a raver so, after the rehearsal that afternoon, he was locked in the dressing room until it was time to go on – in case he went on a binge and either didn't show up or else did something untoward on TV.'

He would be more available for engagements with The Who, The Honeycombs and anyone else short of a sticksman when, roaring drunk at the Manor Lounge in Stockport one night, Prince – lately, a central figure of the first pop drug bust too – 'refused to go on stage until all the bouncers were removed,' sighed Phil May, 'but then some bird ripped the front off my shirt during the first number, and Viv stopped drumming, grabbed her, ripped her blouse and bra off, and punched her full in the mouth. All the bouncers jumped, and we got beaten up, and our equipment smashed. Viv retreated over the road to a pub leaving all this chaos, and I followed him in and sacked him on the spot.'

A minion was sent to fetch the drummer from Hedgehoppers Anonymous – then finishing a show over in Manchester – to rattle the traps for the Things' contract–fulfilling second set. Percussion duties fell once more to Mitch Mitchell, then former Fairy John 'Twink' Alder and, finally, to sixteen–year–old *wunderkind* Skip Alan, already a veteran of Them, The Ivy League and his own trio.

Years passed. Contradictory and far–fetched rumours abounded about what had happened to Viv Prince. Supported by Dick Taylor's comment that 'he has a capacity to upset people that's unparalleled,' someone insisted that Viv had fled Portugal because of a Mafia–like vendetta against him. Another mentioned an unhappy association with the Hell's Angels, but Taylor and May next saw Prince in Sidmouth where, uninvited, they jammed with a tavern's resident balalaika ensemble until police were summoned.

A couple of years Keith Moon's senior, Prince was wilder, fouler and more peculiar, kind of Terry–Thomas to Keith's David Niven. Another role model was a drummer from Sheffield, Kenny Slade who, on first acquaintance in a London musical equipment shop before The Who was formed, found Keith 'real shy, like a little choir boy. You could hardly get a word out of him. Didn't he change!?' [6].

Indeed he did. Three years later, when Kenny, straight from a residency in a Doncaster ballroom and a sideline in drumming tutorials, joined Joe Cocker's Grease Band, Moon seemed to have changed almost beyond recognition when they and The Who were flung together on a short round–Britain package tour.

If Viv Prince was an admired elder sibling, then Kenny Slade was Moon's untamed, over–exuberant northern cousin – though, according to Tommy Eyre, Cocker's teenage keyboard player, Kenny and Keith were more like 'blood brothers just waiting to meet up – such like minds. Moon got hold of some dynamite from somewhere, and him and Kenny blew up the toilet at the hotel in Newcastle.' [7] Thus the highlight of the day wasn't always the show, but the building–up, winding–down and associated deeds of destruction.

By then, Keith's intake of intoxicants and worse was impinging on work – as it had been for Kenny since his tenure as both an asset and a liability in The Messengers, backing combo to Jimmy Crawford, a singer who made hay in the light of his only Top Twenty entry, 1961's 'I Love How You Love Me'. One reported incident had Slade so desperate for a drink in the group's van that he swigged a bass guitarist's after–shave for its alcoholic content. In that state, he was also prone, purportedly, to bawling insults and 'mooning' from a passenger window at the dull watchfulness of pedestrians.

During what was an otherwise surprisingly cordial professional relationship, Jimmy Crawford was driven to punch Slade just prior to a booking in a local US air base: 'Kenny got drunk in the afternoon, and, when I arrived about seven o' clock, he'd been doing a drum solo that lasted hours. Later, the agent comes up to me and says, "What are you trying to do? Muck my business up? Have you seen your drummer?" "No, what's the matter?" In the hall, there's Kenny slowly going crazy – so I had to get a grip on him, and I ended up knocking him through this swing door.' [6]

When Kenny had been approaching puberty, Keith was barely out of nappies, but, on the 1968 expedition, he swallowed dust behind the southern boy in the extra–mural lunaticking (which landed them in a Glasgow police cell one night). Fortunately, Moon had the wherewithal to cover the breakages – in the back passages of theatres, Chinese or Indian diners that were the only ones to serve a late–night meal, and the changeless geography of rooms in Holiday Inns, Trust Houses...

A Ramada in Birmingham was just like a Crest in Glasgow – where Moon and Slade spent a few hours in police custody for some breach of the peace. The Coca–Cola tasted exactly the same – unless, of course, it was laced with something stronger.

Slade was often the butt of Moon's roguish pranks and high jinks with explosives in hotel–suite torpor. 'One night, he seems distraught,' recounted Kenny in Runyon–esque present tense, '"Come here... come to my room," he says. He takes me to the bathroom, and there's this girl laid in the bath just feet and head showing in semi–darkness, and what looks like blood everywhere. I said, "What the hell have you done?" So he switches on the light, and it's a blow–up doll, all covered in tomato ketchup.' [7]

Kenny couldn't help liking Keith, and looked forward to carousing with him again, though their lives were never again to interweave to the same intensity. However, another Sheffield musician, Stuart Moseley was present when Frank White, a parochial guitarist who was promoting a maiden solo album, was travelling to a booking in Manchester with accompanists that included a disinclined Kenny Slade: 'All the way there Kenny was moaning about how ill he felt and how he didn't want to play. Shortly after arriving however, a big white Rolls–Royce pulls up, containing Keith Moon. On seeing this, Kenny makes a complete recovery, saying how great it's going to be with Keith, and loads of free whiskey about. Frank then appears and says there's been a mix–up and they're not playing that night – so all the way home, Kenny's moaning again about how ill he feels, and was totally disappointed about not being able to stay with his pal Moon.' [6]

As Kenny, Frank and Stuart hurtled shoulder–to–shoulder across trunk–road Britain in vehicles shared with their gear, The Who jetted overhead, miles above terrible journeys to loss–making one–nighters. They could afford to wait until they felt like going out on the road again. When they did, what was it to Keith that vandalism didn't pay, and he returned from one coast–to–coast US trek with less than one hundred dollars to show for it? Though his fortunes were by no means as secure as he may have imagined, when The Who took what was effectively more than an entire year off, he spent it just mucking about.

Now that the halcyon days of 'Anyway Anyhow Anywhere', *Stardust* and done–to–death *Tommy* were gone, who could blame him for doing nothing in particular? It was no sin to make a fortune by providing harmless entertainment, was it? A back–street lad who climbed to the top of the heap, who could begrudge him a constant and cosseted pursuit of semi–retired pleasure? Look at John Lennon. He'd been sighted less often than the Loch Ness Monster since the close of his eighteen–month 'lost weekend'. Eric Clapton was venturing but rarely outside his country retreat in the mid–1970s, while Charlie Watts was virtually incommunicado in North Devon.

What Moon could not articulate was that he adored being in the limelight, seldom missing opportunities to be the cynosure of eyes grateful to him for merely existing. How would he have felt if politely brief clapping rather than a howling, foot–stomping ovation had greeted him when he mounted his podium as part of an all–star combo cobbled together to help launch a new album by folk–rocker Roy Harper at London's Rainbow or as he sauntered on, dolled up like a lady, to compere a Sha Na Na recital in New York?

He had no qualms either about leaning on his celebrity to be conducted by the head waiter to the best table in a restaurant or switching on the charm when required – as he did when an element of that lip–trembling pathos some find endearing plus a cheeky grin and autographs settled the matter whenever a squad car pulled over his Rolls–Royce on its way to some fashionable niterie where whirring Nikons would herald his skidding arrival.

Others who were famous for being famous would have preferred to shuffle in unnoticed and be outshone by someone like vibrantly gregarious Keith Moon, ever–present guest at every Variety Club luncheon, Elton John birthday party, big–names–in–good–cause charity dos and 'spontaneous' jam sessions concluding the Rock 'N' Roll Hall Of Fame gala at New York's Waldorf–Astoria.

Unlike hibernating John Lennon or Van Morrison, resentful of his press visibility, Keith did not preserve – or pretend to preserve – an ambition to be unphotographed when stepping from a lift; not have a stick–mic thrust at his mouth every time he walked out of an airport's terminal zone, or have a face that gazed from record shop windows that bloomed with the splendour of his every latest album. He did not envy St. Francis and his 'hidden solitude where I can listen in loneliness and silence to the secret treasures of God's conversation.'

As a showbiz personality, Moon, with his overdeveloped sense of humour and flair for self–promotion, was in the tradition of arch–Dadaist

Arthur Cravan – who paid to box against world heavyweight champion Jack Johnson and was flattened in the first round, who removed his clothes when lecturing to a gathering of appalled high–society ladies, who sailed into the shark–infested Caribbean in a small boat and was never seen again – and 'Louisville Lip' Cassius Clay, better known now as Muhammed Ali, running 'round a Las Vegas boxing ring in 1964, yelling that he was the greatest and the prettiest after knocking out Sonny Liston, who, according to most sports commentators, had been invincible.

More relevant to Moon, however, were Charles Trenet ('The Singing Madman' of Gallic *chanson*), Spike Jones and his City Slickers, Liberace, Lord Sutch, Freddie and the Dreamers, The Barron–Knights, P.J. Proby, Jacques Dutronc, The Bonzo Dog Doo–Dah Band, Gary Glitter and Pete Townshend's *protege*, John Otway, who would have invited professional suicide had any of them attempted a reinvention as a 'musicianly' *artiste* with a self–depreciating image.

It was noted nonetheless, that for all their clowning on the boards, Freddie and the Dreamers did not reach the charts with songs specifically designed to be amusing. Indeed, though he was a sort of Norman Wisdom of 1960s pop, Freddie Garrity's spirited revival with his Dreamers of rhythm–and–bluesman James Ray's 'If You Gotta Make A Fool Of Somebody' in 1963 was half–liked by the discriminating ilk of John Lennon, Keith Richards, Rod Stewart – and Keith Moon, who also identified with Garrity's singular onstage vitality and extreme strategies. On 1964's New Year's Eve edition of *Ready Steady Go*, he was miming one of his smashes in silly hats. Without warning, Freddie – inspired perhaps by the self–immolation of Arthur Cravan – ceased lip–synching, and commenced to cram paper streamers into his mouth.

A more appropriate setting for this idiocy was in pantomime where Garrity and the lads had made their debut as court jesters in Chester Royalty Theatre's *Cinderella*. They were to plunge deeper into this, their natural element, as well as notch up several film appearances, whether in *Every Day's A Holiday* as canteen chefs with 'What's Cooking', a six–minute mini–opera that anticipated The Who's 'A Quick One' by three years – or performing The Hollywood Argyles' 'Short Shorts' – with foreseeable downfall of same – in 1963's *What A Crazy World*.

Extravagant gesture and epic vulgarity had also been the key to Liverpool's Rory Storm and the Hurricanes, led by an indefatigable self–publicist. His 'Mr. Showmanship' nickname was no overstatement as he wound up heterosexual chauvinists with his gigolo wardrobe – which, from mere pink nylon, would stretch to costumes of gold lamé and sequins – and peacock posturing. To illustrate Carl Perkins' 'Lend Me Your Comb,' Storm would sweep an outsize one through a precarious pompadour which kept falling over his forehead, but this was nothing compared to what he did when the group played venues attached to swimming baths. Mid–song, Rory was likely to push through the crowd, clamber to the top board, strip to scarlet swimming trunks and dive in.

When he squeezed even harder on the nerve of how far he could go, Storm's injuries were sometimes self–inflicted as he plummeted from the glass dome of New Brighton's capacious Tower Ballroom and fractured his leg, or was concussed on an equally rash climb to a pillared balcony stage left at Birkenhead's Majestic.

Though Storm fronted the Hurricanes, the others did not skulk to the rear. Maddened by someone's incessant whistle–blowing during one engagement, Ringo Starr, then the drummer, slung a stick towards the offender; striking instead a hulking local gangleader who, mistakenly, enacted a reprisal against Rory. A rowdy bunch with impressive self–confidence, the Hurricanes would sometimes swap instruments for comic relief in which notes chased haphazardly up and down fretboards amid 'free form' clattering.

Sinking into a slough of poverty in 1961, Storm signed on at an Unemployment Benefit Office as a 'rock and roll pianist', a genuflection to Little Richard, another entertainer of the same kidney. To reinforce some argument during a bout of loud piety, Richard flung expensive jewellery into the sea, but is freeze–framed forever in his billowing drapes, pencil moustache and precarious pompadour as he hollered, say, a bombastic 'Long Tall Sally' in 1957's 'Don't Knock The Rock' while punishing a grand piano with parts of his anatomy apart from his fingers.

Of the same vintage, Screamin' Jay Hawkins' was the first modern pop artist to latch onto the notion that if you can't be first, be peculiar. His extravaganzas began with a sulphurous and pedantic emergence from a coffin, bathed in eerie fluorescence. Garbed in, perhaps, turban, zebra–striped formal attire and crimson cloak, he'd produce props like a cigarette–puffing skull and an array of powdery potions, and his singing would flit fitfully from warbling mock–operatics to the blood–chilling dementia of one in the throes of a fit. If the much–covered 'I Put A Spell On You' was his only major smash, the likes of 'She Put The Whammy On Me', 'Feast Of The Mau–Mau' and 'Little Demon' were more blatant blueprints for grosser excesses by Black Sabbath, Alice Cooper and others for whom Screamin' Jay's pioneering feats were to be received wisdom.

Returning closer to home, the chief show–off of Zoot Money's Big Roll Band was witnessed ritually hurling amplifiers and other of the outfit's electronic paraphenalia off the end of Bournemouth pier after one gremlin–troubled performance in its Pavilion auditorium. Yet, de-spite a stage presence akin to that of a psychotic Bud Flannagan as well as a penchant for trouser–dropping and dressing up, Zoot was, like so–many so–called extroverts, quite a shy, self–effacing person.

So was Wee Willie Harris, bruited by his manager as the kingdom's very own Jerry Lee Lewis – though he was less a teen idol than a televi-sion gimmick in loud attire and with hair dyed a funny colour – usually shocking–pink – for regular slots on *Six–Five Special*. Neither was he above banal publicity stunts like a 'feud' with blue–rinsed Larry Page, 'the Teenage Rage' and another 1950s also–ran. If a less enduring pop jester than Screaming Lord Sutch, he resurfaced as a nostalgia act when it transpired that he was still remembered by such as Ian Dury who dropped his name in the lyrics of 1979's 'Reasons To Be Cheerful (Part Three)'. At a memorial concert to the late Lord Sutch at the Ace Cafe in 2002, Harris was received with some affection when he was actually on stage, but cut a quiet, lonely figure afterwards, seated at his merchandise stall.

The late founder of this particular feast had established himself via the discovery that there was plenty you could do with red lipstick and liberal dollops of tomato ketchup – while twenty messy minutes with cold scrambled eggs, cherry food–dye and some old tights will result in glisteningly convincing intestines. Yet Sutch's routines on the boards verged on music hall slapstick, embracing an 'operation' involving the wrenching out of heart and liver (bought from the butcher's that after-noon), and the simulated murder and mutilation of a 'prostitute', i.e. one of his Savages in wig and padded bra.

157

The music was almost an afterthought. After 'Til The Following Night', his singles were divided evenly between rock 'n' roll ravers and horror spoofs such as 'Monster In Black Tights', 'Dracula's Daughter' and 'All Black And Hairy'. While their point was frequently lost without accompanying visuals, the commercial progress of most Sutch A–sides was hindered further by restricted airplay.

The mid–1960s passed with no mainstream 45s comparable to Sutch's – though there were many isolated pot–shots as instanced by the cybernautic 'Look Out There's A Monster Coming' from The Bonzo Dog Doo–Dah Band – who, following Brian Poole and the Tremeloes' less camp attempt in 1963, exhumed too 'Alley Oop', and improved upon 'The Monster Mash'.

More cosmic a ham captivated the crowd during the watershed year of 1967. Owing more than David Sutch to Screamin' Jay Hawkins, University of Reading philosophy graduate Arthur Brown danced in an idiosyncratic sidelong flicker and emitted a penetrating glare when focal point of The Crazy World of Arthur Brown. Robed exotically, he sported a helmet spouting flames (originally a candlestick attached to a sieve). Now and then, things went dangerously awry and both Arthur's drapery, and indeed howling Arthur, were set ablaze to ovations from those who thought it was as premeditated a stunt as the crane that lowered him from a great height onto the podium at some 'happening' during that hot summer.

The toast of London's psychedelic dungeons, The Crazy World of Arthur Brown was as good as it would ever get when, after Track – The Who's label – issued 'Devil's Grip', they went for the jugular with a second 45, 1968's 'Fire' – casting Arthur as 'god of hell–fire' – a *tour de force* that was their only chart strike – a Number One, mind.

Since then, Brown has travelled down many roads – new groups, image transformation, a part as the Priest in Ken Russell's *Tommy*, solo albums, religion...hands–on proprietorship of a building–and–decorating firm in Texas with ex–Mother of Invention, Jimmy Carl Black and, more recently, *Tantric Lover*, a predominantly acoustic offering which provides further evidence that Arthur Brown has always been more than a mere God of Hellfire.

If Arthur Brown was its *de jure* ruler, the fiery furnace's *de facto* overlords were to be Black Sabbath whose initial blues determination had fermented into an apocalyptic brutality which affected a bleak but atmospheric intensity during a season at Hamburg's Star–Club. Sporting inverted crucifixes and similar Satanic fetishist gear, they were smashing out self–penned pieces that exhibited a fascination with the novels of Dennis Wheatley.

However, the scum of internal dissent was to boil down to a clash between guitarist Tony Iommi and vocalist Ozzy Osbourne. Bored silly by painstaking retakes and overdubbing of minor fretboard fills, Osbourne occupied himself with an increasing intake of hard drugs, sexual adventure and other transient kicks such as drawing beads on his farmyard chickens until none were left squawking. Soon, he seemed as nutty as the characters he assumed when giving 'em 'Paranoid' or 1976's 'Am I Going Insane?'.

With Osbourne's departure in 1978, the group started catering more and more for the kind of consumer for whom information that a favoured group's latest album is just like the one before is praise indeed. Sometimes, they'd hear sick–making stories about their old colleague's incarceration in mental institutions and detoxification clinics as a result of his revelling in crapulous debauchery. Allegedly, he evacuated his bowels wherever he felt like it – on the site of the Alamo (for which he was punished with lifelong exile from that district of the Deep South) and in a motel elevator. While doing his business noisily and abundantly, his cheery 'It's OK. I'm staying here' did not reassure other occupants, who got out at the next floor.

Someone else swore that he'd brought a press conference to a standstill by biting off the heads of two doves and gulping them down with the leer of a catatonic Benny Hill. True or false, the multiplying legends boosted sales of collections like *Diary Of A Madman, The Ultimate Sin* and 1988's *No Peace For The Wicked* plus their retinue of 45s like 'Mr. Crowley' and 'Bark At The Moon' with its video of Osbourne as a werewolf.

A fan of Osbourne, with and without Black Sabbath, Frank Zappa had been at the heart of controversy in autumn 1967 when a centre spread in *International Times*, Britain's foremost 'underground' organ, depicted him stark naked on the toilet, albeit with his modesty strategically hidden, years before a full–frontal shot of Keith Moon, lying on his back, appeared in a publication entitled *Rock 'N' Roll Babylon.* [8] Detriot's Iggy Pop was similarly photographed in the late 1970s – albeit vertically – after he'd regularly exposed himself numerous times on stage during his days with the Stooges

Groomed by Zappa, Alice Cooper was to combine theatre, androgyny, and cheap thrills more effectively with a kind of glam–rock from the charnel house. In its fullest flowering, the crux of an extravaganza as slickly contrived as any Broadway musical was that, like Mr. Punch, Alice got sentenced to execution – via gallows, guillotine or electric chair – for all manner of felonies committed from the opening bars of the set. There were a lot of funny activities involving whips, dolls, chickens and a boa constrictor, and repellant fascination was inclined to distract attention from the quality of the music – a melodic, controlled strand of heavy metal underpinning a witty if gruesome lyricism in titles such as 1971's 'The Ballad Of Dwight Fry', which plunged into the inner horrors of a real–life Hollywood thespian whose speciality was ill–favoured underlings, sinister butlers and creepy bit–parts in general. Finally, Dwight the man became a composite of them all.

And so it goes on...

Peddling a hybrid of folk–rock and a brand of pop that conjured up a sort of *Welsh* Who, Y Tebot Piws – formed in the late 1960s, disbanded in 1972 and reformed in 2002 – deserve attention for their Dewi Pws's kilt, tomato–red wig and huge geeky spectacles, and instinctive but coarse grained crowd control, and indeed for their drummer's similarity – on and off stage – to the subject of this tome.

Brewer's Droop, featuring a young Mark Knopfler (who'd have thought), the beer–sodden blues revisionists from High Wycombe, were banned from many venues in their day for the foam–rubber phallus that aided singer Ron Watts' – later an early supporter of The Sex Pistols and sometime assistant to Malcolm McLaren – bawdy jocularity.

Splodgenessabounds' novel 'Two Pints Of Lager And A Packet Of Crisps Please' recitative – hastily–recorded and originally conceived as the B–side of 'Simon Templar' – was a Top Ten entry in 1980. Reflecting the same anarchic, topical and slightly sick humour were two smaller hits. After the group's time was up, leader Splodge performed a rather dubious turn before assembled journalists. This failed, nevertheless, to precipitate a chart comeback.

'Gothic punk' exponents, The Cramps climaxed their shows with bug–eyed singer Lux Interior stripped bare amid dingy light and

Top left **With occasional Beach Boy Brian Johnson and Ready Steady Go presenter Cathy MacGowan**
Top Right **With Viv Stanshall**
Centre **With Abba**
Bottom **With David Frost and Amanda the night before he died.**

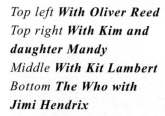

Top left **With Oliver Reed**
Top right **With Kim and daughter Mandy**
Middle **With Kit Lambert**
Bottom **The Who with Jimi Hendrix**

JIMI HENDRIX
&
THE WHO

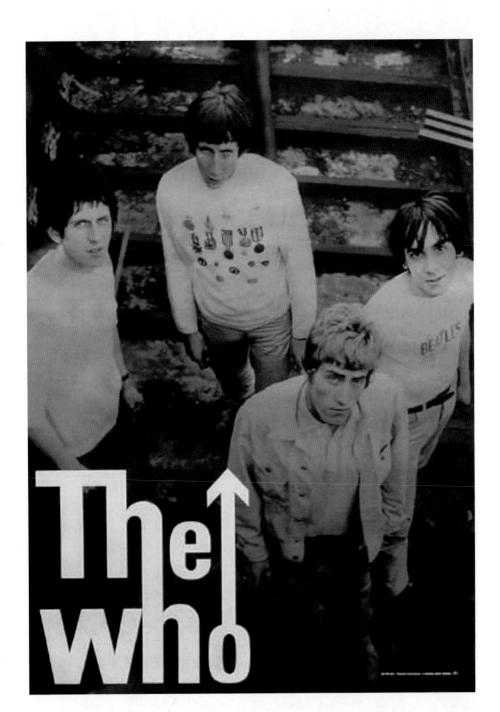

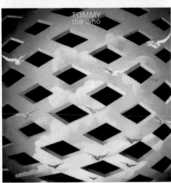

***Keith's recorded output with The
Who and under his own name***
*All covers courtesy Polydor /
Universal*

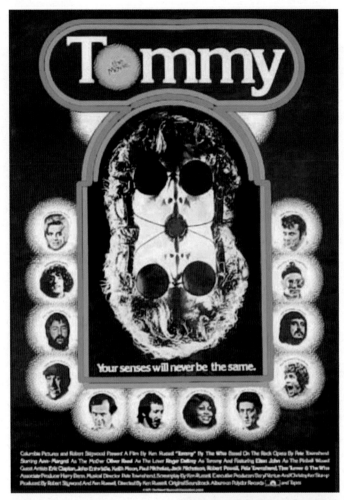

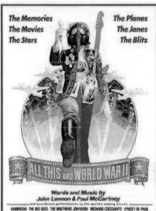

Selections from Keith Moon's movie career

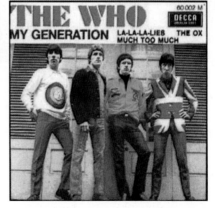

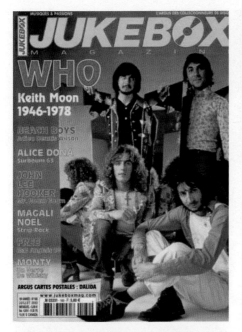

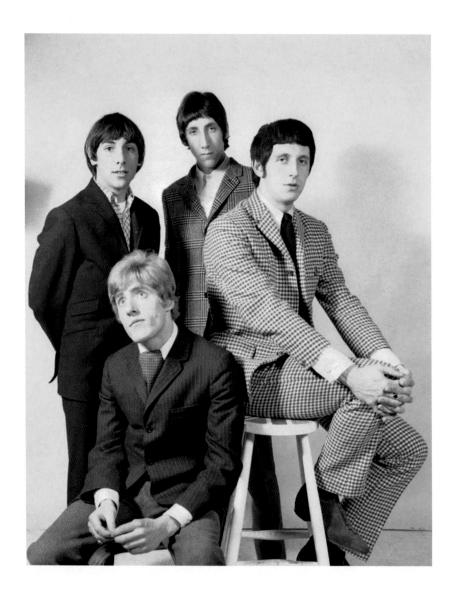

clangorous, stomach–churning chords. Well, I mean, he had a penis, hadn't he?

Bass player Captain Sensible of The Damned had one too. It was there for all to see on the front page of *Sounds* after he'd strolled un-clothed onto a London stage in 1977 when punk rock was fresh out of shock tactics that were traceable to The Who, their chief show–off and the culmination of all that preceeded him.

As the third millennium began not on 1 January 2000, but 11 September 2001 or, if you prefer, Boxing Day 2004, what was the event that divided punk from power pop, New Romantic, Mod revival or whatever it was came next? Was it when hell's magnet dragged Sid Vicious down on 2 February 1979 while awaiting trial for murder? Exactly seven years later when The Damned chalked up their big-gest hit with slushy 'Eloise', lovingly copied from Barry Ryan's vio-lin–soaked 1968 original? A sundered Clash's 1991 chart–topper with 'Should I Stay Or Should I Go', courtesy of snippet coverage in an ITV commercial?

Though the apogee of punk coincided with a barren patch for The Who, perhaps its end may be dated 7 September 1978 and the passing of one who'd absorbed and forgotten more about rock 'n' roll excess than any punk – and probably just about everybody else – would ever know. Few will disagree with that.

Notes

1. The World's Greatest Cranks And Crackpots by M. Nicholas (Octopus, 1982)
2. *Teenage Wasteland; The Early Who* by C. Welch (Castle Communications, 1995)
3. *Loose Talk* ed. L. Botts (Omnibus, 1980)
4. *Hull Times*, 6 June 1966
5. *Rhino's Psychedelic Trip* by A. Bisbort and J. Marshall (Miller Freeman, 2000)
6. *Not Like A Proper Job: The Story Of Popular Music In Sheffield, 1955– 1975* by J. Firminger and M. Lilleker (Juma, 2001)
7. *Joe Cocker: With A Little Help From My Friends* by J.P. Bean (Omnibus, 1990)
8. *Rock 'N' Roll Babylon* by G. Herman (Plexus, 1982)

Steve Gibbons remembers Keith Moon: *'Keith turned up in the dressing room when we were about to appear at the Marquee one night, and asked if he could announce us. He went on in his long fur coat and lion's head medallion, and gave us a huge build–up. Such superstar support certainly helped our career – and so did our general association with The Who. However, there were a lot of hair–raising episodes involving Keith.*

On the European leg of our tour with The Who, we travelled on their chartered plane – which held about fifty passengers. I was quite new to air travel, and shared the overall bemusement when John Entwistle walked down the aisle with the news that Moon was at the controls. Everyone peered anxiously into the front cabin where he was hunched over the instrumental panel, wearing his manic grin. Fortunately, the pilot took over again before we landed.

In North America in autumn 1975, he was trying to curb his drink-ing, but fell off the wagon in a big way as the tour progressed. One night, he was so far gone that there was doubt that he'd be able to play. Nevertheless, he made it to his kit and flopped through the first couple of numbers before he collapsed. The show was cancelled, and had to be re–scheduled for the end of the tour. It made headlines in the national press. There was no way of knowing whether or not it was all a publicity stunt.

Later, Trevor Burton, Entwistle, Moon and I were in some slightly pretentious hotel bar decorated with mock–Tudor furniture and re-productions of old masters. John mentioned that he'd bought a Colt 45 for his collection of antique firearms that afternoon – whereupon Keith produced his purchase from the same place: a low–calibre, loaded, Derringer hand–gun – which he used to shoot holes in the pictures.

There was mayhem at reception the next day, but Keith – via The Who's manager – paid for the damage without argument. This sort of thing happened all the time. Generally though, he never did anything with malice unless something or someone upset him.

Back in Britain, he took exception to the decor in the dressing area at the Glasgow Apollo, and trashed it completely. The police were called, but somehow he placated them, and a photo of him wearing a copper's helmet made the front page of the NME: all further grist to the publicity mill, I suppose.'

'You're Going To Know Me': Moonrise Over North America

'I would like to introduce to you now the most explosive group ever to have come out of England' – the compere's announcement when The Who appeared at the Memorial Auditorium, Dallas on 23 July 1967

The Who had sat on the sidelines during the 'British Invasion' of North America when, for an initial spell of several months in the mid–1960s, most of the UK's major post–Merseybeat groups – and many minor ones – made progress to varying extents in the unchartered United States and Canada. During one 1964 week, two–thirds of the US music trade journal *Billboard's Hot 100* was British in origin. In the wake of The Beatles, the New World went nearly as crackers about The Dave Clark Five and then Freddie and the Dreamers and Herman's Hermits, whose respective front men looked as if they needed even more mothering than Keith Moon.

Other Britons who penetrated the sub–continent via pop–associated styles and trends included John Peel – engaged as resident 'Beatles expert' by a Dallas radio station – Mary Quant, who, pressed by some to autograph her creations–in–cloth, 'began to feel rather like a Beatle' [1], and, since emigrating in 1962, Jack Good, the brains behind *Six–Five Special, Oh Boy!* and other ground–breaking pop shows.

Keith Moon was to be particularly interested in Good's similarly hands–on approach to US television. Once a stand–up comedian, Jack had made his mark as a Hollywood movie stereotype of a bowler–hatted, pin–striped Queen's Englishman, complete with furled umbrella over his arm, when superintending the nationally–broadcast *Shindig*, which held its own in a ratings war against *The Beverley Hillbillies*. [2] On another rival channel, it was fighting a cartoon about an outfit called 'The Beadles', which had them using redundant east London colloquialisms such as 'blimey, guv'nor' and 'blighter', and addressing each other as 'mate'.

In a new teenpic, *Bikini Beach*, Frankie Avalon played it posh as 'the Potato Bug', an English pop–singing 'refugee from a haircut'. Similar in assumed character, Screaming Lord Sutch put it about that he was 'the sixth Earl of Harrow' when 'part of the second wave of the British Invasion in around 1968 with my Union Jack Rolls Royce. It had a trailer painted likewise, full of "I'm Backing Britain" products – mostly records and Carnaby Street clothes. I did mostly trade fayres in between gigs, and put on an upper–class voice.'

Arriving too from the mythical land of Good Queen Bess, Robin Hood, fish 'n' chips, Oxford–and–Cambridge, Beefeaters, monocled cads and kilted Scotsmen, The Who's Great Adventure began in March 1967 with disembarkation at Kennedy airport. If nowhere on the scale of The Beatles' messianic descent on New York almost three years earlier, there were still cameras clicking like typewriters and reporters shooting questions in hopes that the personnel of one of the last unreconstructed British beat groups would crack back at the now stock enquiries about long hair and mini–skirts with a Beatle–esque combination of wit, unsentimentality and unblinking self–assurance. In addition, what with boy soldiers being blown to bits in Indochina, circling media hounds expected sarcastic one–line debates about more inflammable issues than *favorite colors*, preferred foodstuffs and the age at which they hoped to marry.

In a jacket that would have outshone Max Miller, Pete Townshend dominated this expected press conference. Despite having flexed his verbal muscles with the European press, nothing notably droll or even significant came from the lips of a remarkably subdued Moon, but, as it had been with Ringo Starr in 1964, the drummer stole the show in the long term from the others in a society that was later to concede to the adoption of Cabbage Patch Dolls. The Who had in Keith something as lovably affecting; a little–boy–lost, a diminutive snare–drum Cinderella on a lonely pedestal like Ringo, but with an oddball strain that was to proliferate like a psychic rash over his entire personality in ratio to the growing number of comments about it.

He learnt quickly to answer back snappily and impudently to banal enquiries as repetitious as a stuck record – and, if his remarks seemed inane and pedestrian in print, their saving grace on film was the poker–faced *what–are–you–laughing–at* way he told 'em. Neither did the Yanks know how they were meant to take the accent that went with a persona that could switch in seconds from gor–blimey Cockney barrow boy to a proper Lord Snooty, all genteel manners, girly enunciations and a vocabulary freighted with P.G. Wodehouse phrases like 'jolly good', 'dear boy' and 'right–ho!'.

Another much–repeated affectation was the *ooo–arrr* West Country used by Robert Newton in his swaggeringly overplayed and utterly unforgettable role as 'Long John Silver' in the Walt Disney film adaptation in 1950 of *Treasure Island*. Keith picked up on it when Newton–as–Silver's shifty shiver–me–timbers pirate villainy was extended into a long–running series on children's television. Enthralled, the boy never missed a single episode, and entertained the family with his efforts to mimic Silver's manic, eye–rolling facial expressions and his grindingly slow and brandy–slurred intonations: *'aaaahhhh, me old pal, me old beauty...'*

Decisively, Keith caught an edition of *Hancock's Half–Hour* – 'the Knighthood' in March 1959 – in which the comedian delivered excerpts from Shakespeare in the style of Newton in *Treasure Island*, while getting into arguments with the fake parrot on his shoulder. After that, Moon became as well known for his own Jim–lad imitations as Alperton Secondary Modern's school bully and football captain were in their chosen areas. He'd listen so many times to an associated recording of the film, which he acquired in 1965, that he could recite most of Newton's lines from memory – and, as late as 1978, Moon would appear in a brief clip in Long John Silver garb, crutch and parrot too, in the Who documentary, *The Kids Are Alright*. [3]

Moon was amused by the genuine Long John Silver burrs of Reg Presley and Ronnie Bond, respectively singer and drummer with The Troggs, who crossed the Atlantic to support The Who for some of the dates on a summer tour in 1968. The days when The Troggs – who'd scored a US Number One with 'Wild Thing' two years before – might have headlined, were past, and as it was The Who who were going to sell tickets, The Who got top billing. Nevertheless, The Troggs were a hard act to follow, and were to be accorded a standing ovation in Birmingham, Alabama. Yet the ice broke and the two groups became friendly in their common confinement in this bandroom or that chartered flight.

Moreover, the high point of the day wasn't always your spell under the spotlights, but the building–up and the winding–down – and roguish pranks played on each other during the show. Somewhere in America, Moon sawed halfway through Bond's drumsticks and wrapped tape around the cuts so that Ronnie – as fond of practical jokes as Moon – ended up in minutes with only one stick with which to get through three–quarters of The Troggs' set – not that the effect was noticed much as Reg Presley, virtually gulping the microphone, squared up to a public address system constructed for sports commentators. He was to recall a confusing occurrence onstage in Montreal: 'Halfway through the act, everyone started applauding – and I thought that's good because we weren't actually playing at the time. Then we discovered the news of the president's resignation had just reached the auditorium.'

When the troupe crossed the frontier into New York state, they encountered The Yardbirds on their last legs after immortalizing themselves on a lacklustre in–concert album. They all 'played a hilarious gig where a lot of hippies turned up,' noted Reg, 'and they put on an incredible light show before us, making us appear a little dull in comparison'.

Nevertheless, after each show, members of US garage bands might troop backstage to pay their respects to distinguished living artefacts of the British beat boom – who were becoming used to even the most garrulous stargazers suddenly falling silent in an awestriken sense of *deja vu*, mingled with a touch of scepticism – as if The Who and The Troggs couldn't possibly be human beings who picked their noses like everyone else.

'Garage' – or, by original definition, 'punk' – was first used to categorize Anglophile outfits from North America like The Shadows Of Knight, The Sonics, The Seeds, The Monks, The Thirteenth Floor Elevators and ? and the Mysterions, who crawled from the sub–cultural woodwork after they'd grown out their crew–cuts and seized upon whatever easy–to–play aspects of the new Limey idioms they felt most comfortable with.

Certain individuals tried to copy Keith Moon – as instanced by Robert Smith of Rhode Island's boss group The Mojo Hands. His softly–spoken off–stage demeanour was at odds with wild drumming, marred by poor time–keeping and made louder by his copious use of microphones and a wielding of reversed sticks so that the heavier ends battered the kit. Wanton destruction of drumheads and sticks consumed most of his earnings. However, as the other members of the group preferred to model themselves on The Rolling Stones rather than The Who, Smith was fired in 1966.

On an infinitely higher plane than local heroes like the Hands, The Monkees were four youths put together by a cabal of Californian businessmen to play an Anglo–American pop group in a nationwide TV series. Though the project's blueprint was the *Hard Day's Night*-period Beatles, the boxed advertisement that had been placed in the Los Angeles *Daily Variety* on 8 August 1965 had read 'Madness! Running parts for four insane boys aged 17–21', and it was noticed that, though each of the chosen applicants bore some sort of resemblance to one or other of the Fab Four, the balance of personalities could as easily have been based on The Who with elements of Keith in both the 'cute' Davy Jones and the 'zany' drummer, Mickey Dolenz. [4]

This had been endorsed during The Who's maiden appearance on a networked US television show, *The Smothers Brothers Comedy Hour*, in September 1967, which concluded with the most explosive – literally – 'My Generation' ever performed. When hanging about after the afternoon rehearsal, Moon loaded a bass drum with flash powder, which was to be triggered at an optimum moment by his foot pedal. However, like it was during a kitchen scene in Rodgers and Hammerstein's *Oklahoma* musical when members of a household independently and secretively add drops of whiskey to a pudding, so individuals from the studio staff and Who road crew packed further small quantities of powder into the cache over the course of the hours that preceded The Who's slot. The consequent blast blanked the screen, made some woman faint, singed Pete Townshend's hair and purportedly caused permanent ruin to his hearing.

The closing credits rolled in front of teenagers who were as shocked as their parents. Yet, as is their wont, our colonial cousins, convinced of the incredible, exhibited an enthusiasm for it that left more reserved British Who fans swallowing dust. More than their set at the Monterey Pop Festival three months earlier, this was the ignition point of The Who's continued success in North America.

It had mixed blessings. Waking up in a luxurious cage of claustrophobia, Keith would almost expect to yawn and stretch to a standing ovation, so intrusive was the sub–continent's adoration. Where was the sub–continent? There were photographs of him performing in its every territory, but he'd guess he was in Canada only by Mounties that patrolled the besieged hotel, and below the Mason–Dixon line by the chambermaids' cawing Deep South dialect outside his room. The country's richness and immensity was to lie beyond an ocean of faces and flash–bulbs until this particular form of madness subsided.

Notes

1. *Quant On Quant* by M. Quant (Cassell, 1966)
2. Leaving *Shindig* to fend for itself, Good's most intriguing career tangent of the later '60s was *Catch My Soul*, 1968's rock adaptation in a Los Angeles theatre of Shakespeare's *Othello* with Jerry Lee Lewis as a surprisingly effective Iago. For a season in London, P.J. Proby assumed the Lewis role with Good himself as the Moor.
3. *A propos* nothing in particular, Robert Newton appeared in two movies, both called *The Beachcomber*; a 1934 vehicle for Charles Laughton (renamed *Vessel Of Wrath* in Britain) and a 1954 re–make with Newton in the male lead.
4. In parenthesis, Moon was to be the apparent inspiration for the 'Animal' character in the glove–puppet television comedy, *The Muppet Show*, first broadcast in 1977.

Reg Presley remembers Keith Moon: 'Us and the Who were very competitive on stage to the extent that once I turned round and Ronnie Bond, our drummer, was boss–eyed with concentration, trying desperately to keep the beat – because Keith was behind the curtain bashing a tambourine out of time to put him off. He'd also put his hand through the curtain and pull Ronnie's stool back, inch by inch – and pinch the claves he was supposed to play on "Love Is All Around", and make V–signs with them at Ronnie from the wings. However, there wasn't any malice in it, and Keith was always good fun, no matter what it cost.

I was there when he blew up a hotel toilet with a bundle of mini–dynamite sticks he used to carry around with him. After he'd thus caused thousands of dollars worth of damage, he rang up reception and asked, 'Please can you bring me up another room'.

Another time, he rolled a fake hand–grenade down the aisle of a jet, and got The Who banned from ever using that particular airline again.

Then in Greenwich Village, New York, he and Ronnie went into a bar where he made an enormous cocktail by leaping over the counter and filling a champagne bucket with every spirit he could lay his hands on – and the barman let him do it!

Sometimes he'd get so sloshed that he'd tell the road crew not to disturb him under any circumstances the next morning. They'd protest that he had to be on board the tour bus for the next show at, say, ten o' clock, but he'd insist on lying in. So they'd go into his room, lift him gently onto a stretcher and carry him down to the bus where he'd be laid out on the luggage rack. Pete, Roger and John never used to bat an eyelid at anything Keith did. He took excess to excess.'

We Were Paintermen: A Slight Digression Into Some Rival Attractions

'It was The Small Faces who brought me to the Mods as a source of inspiration' – Paul Weller [1]

Let's cross to an alternative universe for three paragraphs. As The Creation cruise by limousine to Wembley Stadium during the UK leg of their record–breaking world tour, their old rivals, The Who, take the stage to a small but appreciative crowd at the Oldfield Hotel in the neighbouring borough of Greenford. With only Keith Moon and John Entwistle left from the original line–up, this was the group's first booking after a long lay–off – one of many during thirty years of bad luck, administrative chicanery, excessive record company thrift and Moon being typecast as a poor man's Jack Jones.

There'd been a place in the pub–rock sun for the latter–day Who back in the mid–1970s, and they'd picked up a neo–punk audience who bought reissues of the old LPs – of which 1967's psychedelic Germany–only *City In The Sky* slipped into the 'alternative' chart in *Sounds* no less. Then a German label commissioned a new Who album, *Who's Left?* – and contributed to the recording costs.

Of course, it couldn't last, and a schedule that had once signified a week's work became a month's. Apart from compilations built round their two Top Fifty entries at the tail–end of the beat boom, the only new Who commodity during the next decade was 1986's *Live At The RMA Tavern, Portsmouth* – though, more recently, Keith shook maraccas on an EP by *Thee Headcoats*, one of the mainstays of the Medway towns indie scene.

You could speculate endlessly about how it might have been – but there was certainly a period *circa 1966* when The Who and The Creation were on terms of fluctuating equality – well, according to the latter group's fan club newsletters anyway. Even the Beatles were seen as a lesser threat to The Who than The Creation and further challengers from the Mod brigade such as The Action, The Untamed, A Wild Uncertainty, The Thoughts [2], The Attack, The Frame and, especially, The Small Faces and The Move.

These were looming on the horizon when, as an indication that the age of publicity photos of groups in The Beatles' image posing on brick–strewn wasteland had drawn to a close, Tony Jackson, lately departed from The Searchers, fronted the newly–formed Vibrations, and become aware by 1965 that 'The Who and all the Mod groups were coming in, so we took that path – a lot of crash, bang, wallop.' Soon, each record company executive, who imagined that he had a finger on the pulse, was either searching for, if not *the* New Who then *a* New Who – or else signing as many acts like them as the traffic would allow, having first asked one of the temps, 'What exactly *is* a 'Mod'?

Hardly a week would go by without another Mod act being thus thrust forward – or so it seemed. Somehow, most of them looked and sounded just like The Who, except that, with rare exceptions, none were committed enough to run up the kind of debts incurred when, say, Keith Moon's wreckage of a drum kit became as foreseeable as the crashing of a Model T Ford in a Keystone Cops movie.

Nonetheless, quite a few Mod ensembles contained at least one key musician who, like Pete Townshend, had attended art school at a time when Pop Art had been predicted by some to be the coming trend, but scorned by the establishment as a novelty. Pre–empting Andy Warhol's soup–cans, the goal was to bring humour and topicality back into Fine Art via the paradox of earnest fascination with the brashest of junk culture, and a mannered relishing of advertising hoardings, comics, beach movies and other artefacts of this Coca–Cola century, ridiculed as puerile, tasteless and fake. In the interests of research, Pop artists listened avidly to Top Forty radio which was, indeed, as Townshend said, 'like the TV – something you can turn on and off and shouldn't disturb yer mind.' [3]

With ex–Moseley Art collegian Roy Wood at the creative helm, The Move came down from Birmingham to the capital in a blaze of publicity stunts inspired by Tony Secunda – their 'Kit Lambert' – and an alarming stage act – of which one of the milder aspects was a novel 'Zing Went The Strings Of My Heart' sung by drummer Bev Bevan. Beset with technical problems, The Who put up a less impressive show than The Move at a *Giant Freak–Out All Night Rave* on 1966's New Year's Eve at the Roundhouse, notable for their Carl Wayne charging onstage with a chopper to hack up effigies of world political leaders before turning to a bank of maybe thirty switched–on televisions.

As its personnel had all served in other outfits that were big in Birmingham but unknown everywhere else, The Move had been well–

placed to amass a strong local reputation with a repertoire that developed from soul and classic rock in 1965 to a diverting mixture of mostly Californian acid–rock and, crucially, Wood's compositions, which included 1967's 'Night Of Fear', an 'A' side that kicked off a five–year run of hits – 'very poppy compared to our more psychedelic stuff,' observed guitarist Trevor Burton – including a British chart–topper with 1968's 'Blackberry Way'.

Earlier Who disciples, The Creation were the flagship act of Planet, Shel Talmy's short–lived independent label, as The Who were Track's (and, later, The Small Faces, Immediate's). Describing their music as 'red with purple flashes', they climaxed their act in more two–dimensional manner than either The Move or The Who by splashing onto a canvas backdrop an action painting that owed less to Jackson Pollock than to Tony Hancock – though one mischievous night, vocalist Kenny Pickett, taking more time than usual, confronted onlookers with a messy exposition of the female nude. Then he set fire to it – and if that's not Art, then I'm sure I don't know what is.

Perhaps the most striking of the Mod groups, The Creation also pioneered the scraping of a violin bow across an electric guitar on a hasty LP, *We Are Paintermen*, issued only in Scandinavia and Germany – where 'Painter Man', the second of the group's modest chart forays at home, had gone to Number One. This triumph – and allegations that their singles had been manoeuvred into the UK Top Fifty by under–the–bedclothes fixing – necessitated virtual exile in Germany for a year.

Moon–like drummer Jack Jones would remember a show at Munich's Circus Krone where 'we set up our painting frame, but we didn't know you needed a special licence with the fire brigade standing by. The next thing, everybody's spraying hoses to put our usual fire out, and the Gestapo arrive in leather coats, hats and dark glasses. They confiscated our passports.' [4]

A contemporary press release, nevertheless, would describe The Creation – with some justification – as 'Germany's third top touring group'. However, somewhere along the *autobahns*, development deferred to consolidation, albeit with some success as exemplified by startling 'Life Is Just Beginning', laden with Sgt. Pepperry strings and horns – and competent covers of classic rock, US soul and garage band standards. Running out of ideas, they quit while they were ahead commercially, after farewell treks round the Netherlands and Germany in 1968.

Other Mod groups left well enough alone, and evolved few characteristics that set them apart. After recovering from the blow of being dropped by The Who, Shel Talmy had taken on The Untamed, harbingers of a non–existent 'Bognor Regis Sound', who'd had a pirate radio 'turntable hit' in 1965 with James Brown's 'I'll Go Crazy', common property of hundreds of other groups. Neither their Talmy–produced cover of 'It's Not True' from the *My Generation* LP and its 'Daddy Long Legs' follow–up could forestall a lingering decline – though today this not untalented also–ran outfit rate much retrospective coverage in all manner of fanzines devoted to the 1960s group boom. [5]

Next up were John's Children, who were thrown off a Who tour of Germany when some carryings–on with chains and feathers caused reaction to be more subdued for the headliners than they'd come to expect, though The Who were still able to whip up a screeching rabble. [6] It should also be noted that The Action's standing in Mod circles was such that their van would be met on the outskirts of Brighton by a cavalcade of Parka–ed scooter–riders, who'd escort them to the venue.

No mid–1960s Mod ever missed The Small Faces either if he could help it. Though the 'real thing' in both appearance and attitude, this East End quartet hadn't anything very exceptional going for them during the brief preamble to their emergence as the best of the bunch. Lambert and Stamp had been 'interested' in them, but ace Small Face Steve Marriott prefered Don Arden, whose son he had known at stage school. Thus Kit and Chris lost the opportunity to manage both of Britain's pre–eminent Mod outfits.

The Small Faces' initial objective was to be like an English version of Booker T and the MGs, but with vocals. Nevertheless, within eight weeks of signing to Decca, they were secure in the Top Twenty with 'Whatcha Gonna Do About It', with a title borrowed from Doris Troy and a chord pattern from Solomon Burke's 'Everybody Needs Somebody To Love'. As with all their 45s, the basic song was a foundation for a sterling studio performance. Over Kenny Jones's round–the–kit drum clatters and an accented two–note unison riff on organ and bass, Marriott's half–strangled, knock–kneed passion matched an electrifyingly slipshod fretboard style lacquered with Who–ish feedback scrawl.

The follow–up, introspective 'I Got Mine', took a dive, but after replacing their original organist with Ian McLagen from Hounslow's Boz People, The Small Faces got back on course with 'Sha–La–La–La–Lee' at Number Three and a lesser smash, self–composed 'Hey Girl' – though both might have better suited Herman's Hermits. After their only Number One, 1966's 'All Or Nothing', and a slight hiccup with 'I Can't Make It' – which lived up to its name – they touched a post–1967 creative peak with 'Here Come The Nice', 'Itchycoo Park' – and 'Lazy Sunday' which summed up the Small Faces' dialectic in its blend of R&B, psychedelia and Cockney chirpiness. Yet it was 'Itchycoo Park' that had been the vehicle of a US advance that was thwarted by Marriott's exit for Humble Pie.

Jones, McLagen and bass player Ronnie Lane carried on as The Faces with Rod Stewart and Ron Wood from The Jeff Beck Group – but, though successful, both they and Marriott's Humble Pie 'super-group' broke up in the mid–1970s, and a Small Faces reunion was a natural regression, particularly as they were one of precious few 1960s combos acceptable to punk. Nevertheless, as indifference towards two 'comeback' albums against Top 40 placings for repromoted 60s singles demonstrated, a contemporary re–birth was not feasible – and Marriott's death in 1991 quelled speculation about any more regroupings that would try in vain to recapture British pop's most unpretentiously optimistic period when singles mattered most.

Notes

1. *Happy Boys Happy: A Rock History Of The Small Faces And Humble Pie* by U.Twelker and R. Schmitt (Sanctuary, 1993)
2. Whose front man on a 1965 Decca single, 'You Don't Own Me', was the ubiquitous Paul Nicholas, then using the stage name 'Paul Dean'.
3. *Beat Merchants* by A. Clayson (Blandford, 1994)
4. *Hamburg: The Cradle Of British Rock* by A. Clayson (Sanctuary, 1997)
5. Among other 1960s recordings by The Untamed was 'Kids Take Over', a Pete Townshend opus deemed unsuitable for The Who.
6. 1970s pop idol Marc Bolan's cautionary tale in pop began in the mid–1960s when he embraced respective careers as a would–be English Bob Dylan and guitarist with John's Children.

Brian Poole remembers Keith Moon: 'In 1965, my very first date with Pam, my future wife, was a trip to the cinema – to see King Rat – and then on to the Scotch of St. James where we ran into Keith and the rest of the boys in The Who. He invited us to a party afterwards in his basement flat. It was brilliant – and it was also the first time I'd come across one of those hubble–bubble pipes you see in films set in Morocco, the Far East and exotic places like that. I got Pam back to her family home at 7.30 the next morning, and her Dad was furious. He forbade her ever to go out with me again. Fortunately, I was able to smooth things out.

About a year later, I was taking part in an Entertainers XI charity football game, and had arrived in my brand–new powder–blue Chevy Impala. Some of the other players and I were standing' round, admiring it when Keith screeched up in a black Rolls, all covered in mud. He jumped out, saw the Chevy, shouted, 'You can't have a clean car like that, Pooley!', and proceeded to chuck mud all over it. It was hilarious! Then he said, 'That's better!' If he'd thought I was upset, he'd have bought me a new one.

Afterwards, we followed his Rolls to a pub he knew. All the way there, his head and arm kept popping out of the sunroof and the driver's window waving us on. You couldn't help laughing at him. He was a total bundle of joy in those days.'

Moon's Bolero

'The Who will never split up. We have arguments all the time, but that is what gives us that extra spark. The Who thrives on friction'
– Roger Daltrey [1]

It wasn't long after the first glow of chart success that the scum of internal dissent was allowed to surface. The Who's passive role in the propagation of Mods–and–Rockers violence became internalised. In the studio, one bone of contention was that Keith did not subscribe to the maxim that if a thing's worth doing, it's worth doing pedantically, and the painstaking Townshend's constant retakes and overdubbing of minor guitar fills were starting to pall. Keith – whose voice was not deemed tuneful enough for backing harmonies – would be bored silly as the other three spent what seemed like half the night attacking, say, three offending notes for 'Happy Jack' from different angles until they matched the 'head arrangement' of one whose boisterous purpose often translated as barely tolerable bossiness.

By late 1966, Keith was weighing up more seriously the acceptance of easy money against the endless hours of merely spectating after the backing track was finished. The time–consuming antics with the road crew and anyone else similarly redundant became unendurably yawnsome, and he began occupying himself increasingly with drugs, booze, sexual adventure and other passing kicks. His not entirely unfounded suspicions that he, not *bete noire* Roger, might be the most expendable Who member musically, were fuelled by the fact that no–one ever consulted him about anything or even considered whether he had any opinions or aspirations beyond being one of the conduits for the outpourings of Pete's imagination.

In the drum isolation booth, his forehead bestowed with pinpricks of sweat, his headphoned ears like mildly braised chops, Keith thumped out take after rejected take, straining to decipher the drone of murmured intrigue amid the tape spools and blinking dials, and emerging occasionally to listen to a playback or, during the interminable re–running of each taped mile, plunge into one of the contretemps that scaled such a height of stand–up vexation and cross–purpose that underlings and hirelings might slope off for embarrassed coffee breaks while defiance, hesitation, defiance again and final agreement chased across the face of Townshend, resplendent as the group's principal creative force.

When each track began to assume sharper definition, Keith could be required to shake the tambourine or contribute something else to a pot–pourri of secondary percussion that listeners might notice after the thirtieth spin of the record. Otherwise, the old ennui manifested itself in him just hovering around during some interminable fiddle–about at the desk. He came to know by sight, individual sweet wrappers and note their day–to–day journeyings up and down a ledge, where an empty can of orangeade might also remain for weeks next to a discarded swab–stick made grubby from cleaning tape–heads.

As he'd been within earshot of the other Who members for every working day since God knows when, he would awake nauseated with the contemplation of further allocated hours with them, shuttered in the studio or grinding up and down motorways.

In turn, Daltrey in particular would wish sometimes that Moon would shut his fucking gob for five minutes or stop filling every minute with sixty seconds of unremitting drivel, his lips moving mechanically and loudly. You couldn't switch them off like a wireless. You'd fall asleep to Moon's twittering and yawn and stretch to it too. Roger would be noticed staring hard at Keith, looking as if he was about to start a punch–up. Sometimes he did – because as well as the drip–drip of hovering off–stage aggravations, the vocalist's periods of pure enjoyment while performing live were marred more and more these days as he fought to be heard against the flat–out thunder of the miked–up drums and the guitarists' gradually more splendid amplifiers.

Paranoia – sharpened by drugs – split Moon's concentration too as flare–ups grew in frequency, but had been shielded from the public so far. Behind the intimacies of off–mike comments and momentary eye–contacts, there was territory impenetrable to outsiders. Matters became so inflammable that a tacit implication in a seemingly innocuous remark might spark off a hastily unplugged guitar and a slammed backstage firedoor.

Such tensions could stimulate the group's inventive resources, but all of a sudden The Who ceased sabre–rattling behind closed doors and were airing personal grievances in the pages of the music press. Longtime animosity between Moon and Daltrey boiled over in the *NME* with Keith's pseudo–plaintive, 'It's Roger. He hates me.' A snigger was almost audible when he added 'because I told him he can't sing. I don't like half our records – and Roger is the reason.' [2]

That emotional and professional solidarity was being shredded was propagated further by Pete sneering that talk like Keith's wasn't far removed from an old woman discussing ailments. Not a week would pass without some upset that had been worth communicating to the whole world. As well as Roger hating Keith, John was jealous of Pete, and Pete stifled John. It should have made the lot of them embarrassed to be alive.

More concrete hearsay reached worried fans who, if fickle in af-fections towards its individuals, found it in them to maintain overall loyalty to the group. Following whispered onstage spite and an overt altercation resulting in injury when he and Entwistle arrived late at a Who booking in Newbury, Keith, purportedly, shot his mouth off to a reporter that he and John were going to carry on as a duo, augment-ing themselves as necessary. There'd be a taste of that shortly in the session for the 'In The City' B–side at which only they were present. Somewhere else it read that Pete and Roger were intending to amalga-mate with drummer Gibson Kemp and bass player Klaus Voorman of Paddy, Klaus and Gibson.

Then Eddie Phillips from Pete's fave raves, The Creation, was asked to join The Who as joint lead guitarist [3] – or was it that Roger was going to be supplanted with their Kenny Pickett? No, it's Boz Burrell of Boz People. Straight up! A mate of mine told me. Are you sure? I'd heard that it was Ray Phillips from The Nashville Teens. He looks so much like Daltrey that – so Ray says here – 'We used to tell people we were cousins, and sometimes they believed us.' [4] Didn't Jess Roden of The Shakedown Sound take a lead vocal on one Who studio date? What's all this on some foreign radio station about Daltrey being killed in Denmark? Maybe it's just wishful thinking by the others.

No–one bit back harder on his anger than Roger – who preferred not to take drugs, and was the victim of intensifying character assassina-tions by Moon, Entwistle and Townshend over venomous pints in a pub's murkiest corner. One night, however, Daltrey, scowling with dis-gust, flushed Moon's supply of amphetamines and further pills down a toilet. Keith came off worst in the consequent fisticuffs before an ebbing away that left him glowering at Roger, and muttering to John and Pete. The incident was hushed up – and so was Daltrey's brief exit from The Who. Then tight coils appeared to unwind, and it made abrupt sense for him to report for duty again, albeit 'with all these conditions. My whole personality had to change, but I hated myself for hitting Keith.' [5]

With Daltrey less domineering to the point of subservience, and Townshend moderating his almost schoolmasterly ruthlessness, a spirit of appeasement prevailed for a while. Yet there remained temptations – particularly on tour – for any one of the four to take himself off to the nearest airport departure lounge or railway ticket office and slip smoothly out of a frequently near–insufferable existence in which a light–hearted mood might persist among The Who for a few fiery–eyed miles before souring to cynical discontent, cliff–hanging silences and slanging matches. Bickering helped pass the time and while The Who's personnel remained unchanged for the fourteen years from 1964 to his demise, Moon, looking after Number One, kept his ear to the ground for openings elsewhere.

When the *NME*'s 'Alley Cat' tittle–tattler reported – without naming names – that two of The Who were leaving to form a group with two similarly malcontented Yardbirds, it was a distortion of old news. When breaks in both groups' itineraries coincided with a mid–week morning during 1966's rainy summer, Yardbirds guitarists Jeff Beck and Jimmy Page – who'd assisted on 'I Can't Explain' and its B–side – 'thought of cutting a track with Keith just to see what would happen,' confided Beck, 'so we rang him up, expecting to get the blank – but he said, "Yeah, I'll be there". Moon was pretty fed up with The Who at that time, but he still had to turn up at the studio so that nobody recognised him. He got out of the cab wearing dark glasses and a Russian cossack hat, so that no–one could see him being naughty with another session.

'We had to have something to play because Keith only had a limited time. He could only give us, like, three hours before his roadies would start looking for him. So I went over to Jimmy's house a few days before, and he was strumming away on his twelve–string Fender electric that had a really big sound. It was the sound of that that really inspired the melody. I invented that melody. We agreed that we would go in and get Moon to play a bolero rhythm with it.' [6]

There remains division about the authorship of this stubbornly chromatic but appealing instrumental with the working title, 'Bolero'. 'I wrote it, played on it, produced it,' insisted Jimmy, 'and I don't give a damn what he says. That's the truth.' [7] Finally, it was attributed to Page on the disc's label.

Nonetheless, just as The Yardbirds' bass player Paul Samwell–Smith believed that, for their much–covered 'Shapes Of Things', 'Jeff should have got a composing credit for the way he developed it when the song was being formed', so Beck's playing brought 'Bolero' belligerently alive. As capable of severe dissonance as serene melody, he overdrove his Stratocaster through a Marshall amplifier to actively create what might have been an aggravating hazard to, perhaps, The Dave Clark Five or Herman's Hermits. For Beck as much as Page – and Pete Townshend – feedback was a deliberated contrivance for sustaining notes and reinforcing harmonics.

Beck also wound on slackened extra–light strings for unprecedented *legato* effect on 'Bolero' as he had on music by The Yardbirds during their two–year golden age as they ventured into areas far removed from their R&B core. 1965's 'For Your Love' precipitated more adventurous smashes – 'Heart Full Of Soul', 'Evil–Hearted You', 'Still I'm Sad', 'Shapes Of Things' and 'Over Under Sideways Down' – all hybrids of instant familiarity and unpretentious musical innovation. Yet, however much certain devotees refuted the idea, by then the outfit had become just as much of a hard–sell pop act as The Dave Clark Five.

Even a 45 by the singer Keith Relf – alone – made the UK Top 50 – and a solo single by Beck then might have done the same – but fast comes the hour when fades the fairest flower. It may be dated from the resignation of the gifted Samwell–Smith in June 1966. The others soldiered on after persuading Jimmy Page, one of the brightest stars in the London session firmament, to step in and revert to a more apt role as co–lead guitarist as soon as general factotum Chris Dreja was able to switch to bass.

The interaction between Beck and Page was compulsively exquisite. From the outset, the concept of one cementing the other's runs with subordinate chord–slashing hadn't entered the equation as, over Dreja's low throb, the two anticipated and attended to each other's idiosyncrasies and stylistic cliches. Yet transcendental moments that would look impossible if transcribed were arousing a green–eyed monster in Jeff. 'Having two guitarists was no longer a great idea by the middle of

1967,' sighed Chris Dreja, 'It had become so undisciplined, and Jeff felt – justifiably – that his space was being invaded.'

It was, however, still all smiles between Beck and Page when they convened at IBC studios to try 'Bolero' and, if time permitted, a vocal item with Keith Moon – and, hopefully, John Entwistle, who Keith had recommended as a suitable singer as well as bass player. It was only when Entwistle failed to show that the three wheeled in John Paul Jones, as seasoned a session shellback as Jimmy – as well as pianist Nicky Hopkins, well known to Keith as occasional Who sessionman.

Simon Napier–Ball, The Yardbirds' then–manager, was the nominal producer, but the *de facto* one was Page, who 'wanted to see a band come out of there, cemented with that one record – but Keith obviously couldn't do it because of The Who, although he led us to believe he was leaving them, probably just to make The Who jealous – and John Paul Jones was a fabulous bass player. It was the obvious solution, going with that band, but it never happened.' [6]

Page, however, had already given it a name: Led Zeppelin. As it was with the composition of 'Bolero', there was dispute over who had originated this. To his dying day, John Entwistle would maintain that it was he who had commented that the line–up was 'so heavy it should go down like a lead *(led)* zeppelin' to Richard Cole, a Who aide who was to work with The Yardbirds. Yet Page ascribed it to Keith, adding 'Cole asked Moon for his permission when we decided to use the name.' [7]

Beck, however, calculated that Moon and Entwistle between them had coined it after the confrontation at Newbury and during the dark murmurings about them breaking away as a two–piece.

Though the trail was going cold by 1967, Jeff and Jimmy continued as if Led Zeppelin or whatever they decided to call it was still a possibility. John Paul Jones wasn't prepared yet to forgo the financial safety net of session work, and, when they discovered what Moon had been up to, The Who chose to treat his cloak–and–dagger hand in 'Bolero' as a registered protest rather than boat–burning. Of them all, Entwistle expressed most sympathy towards Moon, keeping quiet about how flattered he himself had been that Jeff and Jimmy had sounded him out too – though he wondered how long he'd have lasted in the unaccustomed role of lead vocalist.

'After some discussion, we decided to use another singer,' said Page, 'The first choice was Steve Winwood, but he was too heavily committed to Traffic. Next, we thought of Steve Marriott of The Small Faces. He was approached and seemed full of glee about it. A message came through from the business side of Marriott though which said, "How would you like to play guitar with broken fingers? You will be if you don't stay away from Steve."

'After that, the idea just sort of fell apart. Instead of being more positive about it, and looking for another singer, we just let it slip by. The Who began a tour. The Yardbirds began a tour and that was it.' [7]

Though Cream had commenced rehearsals in a Willesden scout hut, the concept of the 'supergroup', that most fascist of pop cliques, was in its infancy then. Nevertheless, it might be interesting, if futile, to speculate on what might have been had a group with Keith Moon and Jeff Beck as its principal selling points smouldered into permanent form, given that Beck was as much a visual asset to The Yardbirds as Moon to The Who. Within his archive of tricks were leaving the guitar squealing against the speaker as he prowled the stage, and turning round abruptly to play it on the back of his neck, above his head or in the small of his back. For a crowning bit of swagger, he might then use a microphone stand or edge of a speaker cabinet to simulate the careen of a bottleneck.

Lately, he'd also become prone to smashing up his instruments *a la* Townshend, and there'd been amusement rather than anger during the taping of 'Bolero' when, grinned Jeff, 'Moon smashed an expensive microphone by just hitting it with a stick. Halfway through "Bolero", you can hear him screaming. He hit the mic and smashed it off, so all you can hear from then on is cymbals.' [6]

At the time, Keith was Jeff's *beau ideal*. 'I didn't really like The Who then,' he confessed, 'They were annoying me because they had *my* drummer!' Yet it is debatable whether Moon had the ability to cope with Beck's mercurial artistic nature. Rather than rehash past glories, he favoured the merits of sweating over something new to keep consumers guessing, while more famous contemporaries – like his Yardbirds predecessor Eric Clapton – churned out increasingly more polished but unastounding albums that devotees feel they have to own to complete the set like *Buffalo Bill* annuals. This would lead Beck to sabotage ostensibly intriguing projects – such as an album with The

Rolling Stones – that might have earned him similar accolades to those won by lesser guitarists like Clapton.

'Whether there's one thing I've done that sums up "Jeff Beck" and my approach to the guitar, I couldn't say,' he estimated, 'I just couldn't do it because as soon as I reach my destination, I'm off somewhere else. I just like to condition my audience to be ready for anything, rather than turn their noses up because I've done a weird album.' [6]

From being tarred with the same brush as Black Sabbath's Tony Iommi, Ritchie Blackmore of Deep Purple and other heavy metallurgists of the late 1960s, the uncompromising Jeff would resurface in the first instance as one of few rock guitarists who could handle 'fusion' convincingly when working with the cream of modern jazz musicians. Where would Keith Moon have belonged in this?

By contrast, how would Jeff have handled being in the same group as someone who'd been born without brakes? While Keith could make Beck's sides ache with laughter over the course of an evening in the Speakeasy, they each went through life on different planes, different speeds. When would Moon have got beyond a joke for Beck? One source of Jeff's huffs when assisting on a Mick Jagger album in the mid–1980s was his inclination not to 'get' certain types of jokes – especially any against himself. Once, he stormed out of the studio when an impish Jagger pretended to instruct an engineer to erase a particularly startling guitar solo.

It's likely, therefore, that the 'Led Zeppelin' responsible for 'Bolero' would have disintegrated sooner rather than later. A more tidy–minded reviewer might conclude by tacking on a phrase like "– which was a great pity", except maybe it wasn't. Perhaps Moon, Beck, Page *et al* were meant to make just this one grand gesture, and then do no more.

After they scattered like rats disturbed in a granary, Jimmy Page urged The Yardbirds to enlist console whizz–kid Mickie Most, labelled 'a protagonist in our downfall' by drummer Jim McCarty. After the group proved incapable of significant commercial recovery, Page waited a decent interval and then, with his New Yardbirds, renamed 'Led Zeppelin', recorded an eponymous debut 1969 album that would have them stereotyped as the ultimate 'high energy' band.

Two years previously, 'Bolero' had appeared on vinyl – as 'Beck's Bolero' and with a contractually mandated production credit to Mickie Most – on the B–side of Jeff's first single as an ex–Yardbird, 1967's

'Hi Ho Silver Lining'. It made Number Fourteen in the domestic Top Twenty, totally eclipsing a rival version by The Attack. Maddeningly catchy, it endures as a regular singalong finale on the 1960s nostalgia circuit.

Reissued, the Beck rendition managed a second and third chart coming in 1972 and 1982, buoyed by its all–star B–side that the first time around was plugged by Jimmy Savile on *Top Of The Pops* when introducing Jeff, who, dolled up in clothes that were a little bit daft, interjected a topical soccer reference ('Up the Spurs!') during his 'live' singing and mimed fretboard picking of 'Hi Ho Silver Lining'.

The vocals on the follow–up, 'Tallyman', were shared with Rod Stewart who Beck, a timid songbird, had enlisted into The Jeff Beck Group, along with Nicky Hopkins, Ron Wood (on bass) and drummer Mickey Waller, for an outstanding US concert debut in the wake of an album, *Truth*, a diverting mixture of mostly workmanlike originals, casseroled blues and oddities like 'Ol' Man River', a song from the shows – which featured timpani banged by a pseudonymous 'You Know Who'.

Notes

1. *New Musical Express*, 4 December 1965
2. *New Musical Express*, 4 December 1965
3. 'No–one directly approached me', Eddie Phillips would recall, 'Maybe they approached my management, but no–one ever said anything to me.' (*Then Play On* by M. Ober) (Brisk, 1992)
4. *The Story Of Top Of The Pops* by S. Blacknell (Patrick Stephens, 1985)
5. *The Guardian*, 28 January 2005
6. *Crazy Fingers* by A. Carson (Carson, 1998)
7. *Led Zeppelin: Heaven And Hell* by C. Cross and E. Flannigan (Sidgewick and Jackson, 1991)

'Smoke Signals At Night': Keith And Viv

'He was so desperate. I always wanted to play drums like that, to get out that frustration, and I think he wanted to be involved in writing – but increasingly he became a social animal' – Vivian Stanshall [1]

With deceptive casualness Vivian Stanshall came into the life of Keith Moon. At first he was just a popular and – when in the mood – hilarious satellite of The Who fraternity. It was probably during one of these cordial chats that seem to lead nowhere in the smoky recesses of the Speakeasy in the later 1960s that Viv and Keith crossed the impalpable barrier between being common acquaintances and friends.

'When I became close to Keith, we were living in each other's houses for about three years,' confessed Stanshall [1] after the two started to seek each other's particular company. If not exactly David and Jonathan, outlines dissolved and contents merged and soon they were dressing similarly, parroting each other's opinions and, overall, outfitting themselves with certain of the other's vestments of personality.

Their mutual admiration appeared superficially to be a collision of opposites as much as similarities. For all Vivian's loutish attitudes when among lads from the wrong end of Leigh–on–Sea where he was brought up, he knew how to behave when among folk of the same genteel background of weeded crazy pavings leading across gardens full of daffodils to front doors with silver letterboxes.

Yet Stanshall believed that 'all of my articulacy, my work, has not resulted from any happy accident. I'm entirely self–educated. I didn't get a single 'O' level. In fact, I was about to be expelled from Southend Grammar, but my silver–tongued mother persuaded the headmaster to recommend me for a place in the local art school. However, my father, who was a chartered accountant who used to galosher his way from Southend to work in Moorgate every day, acquainted artists with gypsies and ne'er–do–wells, and wouldn't give the requisite amount to fund me to go through art school – so I joined the merchant navy.'

As well as not encouraging his son's artistic aspirations, Mr. Stanshall was also minatory about poor table manners and 'common' modes of speech and dialect: 'He was convinced that you couldn't get on in life unless you spoke BBC posh – but if you spoke like that in the streets near where I lived, they'd beat the crap out of you.'

Through his own persistence, nonetheless, eighteen–year–old Vivian, back from the sea, gained a scholarship at the Royal College of Art in Kensington. There, as well as learning painting and illustrating techniques and reading books – rather than Keith's comics – he grasped that 'art schools are levellers. It's not how you talk. It's down to "Are you any good?" It's classless, an emotional commonality. Clever people could also have Geordie and Mancunian accents' – suburban Middlesex ones too.

'Moon always wanted to be Vivian Stanshall,' observed Glen Colson, another Speakeasy drinker, 'and Vivian wanted to be Keith Moon. I watched them, and Moonie so wanted to be that intellectual snob, and Viv would have loved to have been in The Who. He was flattered that a rock star like Keith loved him.' [1]

Though his Who were of greater renown, Moon took the most initiative by hanging around with The Bonzo Dog Doo–Dah Band, in which Stanshall functioned as singer and interlocutor, and on various blowing instruments. Soon, Keith was travelling with them on one–nighters, and getting in on the act. From having simply intrigued him, the Bonzos had taken gradual if unknowing possession of him as, to a lesser degree, US rock 'n' roll revivalists Sha Na Na would in the next decade.

The odd boys of British Beat, they were right up Moon's alley, even if he wasn't a consumer of the trad jazz whose optimum commercial moment coincided with both the Bonzos' formation and original stylistic determination that owed much to The Temperance Seven and The Massed Alberts (a kind of English Spike Jones and his City Slickers). 'We were a little bit trad,' agreed Neil Innes, on a par with Stanshall as the Bonzos' main creative pivot, 'but that was too rigid. We liked The Savoy Orpheans, Jack Hylton, novelty fox trots... We used to go to flea markets and buy up old seventy–eights like "Jollity Farm" – a send–up of a big 1930s hit, "Misery Farm" – "Ali Baba's Camel" and "By A Waterfall", and thus built up a repertoire.

'What we played turned out to be wonderful drinking music, and we ended up doing five pubs a week. Also, Viv and "Legs" Larry Smith, our drummer and tap dancer, were very keen on stage gear, so we all bought these *lamé* suits, corresponding shoes and dreadful ties – and that was "The Look". We cut out speaking balloons, introduced silly gags, and Roger Ruskin–Spear made an exploding robot.' As it was with Keith and The Who, the Bonzos gave Viv an avenue for showing off that generated applause rather than the punishment he might have received at school.

Thus the Bonzos were well–placed to cash in when olde tyme whimsy prevailed in 1966's hit parade, spearheaded by The New Vaudeville Band's 'Winchester Cathedral' – all vicarage fete brass and woodwinds, and clipped, megaphoned vocals. In its wake came such as Whistling Jack Smith's 'I Was Kaiser Bill's Batman', boutiques like 'I Was Lord Kitchener's Valet' and experiments with dundreary side–whiskers, raffish moustaches and similar depilatory caprices that prompted one costumier to market fake ones so those without the wherewithal to sprout their own could still 'Make The Scene With These Fantastic New Raves.' Nonetheless, to no avail, both the Mojos and the Fourmost drew out the agony with respective quaint revivals of 'Goodbye Dolly Gray' from the Great War and George Formby's 'Aunt Maggie's Remedy.'

On the strength of their debut 45, 'My Brother Makes The Noises For The Talkies,' The Bonzo Dog Doo–Dah Band ran in the same pack, but as it turned out they were to defy adequate categorisation. 'We then decided to expand our style,' continued Innes, '1950s rock 'n' roll, flower–power, anything went – and start writing our own stuff. It only took a year to develop. If it got a laugh, it stayed in the act. We became the darlings of the cabaret circuit and then the colleges, and were earning as much as any group with a record in the charts.'

Yet, if the outfit's *raison d'etre* was centred on comedy, they weren't like Freddie and the Dreamers – nor did they conform to one journalist's insistence that they were an English 'answer' to The Mothers Of Invention – though theirs too was a pop–Dada junk sculpture of various musical styles – and that Vivian Stanshall, their ace face, was as intrinsically English an artist as Frank Zappa was North American, donating as he did the most enduring of the Bonzos' verbal gymnastics. By no means snorting at their musical fabric, the lyrics to 'Big Shot', 'Canyons Of Your Mind', 'My Pink Half Of The Drainpipe' *et al* could have led as separate a life from chords and melodies as his evocative sleeve notes to the albums that contained them.

The Bonzos' solitary Top Ten success, 'I'm The Urban Spaceman', however, was composed by Neil Innes. Further hits could be counted on the fingers of one offensive gesture – or less. Nevertheless, they gained both a weekly turn on the anarchic ITV children's series, *Do Not Adjust Your Set*, and prior to that, a slot in The Beatles' interesting–but–boring *Magical Mystery Tour* film – in which Stanshall, quite negating his yellow Custer tresses, moustache and octagonal spectacles, proved a marvellous Elvis Presley impersonator.

Paul McCartney was rowed in to produce 'I'm The Urban Spaceman' because, elucidated Innes, 'Gerry Bron, our producer, was fairly strict about studio time. Viv complained about this to Paul McCartney, who he'd met down the Speakeasy. Paul came along to the 'Urban Spaceman' session, and his presence obliged Gerry to give us more time.' Furthermore, so captivated was George Harrison with Larry Smith's quaint turns of phrase and dress sense – which embraced toy cows grazing on his shoes – that a song about these idiosyncracies, 'His Name Is Legs (Ladies And Gentlemen)', was to be the finale of *Extra Texture*, one of Harrison's albums as an ex–Beatle. It embraced a cameo by Oxford–reared Smith – whose officer–and–gentleman intonations were not – unlike Stanshall's and Moon's – entirely assumed.

Other musicians from 'serious' groups were as charmed by the Bonzos: 'We were liked by people like Eric Clapton,' smiled Innes, 'as a group most of them would liked to have been in – even though we were never mega recording artists.' At one college date in 1970, Aynsley Dunbar – about to join Frank Zappa's Mothers Of Invention – was up there among a percussion artillery of five that included Keith and, of course, 'Legs' Larry Smith.

On the spur of the moment, Traffic's Jim Capaldi stepped in from the VIP enclosure when Stanshall – more Flamineo then than the Falstaff he would become – appealed from the stage for 'someone to thrash the drums' during the Bonzos' set at 1969's Isle of Wight festival, explaining later that Smith was 'off in a helicopter, getting out of his mind with Keith Moon. When Larry eventually arrived, he pushed Jim off the drum stool and gave him a tambourine.' Further unnecessary percussive augmentation was provided by the respective drummers from Eclection and Family plus Keith pattering congas.

Afterwards, Stanshall lingered for The Who's performance in the small hours. His and Moon's activities in the interim included dropping an egg yolk into a *Melody Maker* scribe's cup of tea, and making general pests of themselves. Outwardly, making Art Statements that left targets too nonplussed to give Art Replies, appeared to be the bedrock of their companionship. The notorious Nazi escapade began with a Grand Entrance into the Speakeasy amid the boozy strains of 'Deutschland Uber Alles' from the two, plus Smith, Lord Sutch and a retinue of hangers–on garbed as stormtroopers.

Adrenalin pumping, the sinisterly uniformed pack marched next into other West End watering holes and restaurants, finishing up in a German–themed *bierkeller* in Soho, tankards swinging to the pound-ing rhythms of its *lederhosen*–clad oompah band. Stanshall took a thigh–slapping chance on the dance floor, while Moon's more rampant hand in the hullabaloo terminated with him being flung out onto the pavement by bouncers in feathered Tyrolean hats.

Less chronicled but equally elaborate jokes involved other costumes – notably when Stanshall was a vicar, faking death throes along Oxford Street while a wheelchair–bound Moon pleaded for help from passers–by. There were, too, pranks based upon Sutch–like use of blood cap-sules and, following his instructions, the discovery that twenty–odd messy minutes with cold scrambled eggs, cherry food–dye and some old tights could result in glisteningly convincing intestines.

A costlier party–piece was strolling into a provincial department store to purchase trousers, testing how hard–wearing a pair was by pulling by each ankle, tug–of–war–style. As planned, the garment would rip in half at the crotch, and the sales assistant would call the manager, whose rage would be quietened when the one–legged actor hired by Moon would enter the discussion with 'Hey, that's just what I want. I'll take two!'

On the string of West Country dates where this trick was first per-formed, bass guitarist Lee Jackson would recall his group, The Nice, being benighted in the same hotel as the Bonzos where 'the officious manager told them they had to wear a tie to eat in the restaurant. The following night, the whole band – including Keith – came parading down the central staircase, all wearing ties. They were, of course, oth-erwise naked.' [1]

Guests in a Chipping Norton hostelry part–owned by Moon were less certain of how they were meant to react when, sniggered Stanshall, 'We would both dress as forelock–tugging servants and carry bags, solicit tips, that sort of thing, and grovel. This made Uriah Heep look positively haughty.' [1] The thrill divine was the pre–ordained dropping of a suitcase, followed by quaking with false but hand–wringingly abject terror: 'dreadful mistake...I'm so sorry...never forgive myself...I'm a dirty dog...', babbling, snuffling, cringing and flinging up hands to avert a deserved blow while all but asking to be kicked up the backside.

Moon had an ulterior motive for throwing himself into the part with more gusto than Stanshall. 'Keith would engineer them into the restaurant,' explained Stanshall, 'which boasted the finest wine cellar in the south of England. There were unbelievable amounts of booze, and mussels at outrageous prices, and we'd manage to get these people to spend a lot on a meal, which Keith seemed to think was jolly funny.' [1]

The fun was formalised when Vivian was required to record a short run of Saturday afternoon programmes, *Radio Flashes* – sketches, funny stories, spoofs, 'live' sessions from Greyhound and Gaspar Lawar, items that beggared succinct description, and selections from his eclectic record collection [2] – on BBC Radio One in August 1971 when disc–jockey John Peel, who usually filled that air–time, was on holiday. Naturally, Viv's partner–in–crime was roped in, most memorably in a parody of *Dick Barton, Special Agent*, a detective series on the Light Programme in the 1940s, with himself as master sleuth 'Colonel Knut' and Keith as 'Lemmy', his chirpy Cockney sidekick.

On the whole, such sequences amused the listener accustomed to Peel's laconic delivery and – at that time – 'progressive' taste in music, though sections of some seemed ill–conceived in both content and execution, owing to Moon and Stanshall's pop star indolence, tardiness and inability to stick to a schedule. More than once they'd reel into Broadcasting House the worst for drink and with only the most nebulous – if splendidly confident – certainty about what they'd do and say on air.

Stanshall's rationale was, 'You focus yourself and say, "This is as good as I can be at this time," so you lose fear. I think it's a marvellous idea to be able to flow perfectly. I don't know much about Indian mystics, but I figured that once you've got past a certain age, if you could forget nuts and bolts, you could just play, sing or speak. You wouldn't have to consider your words or the next thing that occurs. You could just do it.'

'Viv was way out of control by then,' countered Lord Sutch, 'but he was still a very creative artist.' Moreover, his cultured enunciation during these broadcasts, even when neither drunk nor sober, must have been a source of pride for his parents, as they would when heard by many millions more on the fade out of Mike Oldfield's *Tubular Bells* in 1973. But whatever had Mr. and Mrs. Stanshall thought when they read of their boy's arrival for a *Melody Maker* interview in 1970 with a shaven head dotted with plastic flies to publicise his first post–Bonzos 45 with The Sean Head Showband? And this just a few months before the second solo offering featuring his now best buddy Keith not just as one of the 'Gargantuan Friends', but with a more personalised label credit as producer of the whole sorry mess.

His mother was still alive when Vivian, as self–destructive as his long–deceased dearest friend, perished in a fire in his lonely Muswell Hill flat in 1995. It was the finish of a race between tranquillizer and alcohol dependency and what was either an accident or, theorized son Rupert, 'a feeble attempt at killing himself'. The last straw might have been when, anxious for company, he befriended local vagrants who betrayed his trust, 'taking half his belongings with them'.

Notes

1. *Ginger Geezer: The Life Of Vivian Stanshall* by L. Randall and C. Welch (Fourth Estate, 2001)
2. Random examples included 78 rpm 'The Lion And Albert' by Stanley Holloway, Charles Penrose's 'The Laughing Policeman' and 'The Farmyard Symphony', coupled with 'The Village Jazz Band' by Billy Hill and his Boys. More unconsciously humorous were more recent items on 45 such as Godfrey Winn's sanctimonious 'I Pass' from 1967.

Ray Dorset remembers Keith Moon: 'After Mungo Jerry made it
in the early 1970s, I used to go to a fairly exclusive watering hole in
Egham where I met Keith a few times. For some reason, he found
someone accidentally knocking a tray of drinks off his table incredibly funny – so much so that he kept ordering further rounds of drinks
to knock them off himself.
He used to get very drunk there, but had some sort of arrangement
with the local constabulary for a squad car to drive him home after
hours.'

The Reel Me: Moon At The Movies

'Keith was a savant, the most amazing mimic. He could vacuum a character off someone in ten minutes, and he would then become them. Not just a caricature, he'd get inside. It was scary. He may have been a little bit autistic. We didn't know about those things then. There was definitely something different inside his head'
– Roger Daltrey [1]

For years, there's been talk – but, so far, only talk – about a Keith Moon bio–pic. At one point, Vivian Stanshall was supposedly co–writing a script, with British comedian John Sessions earmarked for the title role, but the project was jettisoned after an apparent disagreement between Stanshall and Roger Daltrey, who'd commissioned it. Elsewhere, deals have been negotiated, but, like gymkhana ponies refusing a fence, those involved have baulked at the task, having failed to formulate in simple terms exactly what they were taking on. However, in the light of recent commercial successes like *Backbeat* – about Stuart Sutcliffe, The Beatles' first bass guitarist – and 2005's *The Wild And Wycked Life Of Brian Jones*, maybe Keith's time will come, perhaps as some sort of feature–length 'reality' situation comedy.

See, while drumming overshadowed much of Keith's adolescence, he was an avid listener to BBC radio comedy. Initially, he was a fan of the more orthodox *Educating Archie*, *The Clitheroe Kid* and, especially, the inspired *Hancock's Half Hour* – set in a fictitious London borough sliding into seediness. Indeed, *Melody Maker* described Moon as a 'son of Hancock' [2] when he was a guest presenter for four weeks on a BBC programme entitled *A Touch Of The Moon* in summer 1973.

In the sphere of humour, one man's toilet paper is another man's handkerchief. However, as a schoolboy, Keith's taste was sufficiently catholic for him to be also one of those irritating fellows who re–enacted in the playground 'I Was Monty's Treble', 'Bridge Over The River Wye' and further excerpts from *The Goon Show*, whose high summer was reflected in UK hit parade entries in 1956 for its spin–off double A–sides, 'I'm Walking Backwards For Christmas'/ 'Bluebottle Blues' and 'Bloodnok's Rock 'n' Roll'/'Ying Tong Song' [3] – which encapsulated the off–beat humour, topical parodies, incongruous parallels, stream–of–conciousness transmogrifications and casual cruelties of the series starring Terence 'Spike' Milligan, Peter Sellers, Harry Secombe and briefly, Michael Bentine.

As well as ushering in that strata of comedy that culminated in the late 1960s with *Monty Python's Flying Circus*, aspects of the Goons became apparent in the stylistic determination of such as Scaffold, The Bonzo Dog Doo–Dah Band and, less tangibly, The Beatles – particularly in their first two films and in John Lennon's literary output – and The Who, exemplified by the impromptu 'I saw yer!' coda of 'Happy Jack' and, also in 1967, *The Who Sell Out* with outlines dissolving between *bona fide* songs and purposely crass jingles.

Of all The Goons, Peter Sellers seemed to have made the most impact on Moon. At this juncture, I would like to pass on the raw information that Keith was likely to have seen, enjoyed immensely and perhaps been utterly affected by *Two Way Stretch*, a most un–Goon–like movie in 1960 – and one of Sellers' lesser comedies – in which he plays 'Dodger', the most dominant of a gor–blimey trio of convicted career criminals with an off–hand and utterly unconscious cynicism about their delinquencies and its occupational hazards. This mention made, I will make no further comment – except to say that pronounced aspects of "Dodger" reared up in both Keith's public persona as a pop star and in most of the characters he played in his handful of films.

Later, Keith would make a social conquest of Sellers around the time that the distinguished actor–comedian played the Doctor in a 1972 stage performance of *Tommy*. Apparently, he was 'into' Zen macrobiotic cookery and yoga, and recognised by one such as George Harrison as 'a devoted hippy, a free spirit'. [4]

Keith was also a drinking buddy of Graham Chapman, a mainstay of *Monty Python's Flying Circus*. Though Moon was uncredited, the two collaborated on sketches for the show, and Graham's rich pal was among those to whom John Cleese, Eric Idle *et al* turned after nervous investors washed their hands of a proposed *Python* film, *Jesus Christ: Lust For Glory*, retitled *Life Of Brian* – with Graham as the nominal thirteenth disciple. God might have been able to take the joke, but, prodded by pangs of backer Lord Delfont's Jewish conscience, as well as a loss just incurred through signing and hastily dropping The Sex Pistols, EMI's withdrawal of support during pre–production was on the basis of blasphemy.

Rather than jettison *Life Of Brian*, the *Python* team investigated other possibilities for raising the budget required. Chief of these were Keith Moon – and George Harrison, who'd been seen in *Rutland Weekend Television*, a recent BBC2 series starring Eric Idle. Moon's death precluded that line of enquiry, but Idle's man was not so inconsiderate – and so began Harrison's transition from maker of curate's egg post–Beatles albums to paladin of the British film industry after he put forward his own country estate as collatoral to float *A Life Of Brian*.

Purchaser of the dearest cinema ticket in history, it was only fair that George should be fitted into the flick somewhere. While he was content to be noticeable in a crowd scene, it's likely that Keith Moon would have desired more than the 'quiet one' of The Beatles. In the chemistry of the four interlocking public personalities in The Who, Keith vied with Roger as the member with serious potential as an actor, and was designated most often by critics as the one with a destiny as a tragi–comedian.

To what degree his gift for mimicry or his truant afternoons gawping at Hollywood hadn't been wasted was, however, not to be tested very thoroughly, mainly because of appearances in films in which lack of substance was wallpapered over with employment of the famous. Nevertheless, the overall conjecture – with the artist in agreement – was that Keith coped well enough with undemanding roles in which he was recognisable by everyone who thought they knew him. As such, he was advantaged by being amongst friends, most conspicuously Ringo Starr, whose thespian qualities had so improved since his two flicks with The Beatles that he was accepted in as both a joker and a fair 'feed' – a straight man who reacts defensively to phoney insults and humiliations.

To a lesser extent than Starr, Moon had been courted by movie supremos on the lookout for new talent – or was it cynical awareness of the publicity value of printing the words 'Keith Moon' in the credits? In reciprocation, hardly a week went by in the mid– to late 1960s without some pop icon or other fancying him or herself as a 'proper' cinema attraction. Dave Clark, Manfred Mann's Paul Jones, Mick Jagger, even Cilla Black each felt the need to have a go. What did the world miss when eternal Geordie Eric Burdon, allegedly, failed a screen test to star in a film treatment of Evelyn Waugh's *The Loved One* with Rod Steiger?

Yet it wasn't to be some Hollywood big shot who kick–started Keith Moon's screen career in 1970. He and Pete Townshend had been re–laxing in the Speakeasy one evening when Frank Zappa, then leader of The Mothers Of Invention, sat down at the next table. Keith would recount how an eavesdropping Zappa, entertained by their conversa–tion, 'leaned over and said, "How'd you guys like to be in a movie?" We said, "OK, Frank" – and he said, "OK, be at Kensington Palace Hotel at seven o' clock tomorrow morning." I was the only one who turned up.' [5]

That Ringo was involved too, induced Keith to accept formally his modest part in *200 Motels*, this only major film by Zappa, proprietor of a run–down studio near San Bernardino in the early 1960s, where he'd attended to B–feature soundtracks as well as one–shot singles, multi–tracked and released pseudonymously – among them The Hollywood Persuaders' 'Tijuana Surf', which topped the Mexican charts.

This was a point in his favour for Keith, still a keen collector of obscure surf music – as was Frank's joining of his first group as a drummer. Moon also thought that 1967's *We're Only In It For The Money*, the Mothers' third album, was one of the funniest pop records ever released, and a vivid illustration of Frank's well–founded opinion that 'it is theoretically possible to be "heavy" and still have a sense of humour'.

Zappa racked up heftier sales achievements after he'd made his most far–reaching artistic statements in the 1960s. During the next decade, the lyrical wit of the active anti–censorship campaigner grew coarser, and was often sung to apposite arrangements that disguised beautiful melodies. Via a rapid turnover of Mothers personnel and changes in his stylistic determination, he was attracting, for better or worse, a wider audience in his shift towards lavatorial 'humor'.

This was lamentably palpable in *200 Motels* as instanced by Mother Howard Kaylan, who, discussing pornographic literature, utters the deplorable sentence, 'Emanuel the gardener thrust his mutated mem–ber into her slithering slit.' Furthermore, while praised for its spectacu–lar and pioneering visual effects, Zappa's sluggish 'fantasy opera' of his Mothers' sleazy adventures when on tour was riddled with 'balling chicks'–type Los Angeles colloquialisms. A fragile story–line was lost to in–jokes as well as jump–cut cartoon sequences and Frank's affrays with his ill–chosen co–director, Tony Palmer, a sometime journalist for whom pop meant little until a belated admiration for the latter–day Beatles emerged.

Thus, it hardly mattered that Keith made no attempt 'to other be' when, having elected to dress in a nun's habit as 'Pamela' [6], an absonant hybrid of a speed–fuelled groupie and a character not unalike those of Tony Curtis and Jack Lemmon in drag amongst a troupe of uncomprehending female musicians in *Some Like It Hot*. On his official first day's shoot, Moon in his obstructing costume was required to frolic in a bedroom with two topless women, and then peer wildly through the strings of a harp [7], prior to being chased through an assembled London Philharmonic Orchestra by a sex–crazed Ringo made up like Frank himself. Weird, eh?

Another highlight – if that is the word – was 'Lonesome Cowboy Burt', a country–and–western spoof hollered by Jimmy Carl Black, the Mothers' original drummer, whose recurring introduction – as 'the Indian of the group' – had been a characteristic of *We're Only In It For The Money*. 'My part in *200 Motels* was almost as big as Ringo's,' estimated a rueful Jimmy, 'Only the money wasn't.' Nevertheless, cordial encounters with Keith Moon on the set were epitomised by the latter scribbling a note to a Track press officer, directing him to send his new–found friend copies of every Who album in the catalogue.

The light–hearted generosity of such a gesture was at odds with a prevalent mood of depressed forbearance into which the project degenerated; Palmer so removing himself from it that he was to tear *200 Motels* to pieces in his regular column in *The Observer*.

Too much for the common movie–goer, the film faded swiftly from circulation, to be shown occasionally only in film clubs and 'alternative' cinemas where it was watched as an antidote to pleasure on the principal that the more arduous the effort needed to appreciate something, the more 'artistic' it is.

Not worthy of even that was a subsequent disaster with Moon in it, *Count Downe*, renamed *Son Of Dracula*. After acting (and then directing), Ringo Starr also had a stab at producing in 1972 when, in his plush office near London's Horse Guards Parade, macabre props were dotted among the spindly potted trees and smaller accoutrements in the executive suite, and the plaque on its door read 'HQ Dr. Baron

Frankenstein, Brain Specialist.' Ringo was going to make a horror movie.

For this updating of the Dracula legend, he insisted on a last–minute and not especially ample cameo for Keith, having already extended the old pals act to John Bonham of Led Zeppelin and, more conspicuously, to Harry Nilsson, in the public eye then with the million–selling 'Without You' single. He consented to be 'Count Downe' in what was now 'like a non–musical, non–horror, non–comedy comedy,' quipped Starr, 'or it's a horror–horror, musical–musical, comedy–comedy'. [8] Yet, screened only in the States, not even personal appearances by Starr, Moon and Nilsson when the film opened in the bigger cities in 1974 could prevent *Son Of Dracula*'s relegation to 'all the little villages,' moaned Ringo, 'because if we put it on in a town, it got slated.' [9]

That same year, Starr had had more luck outside North America after comprehending that his children were spellbound by T Rex, a medium for singing guitarist Marc Bolan's glam–rock stardom. Coming to admire the foppish Marc's stagecraft too, Ringo had directed *Born To Boogie*, a full–colour cinema documentary about him. It hinged on a T Rex show at Wembley Empire Pool, but contained preordained additional scenes, threaded together with a deadpan catchphrase taken from Wanda Jackson's energetic 'Let's Have A Party' from 1958, and embracing blink–and–you'll–miss–him clips of Keith Moon.

Born To Boogie plugged a gap between an infinitely more impressive celluloid venture by Keith. *Ben Hur* it wasn't, but Moon had cause to be elated by critical compliments for 1973's *That'll Be The Day*, though once more, boon companion Ringo was more prominent. As second male lead, it was so preoccupying that it prevented Starr from giving 'em his interpretation of 'Uncle Ernie' in Lou Reizner's stage presentation of *Tommy* at London's Rainbow Theatre in 1972. This was regrettable but not disasterous as Keith Moon was able to step in with hardly a break in rehearsals, despite his own commitment to *That'll Be The Day*.

It was reported erroneously that Jeff Beck, Eric Clapton and Pete Townshend were also going to be in the flick, [10] but even in the location chosen for its behind–the–times ambience, the more vigilant and hip locals spotted celebrities mooching drowsily to the newsagents for cigarettes; knocking back a quiet lunchtime pint, or browsing in a second–hand bookshop in Shanklin, the terminus of the Isle of Wight's internal railway – and the last bolt–hole where fans and the media would expect to find Keith Moon and his retinue.

'We met and spoke to Nilsson and got his autograph,' remarked David Jones, who loaned his 1950s car for use in *That'll Be The Day*, 'Not many people would have recognised him. We also spoke to Keith Moon, a right nutter.' [11] You'd natter easily to a some bloke taking the air on a promenade bench, only to be told by somebody later, 'That was Billy Fury.' Vivian Stanshall was an everyday sight around the town already, having replaced Ted Wood [12] as stiff–upper–lip vocalist during The Temperance Seven's residency in the auditorium at the end of the turnstiled Victorian pier only a couple of months prior to autumn – what hoteliers call the 'low season' – when a sort of pleasant melancholy descends on resorts like Shanklin.

In the rancid sunlight before dusk, beaches that were once noisy with bucket–and–spade trippers determined to enjoy themselves, emit only seagulls' cries and the constant and pedantic back–and–forth rasp of shingle, like a giant clearing his throat. Yet, for the purpose of the movie, Shanklin's quietude limited the potential for chaos that the presence of pop stars in public places could summon. What's more, the overcast skies and 'bracing' wind could pass for summer, taking into account the meteorological whims of British Augusts, even if 1959's – the year the film was set – was one of the most glorious of the century.

Into the bargain, within the island's boundaries too, were a holiday camp bereft of holidaymakers; a grammar school emptied by a half–term break, and Shanklin's almost–but–not–quite olde–worlde theatre, cafes and amusement arcades – all the required locational elements to convey the poignant impression of a provincial England in the late 1950s where the last fish–and–chip shop closes at 10 p.m., and its greasy merchandise devoured with the fingers from pages of last month's *Daily Herald*.

The logistics of finding extras were resolved easily too – by a single advertisement in *The Isle Of Wight County Press*. Most of them had been selected by the time Keith Moon's helicopter touched down on the roof of the hotel allocated to the cast, its down–draft blowing away onto the beach below the kitchen towels laid down to direct the pilot. Moon emerged in full Red Baron flying rig, commenting, 'It's the only way to travel, man. I was on my front lawn in Chertsey twenty minutes ago, and now I'm here.' [13] While heading next towards the stairs leade-ing to his suite, he ordered a large brandy.

'He was drunk, out of his head,' gasped David Wells, one of the star–struck onlookers when Moon came on set the following morning, 'He gave an impromptu drum performance there: a real crashing solo. Then he climbed up this step ladder leaning against the stage, and shook it violently before he collapsed over the top of it, and fell into his kit. The director was furious because it put back the whole day's schedule.' [11]

Moon was also impatient with himself. Vic Scovell remembered, 'He had a one–liner. He had to do it about twenty times. He was get-ting really fed–up.' [11]

Scivell and some of the other auxiliaries were peripheral guests at a typically extravagant party thrown by Moon at Shanklin's Eastcliff Club when all the work was done. Buried in the uneuphonious up-roar were the strains of 'My Generation' and 'The Kids Are Alright'. Yet, from smiling indulgently, Phil Gould, later Level 42's drummer, stiffened and looked daggers at the stage as a near–re–run of the Will Birch affair in Bishop's Stortford got underway: 'My brother John or-ganised the party and said, "Bring your drums down". Keith Moon proceeded to demolish my kit, thrashing the living daylights out of it. There were dents in the heads, a cracked cymbal. It was a dishevelled mess. The whole novelty of having a superstar demolish my kit quickly wore off. The Who's tour manager gave me a pound. That was my first brush with stardom.' [11]

Perhaps Moon couldn't shake off what some might have seen as a type–casting as 'J.D. Clover', stage alias of Arthur Twigg, gap–toothed, poorly–educated and scatter–brained drummer in Bickerstaffe Happy Holiday Camp's Blue Grotto's resident rock 'n' roll combo, Stormy Tempest and the Typhoons. It was apparent that there was bad blood between Clover and Tempest who, in silver jacket and hair stiff with lacquer, was played by Billy Fury, the now–ailing rock–a–balladeer, soon to undergo a second heart operation. Like The Who, he'd never scored a Number One, though there'd been a few close shaves.

With his days as a waiter on the Mersey ferry holding him in good stead, Fury's former Liverpool primary school classmate, Ringo–as–Grotto barman Mike Menarry's scripted views on the Tempest outfit included an outlining of their after–hours carnal pastimes and a dismissive 'but there's no future in being a Typhoon. I mean, where does it get you?'

Short but memorable, J.D. Clover's main dialogue in the film is an inconsequential chat – about why the Typhoons didn't compose their own material – with 'Jim MacLaine', namely David Essex in a motion picture debut after years of struggle which had started with him drumming in London R&B outfit, The Everons – later, The China Plates. By the time the Plates shattered in 1966, David had been recognized as the group's X–factor, and was persuaded to concentrate solely on singing. He also branched out into acting, 'arriving' in 1971 as 'Jesus' in the rock musical *Godspell*.

Essex was granted a seven–week leave of absence from the show to film *That'll Be The Day*, an opportunity, he said, to prove he could be a bastard as well as beatific. Moreover, as it had been with Anthony Newley and *Idle On Parade* in 1959, a parallel career in pop seemed a natural progression.

When *That'll Be The Day* premiered at the ABC, Shaftesbury Avenue on 12 April 1973, Moon's arrival attracted more snip–snapping media attention in some quarters than those like Essex with better claim to it. Nonetheless, Keith was to have more lines to learn as an older J.D. Clover in the sequel, *Sooner Or Later* – which became *Stardust* by autumn 1973. With MacLaine, Clover was now in a beat group called The Stray Cats. His incorrigible fecklessness was captured most subtly in an inattentive fiddling with some desk ornament during the group's all–important audience with a music industry mogul, droning on about 'something you desperately need in the way of... shall we call it professionalism?', accompanied by a pointed glance at Clover.

Harking forward to the Swinging Sixties, Adam Faith assumed the role of Mike Menarry [14] – now road manager for The Stray Cats and confidant of self–interested MacLaine, who has been casting covetous eyes at 'Johnny Cameron', hogging the lead vocal and guitar spotlight. Menarry engineers the ousting of Cameron, and MacLaine becomes, to all intents and purposes, a solo performer, the other Stray Cats fading into the background from the moment he sniffs fame.

Moon was all too *au fait* with the realism of *Stardust*'s behind–the–scenes portrayal of the drugs and sex that were common currency in the midnight–to–six hours he'd kept since first surveying the planet from the Olympus of chart acclaim in 1965. Helping him get into character too was the off–screen unity of those Stray Cats who, with Keith–JD most effective as their sozzled but hard–talking spokesman, would rid themselves of Essex–as–MacLaine after he became a being apart. They tended also to distance themselves from Paul Nicholas – 'Johnny Cameron' – even though he and Moon had been acquaintances since paths had crossed along a backstage corridor at Wembley Town Hall the night that Keith had first encountered Screaming Lord Sutch and the Savages.

After leading the support group that night, Nicholas was superceded by Nicky Hopkins as Sutch's pianist. With the candour of middle age, Paul would maintain that he owed a lot of his dramatic skills to his tenure as a Savage. 'He was good–looking with long hair,' added his Lordship, 'So he was the ideal choice to be the "prostitute" – to run around the stage and get his heart and lungs ripped out during the mock operation in "Jack The Ripper" with the others holding it together musically. This bought Paul out of his shell.' [15]

While cutlery clattered on plate at Nicholas–Cameron's separate table, never did it occur to Keith and the other Stray Cats not to eat together in the studio canteen – as if their corporate joys and sorrows also bound them in real life. As it was before the cameras too, Keith formed a specific, almost protective, attachment to Dave Edmunds, wild man Clover's antithesis as the monosyllabic 'Alex'.

If lacking 'image', this Welsh singing guitarist had, nevertheless, maintained a certain steady artistic consistency when weathering whatever rock trends came his way since breaking free of the trivial round of engagements in and around his native Cardiff. After peaking in 1970 with a UK Number One – a trundling revival of bluesman Smiley Lewis's 'I Hear You Knocking', on which the talented Dave had superimposed all instruments and triple–tracked vocals – the going got erratic, but he ticked over with workmanlike albums, and his role in *Stardust* – for which he also organized the tie–in LP with assistance from pub–rockers Brinsley Schwartz.

They were also engaged to warm up the crowd – drawn from David Essex's fan club subscribers – before an all too realistically riotous Stray Cats concert sequence at Manchester's Belle Vue, scheduled to begin at 6 a.m. on the morning after 'we got drunk with Keith Moon at the Post House,' recounted their Nick Lowe, 'He sent out for copious quantities of curry, which he dumped over actor Karl Howman's head'. [16]

Despite leading Brinsley Schwartz astray [17] ; a mishap in Belle Vue's bowling alley whereby Moon disappeared into the mechanism beyond the ten–pin clearing–gate; a champagne–sodden celebration of David Essex's first US chart–topper, and a couple of strike–happy fits of pique – which brought Keith on one occasion to a near–punch–up with the scriptwriter – all's well that ended well, but even with excellent notices for his shabbily likeable J.D. Clover, Moon had had his fill of the pre–dawn starts and memorizing dialogue. Thus he never got round to anything halfway as appealing as *Stardust*, not even Oscar–nominated *Tommy* in which an initially nervous Moon brought a visual dimension to perverted, spivvy 'Uncle Ernie' that earned surprised praise from director Ken Russell: 'Keith cherished that role. He brought something to it that no actor could have done.'

As Frank Sinatra had pleaded for his Oscar–winning part in *From Here To Eternity* because he 'might have *been* Private Angelo Maggio', [17] so Moon *was* Uncle Ernie as he improvised round the more unsavoury aspects of his own character and public persona – often with an unprecedented subtlety – in what some critics agreed generally were among the most rivetting scenes in a film in which style rode roughshod over substance.

If he'd been ten years younger, Keith could have made as fair a fist of 'Jimmy Cooper' in The Who's Mod retrospective movie, *Quadrophenia*, as the Royal Shakespeare Company's Phil Daniels, who actually landed the part. Had Keith lived, he would have been even more suited to Daniels' verminous, pill–pushing and out–of–control 'Jack The Hat' in 2004's BBC television production of the Swinging Sixties crime drama, *The Long Firm*.

Yet, instead of maturing as an actor, Keith Moon rotted. Favouring minor supports that required little preparation, he featured in just one rather daft scene – as a scientist with a sanitary towel as a moustache – in *Sonic Boom*, a comedy short directed by a Los Angeles university student he had befriended. Neither could Keith say no to something infinitely bigger to tell his widowed mother, even if it was only another bit–part. This time, he was a dress designer who laced feyness with touches of Hancock and broad *ahharr–harr–harrr* Long John Silver – in *Sextette*, a mediocre epitaph in 1978 for Mae West, the celluloid legend who'd 'never needed Panavision and stereophonic sound to woo the world, I did it in black–and–white on a screen the size of a postage stamp. Honey, that's talent.' [18] In this bawdy farce, the octogenarian Miss West, wisecracking in her sexy serpentine husk, wasn't bothered in the slightest about the starring role of Marlo Manners, a Hollywood screen goddess who'd just plighted her troth to her sixth husband.

Crotchety she might have been, but West turned out for the post–production blow–out to receive the plaudits of male co–stars which, with Moon, included Tony Curtis and George Hamilton. On hand too were Alice Cooper and the omnipresent Ringo Starr. Yet disappointing reviews would cause *Sextette* to disappear with indecent haste from general release after booming in half–empty mid–Western drive–ins.

Keith Moon's movie career swirled down a metaphorical plugh-ole too. It's possible that he may have developed into a well–loved, if rather one–dimensional, character actor, replete with the predictable mannerisms and variations on a familiar performance – like a conju-ror reproducing a popular effect to amuse children. Thus he may have become not just the master of his field, but its only occupant. Already, he'd demonstrated that he was quite capable of upstaging a supposedly bigger box–office attraction with just the raising of a Robert Newton eyebrow. Events would prove that, though he wasn't to investigate fur-ther opportunities to do so, it wouldn't be his fault entirely.

Notes

1. *The Guardian*, 28 January 2005
2. *Melody Maker*, 19 August 1973
3. You may be surprised at how many British comedians were cred-ible pop artists. The Goodies, for example, are on a numerical par with Stereo MCs or Suede as UK singles chart entrants; Hylda Baker and Arthur Mullard made the Top 40 as a duo – and so did Tommy Cooper, Bernard Cribbins, Peter Sellers, Bruce Forsyth, and Dick Emery; Charlie Drake was a fiercer rock 'n' roller than most of the Larry Parnes stable – and then there's Benny Hill, rated by no less an authority than psych–journal *Ptolemaic Terrascope* as 'one of the fin-est comic songwriters this country has ever produced.'
4. *Musician*, November 1987

5. *Frank Zappa* by Barry Miles (Atlantic, 2004)

6. A role Zappa had earmarked originally for a disinclined Mick Jagger

7. The original harpist had walked out, refusing to have anything to do with an opus entitled 'Penis Dimension', but had left her instrument behind.

8. *Rolling Stone*, 30 April 1974

9. *Rolling Stone* 23 May 1974

10. *Cashbox*, 16 October 1972

11. *Isle Of Wight Rock* by V. King, M. Plumbley and P. Turner (Isle Of Wight Rock Archives, 1995)

12. Brother of both Art (of The Artwoods) and Ron, then one of The Faces, but soon to join The Rolling Stones. Ron was also present during the filming of *That'll Be The Day*.

13. *The David Essex Story* by G. Tremlett (Futura, 1974)

14. Starr felt that his continuance as Menarry would be to condone a story–line too close for comfort to that of the Beatles.

15. Nicholas went straight from *Stardust* to playing Richard Wagner in Ken Russell's *Lisztomania*, starring Roger Daltrey.

16. *No Sleep Till Canvey Island* by W. Birch (Virgin, 2000)

17.Perhaps a slight exaggeration, The Brinsleys being from a pub rock background, a genre not normally associated with sobriety – as adequately illustrated by bass palyer Nick Lowe's own consumption, which in the 1980's reached levels dangerously close to those of Moon's in the previous decade.

18. Sinatra to Tony Scaduto

19. *Loose Talk* ed. L. Botts (Omnibus, 1980)

Nick Garvey remembers Keith Moon *(Ducks Deluxe/ The Motors):
We were playing a gig in Manchester with Brinsley Schwartz when they
were involved with* Stardust. *At some party or other afterwards, Keith
Moon opened a bottle of Newcastle Brown with his teeth. It smashed in
his mouth, causing him considerable oral injury. Only with the aid of
heavy make–up could he appear on set the next day.*

Moonlighting With Heavy Friends

Keith thought a great deal of David Sutch, and used to laugh un-controllably from the wings when he was on stage' – John Schollar (Clyde Burns and the Beachcombers) [1]

In the early to mid–1970s, The Who realised that they could wait until they felt like going out on the road again or making a new record. A consequent cutting back on the diet of tour–album–tour sandwiches, incumbent upon poorer groups, enabled Keith to earn a few credits on album sleeves of friends.

Yet the most prominent extra–curricular project in which he was involved is memorable for his minimal involvement. Early in 1970, a small army of renowned ex–Savages did their duty by their old boss after Screaming Lord Sutch landed a profitable two–album deal with Atlantic Records, following a well–received season at Thee Experience on Sunset Strip.

'I was using an American backing band,' Lord David recalled in his last ever interview, 'doing my standard act – 'Jack The Ripper', 'Dracula's Daughter' and a lot that I'd composed myself – and Mario, the owner, was impressed enough to sort out off–peak sessions at Mystic Studio with an apprentice engineer. Next, after I wormed my way backstage at a Led Zeppelin concert in Los Angeles, Jimmy Page volunteered to play on what was to be the first *Heavy Friends* album. He ended up co–producing. John Bonham asked if I'd mind if he came along too. I said I'd be delighted. I'm told John Paul Jones wanted to come too, but their manager wouldn't let him. Noel Redding was com-ing through town too – and he ended up on it. Mitch Mitchell was on some stuff. Jeff Beck and Nicky Hopkins were there as well.'

While the resulting *Lord Sutch And His Heavy Friends* was des-ignated as the worst rock album ever made in a 1999 poll amongst Britain's more unimaginative radio presenters, Sutch's public image diverted attention from the quality of a controlled, melodic vein of early heavy metal underlining a witty if gruesome lyricism.

The follow–up, 1972's *Hands Of Jack The Ripper*, however, was a cheapskate me–too affair. The heart of it was a tape–recording of a showcase performance in April 1970 at an over–crowded Hampstead Country Club during which Sutch was backed by his usual Savages plus a clutter of available luminaries, some more luminous than others, but billed as his 'Heavy Friends'. As well as guitarists Ritchie Blackmore and Spencer Davis, Procol Harum's Matthew Fisher on keyboards and, again, Noel Redding, past and present members of Deep Purple, Cliff Bennett's Rebel Rousers and The Aynsley Dunbar Retaliation weighed in too – and so, briefly, did a tipsy Keith Moon, providing what one reviewer described as 'periodic accompaniment' [2], that is, playing standing up at a drum kit shared with his old tutor, Carlo Little.

Perhaps you needed to have been there – because, on disc, Moon's contribution to just a couple of salaams to classic 1950s rock can't be distinguished in the general racket. Nevertheless, the mere presence of Moon – who'd been unaware that the show was being taped – was sufficient for his bemused name to be prominent on the album's packaging, and, before that, for publicists to imply that he would be among the all–star 'surprise guests' during his Lordship's early evening spot on the Saturday, at the Hollywood Festival in Newcastle–under–Lyme, over May 1970's bank holiday weekend, when he was up against the likes of Steppenwolf, Black Sabbath, Traffic, The Grateful Dead and Family. Nevertheless, though he and his Savages gave a worthy account of themselves, no–one famous took the stage that day with David Sutch.

So passed – on a sour note – Keith's last significant encounter with both David and Carlo – though Sutch and The Who were on the same land mass at the same time late in 1971 when the former was touring a double–header in the States with Vivian Stanshall, at a loose end following the break–up of The Bonzo Dog Band. The previous summer, the 'woman tone' guitar of Eric Clapton, an acquaintance from art school days, had been heard on Viv's runaway Sean Head Showband's single, 'Labio–Dental Fricative' – and Stanshall's next effort featured Moon as one of his 'Gargantuan Chums'.

As well as drumming, Keith was also nominal producer of this joke revival of Terry Stafford's 'Suspicion', a minor British hit in 1964, [3] but recorded too by Elvis Presley in characteristic hot–potato–in–the–mouth manner. [4] While overdoing the inherent melodrama, Viv also conveyed the impression that he was as aware as any listener of his own ridiculousness.

Keith also assisted on the B–side – attributed to biG Grunt (*sic*) – a Stanshall ditty entitled 'Blind Date', which had been intended initially for British balladeer Matt Monro. 'I sang it through to his manager,' laughed Viv, 'who collapsed under the desk. I just couldn't write a straight song.'

While The Bonzo Dog Band was in abeyance, 'Legs' Larry Smith had also tilted at the charts, likewise under a pseudonym, with Topo D Bill's 'Witchi Tai To', a cover of an opus by US singing saxophonist Jim Pepper, with the same naggingly hypnotic effect as the extended fade of Steam's contemporaneous 'Na Na Hey Hey Kiss Him Goodbye'. Moon had had a hand in the Smith recording 'at a terribly drunk session at Trident,' grinned Larry, 'It was a Red Indian chant that once it got into your head, you couldn't get rid of it. It was Record of the Week on Radio One, and was very big in France.'

Drinking from the same pool as Smith, Stanshall and The Bonzo Dog Band, Scaffold, formed by Mike McGear – Paul McCartney's younger brother – and fellow Liverpudlians, John Gorman and Roger McGough, mingled poetry and satirical sketches. [5] They'd stormed into the domestic Top Ten previously with the vexing catchiness of 'Thank U Very Much' and 'Lily The Pink', and were hoping to do so once more with 1971's 'Do The Albert', commissioned by the BBC for a slightly belated television programme about the centenary of the Royal Albert Hall in July 1971. [6] As well as reeling in Moon on drums, and Stanshall to growl a fustian *basso profundo*, Scaffold also called upon another ex–Bonzo Dog Bandsman, Neil Innes to plink piano, and, from Stone The Crows, guitarist Les Harvey. [7]

That same year, Keith banged percussion on 'Number 29', and sang backing vocals on 'I Believe In Everything', items on John Entwistle's first solo LP, *Smash Your Head Against The Wall* – and all The Who's three instrumentalists (as Tommy and the Bijoux) appeared on 'Warm Heart Pastry' from *Smiling Men With Bad Reputations*, a solo offering by Incredible String Band mainstay, Mike Heron.

Leo Sayer's departure from the context of a group – Patches – was permanent, however, but before he became the late Adam Faith's hit-making *protege* – and the composer of Roger Daltrey's first A–side in his own right, 1973's 'Giving It All Away', Patches had won *Melody Maker*'s yearly Battle Of The Bands tournament, and had been taken under the managerial wing of Dave Courtney, who'd succeeded Robert

Henrit in Faith's Roulettes. In 1969 too, the combo had released a single, 'Living In America' – with Keith Moon present in the studio, and behind the kit on some of the takes.

When 'Living In America' found its way to the deletion racks, that was just about that for Patches – and Sayer would bide another four years before making commercial headway. His donning of a pierrot costume for the required *Top Of The Pops* plugs might have been contributory to his 'The Show Must Go On' commencing an almost unbroken run of hits until 1979, leaving the majority of Britain's more conservatively–attired singer–songwriters swallowing dust. Among these was Dave Carlsen, a Celt who had worked the folk club circuit prior to moving to London and attempting to 'go electric' as Bob Dylan and, more recently, Mike Heron had done.

The story goes that, in January 1973, Carlsen had been embroiled in a late night session for 'Death On A Pale Horse', a track for an album contracted by Spark which, if a label of no great merit, felt that an artiste of Dave Carlsen's calibre deserved nothing less than the finest available musicians that could be gathered in a studio a stone's throw from the still–trendy Speakeasy. It had already turned into something of a 'supersession', what with Henry McCullough from Wings on guitar, and Noel Redding thrumming bass. A gofer was despatched to round up a drummer, and stumbled upon Keith Moon, almost–but–not–quite in an inebriated state in the Speakeasy.

With nothing better to do, Keith was willing enough to help Dave out. However, after 'Death On A Pale Horse' was in the can, another number was abandoned during an altercation with the studio manager that concluded with a thirsty and irritated Moon's abrupt return to the club. Nevertheless, he'd done enough for a negotiable mention on the jacket of what would also be titled *A Pale Horse*.

Fame proved as elusive for Dave Carlsen as it would for another Spark signing, Keith David de Groot, whose LP for the company was to be reissued on CD in 2000 with the names of renowned helpmates such as Jimmy Page, Nicky Hopkins and Clem Cattini in bigger lettering on the packaging than his own. The world, however, is still waiting for *A Pale Horse* to receive the same treatment.

Carlsen may have had the musical talent, but not the same capacity for self–hype that was Roy Harper's. This Yorkshireman's climb to a qualified celebrity had been punctuated with grave physical ailments and sojourns in mental hospitals and prison, which had all left their lyrical mark on his compositions. As a consequence, he was far less twee – and far less marketable – than the Elton Johns and Al Stewarts down south, even if his hitherto primarily acoustic albums also appealed more to self–doubting adolescent diarists than enthusiasts of heavy metal, jazz–rock and like genres that dominated the early 1970s scene.

Promoted in like fashion to fellow northerner Kevin Coyne, as an 'anti–star', he was appreciated as a 'songwriter's songwriter' by such as Led Zeppelin – to the extent that he had been the subject of 'Hats Off To Harper', the finale of 1970's *Led Zeppelin III*. What's more, Jimmy Page had been only too pleased to accompany Roy during what was billed as a 'St. Valentine's Day Massacre' on Thursday, 14 February 1974 at the Rainbow. After an initial set solely by a seated Harper, Page heralded his entry stage left by pressing an amplified 'Avon Calling' ding–dong doorbell. As the concert progressed, the proscenium was filled by other renowned players including Ronnie Lane from The Faces, John Bonham (on acoustic guitar!) and, for three numbers – 'Too Many Movies', 'Male Chauvinist Pig Blues' and 'Home' – a clearly ill–prepared Keith Moon.

Harper didn't mind – and his fans loved it. Moreover, in contrast to his attitude towards *Hands Of Jack The Ripper*, Keith was quite amenable to his bits being selected for Harper's in–concert double–LP, *Flashes From The Archives Of Oblivion*, even to 'Home' being its loss–leader first single. After all, it was he who'd played on the studio version of 'Male Chauvinist Pig Blues' on *Valentine*, the album that the show was launching. [8]

Publicity stemming from the Rainbow event was to tip *Valentine* into the Top Thirty the following month. By then, Moon was beginning his 'American period'.

After he was ensconced in the ego–massaging environs of southern California, his friendship was cultivated by Love, once admired for their fusion of British beat, gorgeous jingle–jangling folkish–rock and elements peculiar to themselves, but now dying on their feet as merely a backing outfit for mainstay Arthur Lee. Thanking Keith Moon for non–specific services in the notes to their *Reel To Real* album didn't slow a rapidly accelerating decline.

Of the same mid– to late–1960s vintage, Alice Cooper was no longer functioning as simply the front man of the group of the same name, having rid himself of the musicians who been with him since his Arizona schooldays. One of his cast–off collegues, multi–instrumentalist Michael Bruce, tried to go it alone too via albums such as 1974's *In My Own Way*, which, in the context of this discussion, is notable for Moon's drumming on 'As Rock Rolls By' as his tambourine–bashing would be in the same Los Angeles studio a few weeks later on 'Bo Diddley Jam', a number underlined by Diddley's incessant 'tradesman's knock' rhythm on *The Twentieth Anniversary Of Rock And Roll*.

Though as fleeting, Keith's role in *Flash Fearless Versus The Zorg Women Parts 5 & 6!* was at least a cameo – in Robert Newton–Long John Silver mode – rather than an unremarkable if fevered stint on minor percussion. A glorious failure, this laboured sci–fi musical project had evolved during the making of John Entwistle's fourth solo LP, *Mad Dog*, in 1975. While the brainchild of its producer, John Alcock, the concept was realised on an album arranged by both him and an apparently disinclined Entwistle for a hand–picked crew as variegated in its way as that on a passenger aeroplane in a disaster movie. Among them were Alice Cooper, Steeleye Span's Maddy Prior, The Thunderthighs female chorale, Justin Haywood of The Moody Blues, Nicky Hopkins, Kenney Jones, and, blowing sax just like he had in Merseybeat outfit Derry and the Seniors, Howie Casey.

In the end, Keith Moon's extra–mural musical activities didn't amount to much, not in terms of quality anyway – although there was to be a post–script of more substance than anything that had gone before, in the soundtrack to a Beatles–inspired 1976 movie, *All This And World War Two*, which contained amongst its Lennon–McCartney works by the likes of Bryan Ferry, David Essex, Leo Sayer, Rod Stewart and Status Quo, a charming 'When I'm Sixty–Four' by Keith–as–upper–crust–twit over tea–dance strings. With all the attributes of a box–office smash, but none that actually grabbed the public, *All This And World War Two* pulled all of nine customers on its first night at the ABC in Aldershot.

Notes

1. *The Man Who Was Screaming Lord Sutch* by G. Sharpe (Aurum, 2005)
2. Disc And Music Echo, 30 April 1970
3. Nevertheless, it eclipsed a native cover version by Millicent Martin.
4. His arrangement of 'Suspicion' reached the UK Top Ten over Christmas 1976.
5. The following year, Scaffold would amalgamate with former Bonzo Dog Bandsmen and others in Grimms, a poetry and comedy presentation with solo spots for all the principals. Sometimes, Keith Moon would join them on stage.
6. Queen Victoria laid the foundation stone in 1868, and the Hall was declared open two years later.
7. For whom 'Do The Albert' was his final recording. A week later, Harvey touched a microphone at a venue in Swansea, and, because persons unknown had been up to no good with the wiring of the PA system, promptly absorbed more than enough high voltage to kill him.
8. It was also the flip–side of the spin–off 45, '(Don't You Think We're) Forever'.

Gerry Conway remembers Keith Moon *(Fairport Convention): When I was drumming with Grimms, we took part in a charity football match over an Easter Weekend against a team from Monty Python's Flying Circus. Towards the end, Keith turned up in full Nazi regalia, and sort of presided over the rest of the game.*

People tend to think that his drumming too was all show, but I was surprised recently at how technically accurate he was on a Mike Heron album – in which I was also involved. The track was quite complicated, but Keith managed it. Nobody else could have played with the same abandon and still made it work.

'Success Story': The Prime And The Stagnation

'When the greatest show on Earth comes to town, I've got to get a little excited' – Robert Hilburn of the Los Angeles Times [1]

The 1970s began as a re–run of 1967 without colour, daring, humour or, arguably, originality. *The* hit song of 1970 itself was Free's 'All Right Now', which had appropriated the salient points of The Rolling Stones' 'Honky Tonk Women', their final UK Number One – while, beyond *Top Of The Pops*, were albums or album–enhancing 45s from Humble Pie, Led Zeppelin, Man, Budgie, Black Sabbath and other 'heavy' ensembles, who appealed mostly to male consumers, for whom information that a favoured act's latest is like the one before was praise indeed.

Too many of the old heroes of the beat boom had gone down. The Yardbirds, The Small Faces, The Animals, The Byrds, The Spencer Davis Group, The Dave Clark Five, Manfred Mann, The Zombies and The Beatles had all either disintegrated or were about to disintegrate, leaving a residue of mostly tedious splinter groups, supergroups and solo performers to add to a growing pile. Other Swinging Sixties behemoths such as The Searchers, Herman's Hermits and Wayne Fontana were soon to embark on the first 'British Invasion' nostalgia tours of the States, while The Who, The Kinks and The Rolling Stones were also focussing principally on the more lucrative North American market where they were deferred to as Artists rather than it being taken for granted that they and their kind existed only to vend entertainment with a side–serving of cheap insight.

While sustaining interest in their latest output across the Atlantic more than anywhere else, The Who's release schedule also included repackagings and 'best of' singles collections from the archives. All of them were compiled with a pronounced pre–1970s bias, mainly because chart entries that followed the first serious flop, 1968's 'Dogs', tended to depend entirely upon commercial viability. The Who were no longer assured of a hit with whatever was released under their name – especially at home where a typical consumer began to care less about The Who as musicians.

Of greater fascination was the flow chart of tit–bits, true and untrue, that splattered vivid and often scandalous hues onto their private lives

– as instanced mildly by Keith ringing a slumbering and then annoyed Pete in the middle of the night. After Moon forgot to hang up, the rumble of his own snorezzzzzzzzz were heard when Townshend next picked up the receiver the following afternoon. This may have been deliberate, a bit of a lark.

It was hardly surprising, therefore, that the professional bonds between the personnel were loosening. As they'd been within earshot of each other for every working day since God knows when, it was refreshing for, say, John Entwistle to record his first solo LP, *Smash Your Head Against The Wall*, in 1971 or Keith Moon to wonder if he had true possibilities as a screen actor. Oil was poured on frequently troubled waters, and dark nights of the ego lightened by the insistence that the very separateness of individual projects, 'Enriched The Group As A Whole', just as another publicist's cliche, 'Musical Differences' could be brought into play – if the circumstance arose – as a reason for someone leaving.

What no–one could deny was the bleedin' obvious: that the opportunities for extra–curricular activities had been made possible by the day–to–day mundanities of income generated by The Who. These days, this emanated not so much from record sales as concerts where it was no longer sufficient to deliver an half–hour slot when headlining – as they had in 1966 – on ostensibly something–for–everybody scream–circuit packages with Lord Sutch, The Merseys, The Fortunes and The Graham Bond Organisation.

Now it was three hour performances in sports stadia and exposition centres that could rake in the most loot with the least effort, by accommodating tens of thousands in one go, and in which onstage silences and pianissimos were undercut by a ceaseless barrage of stamping, whistling, discomforted snarls and, worst of all, bawled requests for the good old good ones like 'I Can See For Miles' or 'Magic Bus', anything loud.

Such occupational irritations weren't peculiar to The Who. 'Suddenly, shows were incredibly long,' noticed Charlie Watts, 'and when they miked drums up, it became a whole other world. When you get a guy mixing you, it's very loud but flat.' [2] Sometimes, there were worse tribulations than dissatisfaction with onstage sound. Maddened by noise and body pressure, one hot–headed riot squad had been so goaded by Ginger Baker's reprimands for their arbitrary manhandling of fans during Blind Faith's US tour in 1969, that the 'high priest of percussion' [3] himself was a recipient of their punches and kicks. Was Baker berating the uniforms that guarded him as the supergroup's initial low volume led dismayed bottles, cans and even plates of food to be hurled stagewards? In a travesty of legitimate admiration, homely, receding Ginger was once scragged behind his kit by maverick souvenir hunters who fled with his sticks as the tardy cops waded in.

The Who's security was too tight for Keith to be victim of such undignified assault. In other respects too, he had fewer complaints than Baker and Watts, having developed a swift acceptance of the new regime's attendant increase in onstage volume and the advent of monitor speakers – and headphones where necessary – as he battered his kit in North America's stadiums to snow–blinded acclaim. Tinnitus–inducing rock on stage was accompanied by turmoil as, instanced by an attendance of nearly twenty–eight thousand at Saratoga Performing Arts Centre on an off–peak Monday in 1971, The Who took the sub–continent for every cent they could get. Dollars danced before the gleaming eyes of The Who and their business associates as telephones rang with merchandising deals, advances against takings, and estimates spewed out at a second's notice by entrepreneurs yelling 'Klondike!'. The asking prices per concert were reported to be comparable in real terms to the million greenbacks pocketed by David Bowie for one notable US recital in the subsequent fatter decade.

As these blizzards of notes subsided into wads, market research showed that loud had become louder and then loudest. Present at Madison Square Garden for a Led Zeppelin *blitzkrieg*, once and future Yardbird Chris Dreja remembered the PA system and flat–out amplifiers 'literarily moving the concrete in front of fifty thousand people. Having not been to many such events since The Yardbirds, it completely freaked me out.'

Hell, The Who could equal that – and the limousines, private jets, portable stage, backstage area theoretically as impenetrable as Fort Knox, and the general protective bubble amid the howling publicity and celebrity guest–lists. They could also match the 'festival seating', which at many venues often meant 'no seating' – so when the stadium doors were flung open, everyone with the same–priced admission would grapple for a clear vantage point. Outside, would–be gatecrashers were beaten back by police, the consequent injuries and arrests blamed upon hundreds of forged tickets.

In one of pop's slow moments, there were few other overt focuses of adoration in the States in mid–1972, nothing too hysterical or outrageous. With David Bowie only a marginal success then, glam rock was no more than a trace element in the *Hot 100* – while rotgut spirits, Mandrax, headbanging and streaking were among desperate diversions that were catching on as the 1970s trundled past the half-way mark, and precedents were yet to be forged by the likes of The Ramones, Television and The Shirts in New York's twilight zone, and The Sex Pistols' exploratory rehearsals in London.

Yet there were indications already of disenchantment with contemporary pop, even in the States. In the year that *That'll Be The Day* emerged from Britain, *American Graffiti* recreated 1962 in a Mid–Western town. On both sides of the ocean, rock 'n' roll revival acts thrived, whether Sha–Na–Na and Flash Cadillac across the pond or Shakin' Stevens and the Sunsets and Crazy Caven back home. These 'retrogressive' trends and the snowballing of specialist 'fanzines' chronicling them encouraged many hearts to pound in anticipation while squeezing between jumble sale hags blocking passage to a pile of scratched 45's and brittle 78's on a 'White Elephant' stall. Such expeditions for overlooked artefacts from earlier musical eras helped to keep a ghastly Melanie–'Bridge Over Troubled Waters'–*Eric Clapton At The Rainbow* present at arm's length. Haphazard cells of archivist–performers grew in impetus and became more cohesive a reaction against the distancing of the humble pop star from a home audience that would soon be ripe for pub–rock and the shouting and banging of punk – street–level developments that by theoretical intention precluded pop stardom, even if there'd be places in the pub–rock sun too for The Searchers, The Troggs, surviving personnel from Johnny Kidd's Pirates and a reconstituted Downliners Sect.

How much more gratifying it was to spend an evening in the warm, jolly atmosphere of licenced premises where such as Kilburn and the High Roads, Roogalator, Joe Srummer's 101ers or Dr. Feelgood played with more dignity and thought for the paying customer than any big–time group at Wembley or the Rainbow, who were otherwise forever in America, where the drummer had just thrown a Green Room tantrum because of a misconstruing of an amenities rider in the contract about *apricot*, not *cherry* brandy! Can't you bloody read, you dozy Yankee bastard!? No, I don't suppose you can – because it also stipulates *Remy Martin*, not *De Kuyper*!!!

Even as an abruptly radical *NME* lampooned 'dinosaur bands', foreign territories, especially the States, would stay amenable to such as The Who – though often the group's deliverance of the expected high–energy brutality was merely an excuse for buddies to get smashed out of their brains together after heading for the toilets during the support act to partake of various illegal drugs on offer. Blood splattered a water–closet ceiling where someone had been shooting up heroin inexpertly. Back in the arena, urine–filled beer–cans would be hurled stagewards if the band didn't boogie. Few of these odious projectiles, however, landed within the spotlight's glare, where matchstick men with electric guitars and the hugest drum kit ever assembled cavorted, making a gradually more distant noise, and completely oblivious to the squalor before them.

Yet every tour was a sell–out – and always would be – affirming in terms of box–office receipts, The Who's resonance as both figureheads and grey eminences of late twentieth century pop, but, forgetting the glowing reviews and the upward curves on profit graphs, where did Keith Moon belong in all this? He wasn't the sort to take a good book to kill time or sit quietly in the corner at some post–concert shindig or other that was not so much *Satyricon* as a BBC play mock–up of an imagined pop group drugs–and–sex orgy. Wearing halos of marijuana smoke, pushers, groupies, socialites and other loud–mouthed periphery would compete to actuate inane dialogue with Townshend while, over on a makeshift stage, Moon and Entwistle were life–and–soul of an interminable blues jam. Daltrey, meanwhile, had gone to bed early.

After the main party was over, certain round–eyed rumours of – frequently narcotic–fuelled – escapades would be founded in hard fact. The most documented on an early 1970s trek across the States took place at its very beginning in New York's Navarro hotel. From an adjoining room, Keith had been unable to awake a road manager from whom he wished to borrow a cassette tape. After a musing moment, the devil in Moon started an exploratory picking with a table knife at the plaster of the separating wall, maybe nine inches thick. Grains, flakes and larger particles of the stuff fell away, forming spreading mounds of mini–rubble on the carpet.

It was slow and laborious, but eventually Keith reached a brick, which was dislodged after an ecstasy of chipping at its surrounding cement. His fingers were blistered, but that was a minor discomfort compared to the overall ache in his hands and wrists. Nevertheless, creating a body–sized hole, he crawled through and, shrouded in a haze of white powder, located the tape to the rabbit–in–headlight mesmerisation of its now bolt–upright owner, and strode out. [4]

In the desecrated privacy of his own room too, Moon, if an admirable young man in many ways, demonstrated that he had his quota of young men's vices. He had his fill of the casual, unchallenging and sometimes rather experimental sexual gratification procurable from pulchritudinous and often notorious females practiced at evading the most stringent security barricades to impose themselves on well–known musicians. Stray intimations about Keith's bedtime proclivities – almost as much as his consumption of hard drugs and customary destruction of other people's property – filtered via gossip columns and word–of–mouth to other time zones. Feted wherever he went, the most debauched Roman emperor might never have had it so good.

His high standing on the groupie celebrity bulletin was partly down to the consensus was that The Who were putting on a far better show than rival attractions like George Harrison, whose trek round North America in 1974 left him exhausted and foul tempered while The Who had filled Madison Square Garden on four consecutive nights that June, the second of which was described in *Billboard* as 'one of the finest concerts ever in the Garden' [5] against 'a little disappointing' in the *New York Times*. [6]

The same review was long–faced too about the lack of new material. Yet The Who, in coming to terms with both their past and present situations, were realising that all an act, still intact from the 1960s, needed to do to please the crowd was to be an archtypal unit of its own, spanning every familiar trackway of its professional career – the timeless hits, the changes of image, the bandwagons jumped – and that giving 'em a latest single or a track from an album yet to reach the shops was regarded as an indulgence, an obligatory lull requiring a more subdued reaction than that for when 'My Generation', 'Pinball Wizard' or 1971's 'Won't Get Fooled Again' makes everything all right again.

Pop's history was becoming as lucrative as its present. A pop memorabilia auction had been held in New York as early as October 1970, with Townshend's broken guitar and a Cadillac that had once transported The Beatles its dearest lots. Already, there was a sense not so much of nostalgia as impending hangover after the Swinging Sixties.

Back in Middlesex, the likes of Doug Sandom and what was left of Clyde Burns and the Beachcombers had returned to secure anonymity. Some, however, would reappear at the parochial venues from whence they had emerged. Yet real or imagined horrors about this unmarried mother or that incensed Mr. Big obliged other ex–beat group musicians to renege on their past and start at shadows.

Dame Fortune granted a few another bite at the showbusiness cherry. Shane Fenton, for example, had found himself back in the British Top Thirty during a swing back to the flash and cheap thrills of the Big Beat. This was thanks to Marc Bolan, Slade, Alice Cooper and the Sweet paving the way for the theatrical 'glam rock' excesses of Alvin Stardust, Gary Glitter and Roxy Music. Woodstock Nation denim–and–cheesecloth was *chic* no more. In the ascendant were sequins, lurex and mascara–ed gentlemen dressed like ladies.

On their only appearance on BBC2's *Old Grey Whistle Test*, The Who, with certain members sporting T–shirts and scrappy beards, had embraced elements of what was anathema to both glam–rock enthusiasts and the sort of viewer who could reel off the personnel on the latest Return To Forever, Billy Cobham and Weather Report jazz–funk albums. For Top Drummer in *Melody Maker*'s 1975 poll, he'd probably favoured technique over instinct by voting not for Keith Moon or Ringo, but either Cobham, Bill Bruford, Phil Collins of Genesis or Alan White who replaced Bruford in Yes.

Moreover, while the group's television slots were always special to moth–eaten former Mods, saddled with mortgages, they were intrigued when a daughter at art college couldn't stop talking about something called The Sex Pistols.

Notes

1. *Los Angeles Times*, 10 December 1971
2. *Rhythm*, June 2001
3. *Zigzag*, Issue 40 (undated)
4. Steve Marriott, then of Humble Pie, was to claim that it was he, not the road manager, who'd been the victim of this disturbance.
5. *Billboard*, 22 June 1974
6. *New York Times*, 12 June 1974

Ian 'Tich' Amey remembers Keith Moon *(Dave Dee, Dozy, Beaky, Mick and Tich): We arrived at a dance hall in Bath once, where the toilet door in the dressing room was off its hinges. The promoter explained that that was because The Who had been there the previous week.*

My best friend, Nigel, had an encounter with Keith Moon in the early 1970s when he went to a preview of one of the David Essex films in which Keith had a part. He found himself sitting next to Keith in the cinema. All of a sudden, Keith turned to Nigel, and asked, "Do you like brandy?" "Yes," replied Nigel – so Keith says, "This is for you", and handed Nigel a huge bottle he pulled up from under his seat.

Nigel thanked him but felt he couldn't take such an expensive gift from a stranger. "That's OK," explained Keith, "I've got another one for me. Cheers!"

225

Dave Dee remembers Keith Moon: When I was recording manager for Antik in the mid–1970s ,I was in the same hotel in Frankfurt as Rod Stewart and the Faces – and Keith, who'd come with them. We were in the bar into the early hours, and Keith asked if I wanted a drink. I requested a vodka and tonic, but the barman said he was about to close. 'I want to buy my friend David a drink,' insisted Keith, 'and if you don't serve me, I'm going to set fire to the bar.' Rod muttered, 'Time to leave' – because he knew that if Keith said he was going to do something, it was no idle threat.

Sure enough, he rolled up the carpet, stuffed it with newspaper and was on the point of applying a lighter to it...

Hooray For Hollywood!: The Lost Weekend With Lennon

'LA is a meat factory that grinds people into neat little packages. I don't want to be a neat little package' – Keith Moon [1]

During an *NME* interview in 1966, Pete Townshend said he regarded the interlocking personalities of The Beatles as the beat group's chemical prototype. While casting himself as The Who's 'Paul McCartney', he reckoned that Keith Moon was their 'John Lennon' for his overall craziness.

Lately, however, press conference chats with the chief Beatle had been inclined to draw less wry one–liners about mini–skirts and hair-cuts than two–line debates about wider issues. In the aftershock of an incident in Manila International Airport where The Beatles were jostled by an angry mob, a battering psychological rather than physical fate awaited them on their forthcoming North American tour, courtesy of Lennon's off–the–cuff comments in London's *Evening Standard*. When reprinted in the US teenage magazine *Datebook*, his opinions that The Beatles 'are more popular than Jesus right now' and that 'Christianity will go. It will vanish and shrink' were interpreted as 'blasphemy' – particularly by 'redneck' whites in the Deep South who so strongly laced a right wing militancy with God–fearing piety that a backlash of moral opprobrium precipitated hellfire sermons vilifying The Beatles, bonfires of their records, their removal from radio playl-ists, picketing of shows by the Ku Klux Klan, hostile audiences and even speculation about the possible in–concert slaughter of Lennon by divine wrath – or someone acting on the Almighty's behalf.

That particular storm passed, but The Beatles still downed tools as a working band and retired to the studio. Nonetheless, in the eyes of the world, the zenith of 1967's Summer of Love was when the group con-vened before the BBC's outside broadcast cameras in Abbey Road's cavernous Studio One to perform 'All You Need Is Love' as Britain's contribution to *Our World*, a satellite linked transmission with a glo-bal viewing figure of four hundred million. At The Beatles' feet for the *omnes fortissimo* chorus was a turn–out of selected friends and relations including drummer Gary Leeds of The Walker Brothers, Cream's Eric Clapton, Pattie Harrison, Mike McCartney, Mick Jagger – and Keith Moon.

He'd entered their orbit when his standing as one of the hitmaking Who enabled him to be scrutinized through spy–holes and be allowed to hold court with a whiskey–and–Coke close at hand in the Bag O' Nails, the Scotch of St. James and maybe four other London watering holes.

Of all The Beatles he encountered within these walls, John's sense of humour was closest to his own, though Ringo Starr's ready wit was as guilelessly amusing as his colleague's was cruel – and, of course, Starr was a drummer as well. Keith's cultivation of an ultimately closer bond with Ringo may have been interrelated with the behaviour of Lennon after Japanese–American 'concept' artist Yoko Ono replaced McCartney as John's artistic confrere in 1968 as she had Cynthia, his first wife, in his bed.

Through Yoko's catalytic influence, the planet was to be confronted with a John Lennon it had never known before, one for whom The Beatles – and, for a time, everybody else – would soon no longer count. The pair seemed so bound up in themselves that every occurrence and emotion was thought worth broadcasting to as wide a forum as possible. To the man–in–the–street, Yoko had appeared as if from nowhere not long after the death in August 1967 of Brian Epstein, The Beatles' painfully committed manager. For her part, Ono had been unaware of any serious integration of modern art into pop – rather than Pop Art's *vice–versa* – to the degree that The Who's 'auto–destruction' and the connected strategies of The Creation and The Move had been unknown to her prior to her arrival in London late in 1966.

She'd been sniffing round Ringo for his patronage, but he'd been unmoved by her wrapping Trafalgar Square statues in brown paper; her inane *Grapefruit* book; her *Four Square*, a re–make of a film entitled *Bottoms* (that consisted entirely of what you think it did), and anything else she considered necessary to hold his interest.

Ringo's bemusement with Yoko contrasted with John's jealous imaginings after he brazened it out by escorting her to a drama at the Old Vic playhouse. A perturbed *Beatles Monthly* passed her off as his 'guest of honour' but nothing could cover up Lennon's flaccid Beatle member on the sleeve of *Unfinished Music No. 1: Two Virgins*, first of a trilogy of self–obsessed albums with Ono. Its release date had been postponed for months while appalled advisors tried to dissuade one with whom penis display had hitherto not been associated, from

228

making what was, so he explained, an Art Statement. Average Joe was too nonplussed to give an Art Reply to this and other of old John's bewildering pranks with that creepy Yoko – like the Bed–Ins, sending acorns to world leaders, 'Bagism' and *Self–Portrait*, a flick starring John's now–notorious knob.

Having pledged himself to Yoko more symbolically than a mere engagement ring ever could, John had married her in March 1969. Next, his second hit without The Beatles, that autumn's 'Cold Turkey' – with accompaniment by the ad–hoc Plastic Ono Band' – was B–sided by Yoko's 'Don't Worry Kyoko', which her new husband declared as potent as his adolescent self had Little Richard's 'Tutti Frutti'.

Work–outs of 'Don't Worry Kyoko' and 'Cold Turkey' filled his last stage appearance in Britain – at a charity knees–up at London's Lyceum ballroom in December after trawling what a reviewer would describe as 'a jamboree of pop talent' [2] to constitute a sprawling 'Plastic Ono *Supergroup*'. The most renowned among them were guitarists Eric Clapton and George Harrison, the latter's protege Billy Preston and Nicky Hopkins on keyboards, and, in an artillery of drummers, 'Legs' Larry Smith and Keith Moon. For most spectators it was sufficient that they were simply there, but as 'Don't Worry Kyoko' plunged into its twentieth cacaphonous, headache–inducing minute, it was noticed that some within the jamboree of pop talent were exchanging nervous glances.

Joining in the impromptu racket too were Delaney–And–Bonnie–And–Friends, consisting principally of Los Angeles session musicians on the make, who were about to score in the UK singles chart for the first and only time after Eric Clapton had rendered practical endorsement with finance for a European tour. Most had endured an age of anonymous studio drudgery before ascertaining that hanging around with The Beatles, the Stones, The Who and, later, Traffic was a springboard to, if not fame, then a stronger negotiating stance for more extortionate fees to supply their services.

If he found much to praise about drummer Jim Gordon [3], and his successor Jim Keltner, Keith – unlike Clapton, Harrison and Ringo Starr – wasn't overwhelmed by the Friends' aggressive friendliness. Indeed, he chose to distance himself from their magnifying of the gap between themselves and the common herd. Such an attitude epitomised this so–called 'Blue–Eyed Soul School' who, crowed one of their saxophonists, 'went on to back all the players that really do have a lot of influence'.[4]

When he left his country of birth forever in autumn 1971, John Lennon was wary of them too, preferring to dwell in New York where he and Ono were to record *Sometime In New York City* with local musicians. [5] The kindest critics agreed that it was documentary rather than recreational. Adding injury to insult, *Sometime In New York City*'s anti–government sentiments – and, protested John, that President Nixon believed he was intending to campaign for the wrong side in the next US election – provoked, purportedly, ceaseless official harassment that hindered Lennon's attempts to settle on US soil, and was among factors that led him to leave his wife in 1973 and plunge into a fifteen month 'lost weekend', some of it spent in and around Los Angeles, where he cohabited with May Pang, Yoko's Chinese secretary.

His presence sent an electric thrill through the Blue–Eyed Soul School and the rest of the region's close–knit music community – and so did that of Ringo Starr who, experiencing similar marital upheavals in England lived there too. With his own marriage floating into a choppy sea as well, Keith Moon was to plump down the next stool for three–in–the–morning bar–hopping and late afternoon mutual grogginess by the swimming pool in the grounds of a disorderly, if very well–appointed, ocean–side chalet on Stone Canyon Road in smart Santa Monica, beneath the cedared sweep of the Hollywood hills.

Ringo, Keith and, briefly, John – plus additional occupiers drawn from their intimates – had decided to rent the place jointly in order to stay the phantoms of what was by pop standards, approaching middle age. The instant fortune that had come his way since joining The Who in 1963 permitted Moon to shrug off what was a costly indulgence. However, Malcolm 'Big Mal' Evans, The Beatles' road manager and general runaround, was obliged to be more circumspect when, missing the activity and reflected glory, he deserted his wife and children in Surrey for sunny California where, thinking his former masters needed him still, he rented an apartment in seedy downtown LA, the closest he could get to them, financially and geographically.

Keith grew as fond of Mal as Ringo and John were already, but his special friend from among the natives was a Harry Edward Nilsson III, one of pop's great enigmas: the much–covered composer whose two most enduring smashes were penned by others, and the singer who had never been seen before a public audience.

Shortly before Keith's flight to California, it had been in the grey of a winter morning amid the slip–slapping wharfs of London's docklands where the two had been readying themselves for a shoot for *Son Of Dracula*, an all–pals–together movie made under the auspices of mutual buddy Ringo. Someone brought along an outsize bottle of brandy. Others present demurred – too early in the day – but when Nilsson poured a half–pint of the stuff down his neck, 'I knew at that moment it was destiny put us together,' grinned Moon, 'We were drinking brandy at nine o' clock and, thanks to Mal Evans, white wine all the rest of the day.' [6]

Six years earlier, during one of his bouts of deriving deep and lasting pleasure from studying raw data on record labels, Keith had perused a long–player by the pre–packaged Monkees, who had been thrust together to play an Anglo–American pop group in a world–wide TV sit–com, aimed at pre–teens. Nevertheless, Moon's taste was sufficiently catholic to be a fan in a chin–rubbing kind of way. He noted 'Nilsson' bracketed as composer of a track entitled 'Cuddly Toy'.

There remains much division over the creator of this masterpiece of song. Was he an inconsistent genius who defies categorisation or a tiresome *bon viveur*, content to have fulfilled only a fraction of his potential? Certainly, the final episodes of Nilsson's career were less impressive than the first. A Brooklyn–born bank clerk of Scandinavian extraction, he was prey to the psychological ups and downs of the classic 'artistic temperament'. While gaining promotion to computer department supervisor at work and appearing to be on the verge of 'settling down', he made two albums – *Pandemonium Puppet Show* and *Aerial Ballet* – that became, with *God Bless Tiny Tim* and Captain Beefheart's *Safe As Milk*, the toast of the London in–crowd.

Nicknaming him 'The Fab Harry', John Lennon nominated the new cult celebrity as the Beatles' favourite American artist – quite a feather in his cap – and took an initiative by telephoning Nilsson at work. This began a lifelong amity between Lennon and then Starr. Next, Nilsson's mystique accumulated through a reluctance to be interviewed, and out–of–focus publicity photographs. After a chartbuster with 'Everybody's Talkin', more – mostly US – hits followed until the going got erratic for a while.

Nilsson bounced back with the score to and 'treatment' of to *The Point*. Animated by Dean Torrance (the 'Dean' of Jan And Dean), this was the first ever feature–length cartoon film for television. It won many awards, and yielded another US chart entry in 'Me And My Arrow'.

Next, Nilsson enjoyed a major international breakthrough with 1971's *Nilsson Schmilsson*, recorded in London in 1971 with help from illustrious pals. This contained three hit 45s including the million–selling 'Without You'. The subsequent *Son Of Schmilsson* proved to be Nilsson's commercial tide–mark as he embarked on dilettantish perpetuations of an arrogance that encapsulated the disdain of the real or self–imagined 'superstar' for the paying customer at its most loathsome.

Constructively, there wasn't much else to do in the Santa Monica villa. Lennon and Starr were above the tour–album–tour treadmill incumbent upon poorer stars – and so, up to a point, were Nilsson – and Moon, whose Who were on a comparatively lengthy sabbatical. Lacking both application and financial motive, Keith didn't relish the prospect of going on the road again anyway. Hadn't science advanced enough to transmit and reassemble his atoms on a stage in Canberra and back again? This would have meant no soundchecking with an eye–crossing headache after a day's air–mile–consuming, drinking, smoking and laugh–a–minute roistering that would continue in the fug of dressing room and artists' bar. His psyching up process would keep the second house waiting, and a slow handclap might accelerate into applause spiced with a sort of triumphant testiness, and then cut to an unsettling hush when he finally positioned himself behind the kit to count in 'I Can't Explain'.

What was a minor territory such as Australasia to Moon now that Mammon had started to spirit him away to the west coast of the New World? If on the slide elsewhere as a mere pop star, he was lionized almost like he was an Artist over there, and, rather than the thrills and spills of another Who tour, it was less grief to get smaller kicks with one–off events like a big–names–in–good–cause fund–raiser in Hollywood, where petals from the very flower of Californian pop were sipping posed cocktails like melted crayons, when a buzz filtered through the hundreds of guests that Keith Moon had just breezed in. This wasn't television or a picture in *16* magazine. One of those impossible yardsticks of teenage escapism and aspiration, Keith Moon was actually within, asserting his old power in abundance in his involuntary lure for the younger *conquistadors* and their acolytes who buzzed round him like wasps to a jam–jar.

At the crest of his own celebrity as the overlord of glam–rock from the charnel house, Alice Cooper was delighted to breathe the groovy air round Keith in a living room along Stone Canyon Road where Moon was as likely to fling a bottle at the television screen as rise from an armchair to switch it off. After all. shot–up TV sets were quite the norm around Elvis Presley's Graceland mansion in Tennessee and his home–from–home in Bel Air. Besides, Keith had more than enough credit to make light of the proviso that he and the others meet costs of all repairs to the Santa Monica premises and its contents that included the gold discs of more regular tenants like singer–songwriter Carole King, and portraits of John F. Kennedy.

From his frames, the assassinated president gazed down reproachfully at rooms littered with junk food leavings, empty crates of liquor, overflowing ashtrays and drunken layabouts. Now, the building that had once belonged to his family was open house for its present incumbents' circle of friends–of–friends as well as Bobby Keys, Jesse Ed Davis and like former 'Friends of Delaney–and–Bonnie'; personnel from Rick Nelson's Stone Canyon Band, and more fabled and fleeting callers like Cooper, ex–Monkee Mickey Dolenz, Phil Spector, Peter Frampton – who'd made a small beginning as a solo attraction in North America after a walk–on in *Son Of Dracula* – and ace guitarist Joe Walsh, a New Yorker who had lately joined The Eagles. Fanning dull embers for Beatle watchers, Paul McCartney and, more frequently from a Beverley Hills *pied a terre*, George Harrison popped by too.

Hollywood breeds many insecurities but the cardinal sin is to show them. Visible desperation is too nasty a reminder of the impermanence of stardom and wealth. Since accidentally running over and killing his chauffeur in 1970, Moon had been as a kite in a storm – and was now more lost than ever as an attention–seeker amongst attention–seekers in the principal industry, voracious for new sensations to exploit. He was centreless in a centreless modern city, founded on the premise that entertainers are commodities to be bought, sold and replaced when worn out in a haze of ruthless backstabbing, fake sincerity, crippling protocol of cool and the spieling emotional shallowness from those for whom reality was a column of figures.

Natural sleep was a sanctuary, moreso than worsening black–outs as Moon watched the the human driftwood bobbing through the liberty hall where he now dwelt, and who observed him in a black velvet monogrammed dressing gown, washing down his breakfast with Buck's Fizz from a mug. Within an hour of dressing, he'd punish up to four decanters of spirits 'just to get things moving.' [7]

With artificial adrenalin pumping, he fought too hard – as he had when the youngest and newest Beachcomber and then one of The Who – to gain and cling to a position as life–and–soul of the party. In North America, he was aided by his stubborn and fascinatingly alien calling–card Englishness – for, unlike Ringo, keeping such company did not cake his speech with words like 'gotten,' 'sidewalk,' 'candy' (for 'sweets'), 'pants' ('trousers') and 'elevator'('lift'). He continued to go to the toilet rather than the 'john', and it never become his habit to celebrate Thanksgiving – the commemoration of that sacred day when the Pilgrim Fathers broke bread with the real pioneers of this vast new world, prior to their desecration of the 'Red Indians' way of life

Yet it wasn't always easy to imprint his pre–eminence in the after–hours revels in Los Angeles as the Stone Canyon Road mob and their hysterically chattering hangers–on sauntered into topless bars; gatecrashed parties and local radio shows; raced by moonlight to the Malibu surf, and kerb–crawled in phallic Lincoln Continentals with deafening sound systems. It wasn't uncommon for any one of them to stir with the mother of all hangovers in a strange bed, unable to recollect the circumstances that had brought him there.

If futile and public, most of their escapades were harmless enough not to warrant media attention. Moon's predictable frenzy of explosives, self–harm, naked cavorting and material wastefulness tended to evoke laughter rather than participation from the rest. Yet, perhaps slightly star–struck by his Liverpudlian housemates, both several years his senior, Keith was an onlooker, a bit–part player at most, in some of the more conspicuous of the short–lived Santa Monica cabal's larks.

Ringo was pictured with a cigarette inserted up his nose in Sunset Strip's Playboy Club – and that was nothing to his jumping three traffic lights on 'Stop,' and a subsequent court order to attend a two–nights–a–week course on the US highway code. At the centre of it all, however, was Lennon, ejected – with a sanitary towel fixed to his forehead – from West Los Angeles' Troubadour where he and Nilsson had been constantly interrupting a show by The Smothers Brothers, with comments that included swearing and a recurrent 'I'm John Lennon!' There were also allegations that he had assaulted both the comedy duo's manager and one of the night club's waitresses, who filed a complaint against him to the district attorney. Once outside the building, he instigated a scuffle with a waiting photographer.

Less widely reported was an excessively worshipful and inebriated backstage audience with Jerry Lee Lewis – whose graver immoderation, marital ructions and brushes with the law had likewise gilded the legend. Sozzled again that same week, Lennon trashed a memorabilia collection so precious to a prominent record mogul that even Keith Moon would have thought twice about so much as touching it.

For John's birthday celebration, Ringo secured Cherry Vanilla, a singing actress much given to exposing her breasts, to recite Shakespeare in her New York twang, while for Starr's thirty–fourth, Moon ordered up a sky–written 'Happy Birthday, Ringo!' across Tinsel Town's rind of smog. A more practical gift was the drum set Keith had no clear memory of buying Ringo's visiting elder son, Zak, for whom Moon was the god of percussion, 'the very best in the world,' thought Zak.[8] If prompted, he'd concede that 'my old man's a good timekeeper but I've never thought of him as a great drummer.' [8]

To Zak's old man, no recent hedonistic extreme had been 'more satisfactory than playing. It still feels magic to create something with somebody in the studio.' [9] Yet there was nothing too absorbing or original on either Nilsson's slovenly *Pussycats* – produced by Lennon – or his swift follow–up, *God's Greatest Hits* – renamed *Duit 0n Mon Dei* to placate his record company. The first had come simply because he, his Irish girlfriend, John and May Pang 'were sitting around with nothing to do, so we said "Let's do an album." We picked songs off the top of our heads and just did it.' [10]

With Starr, Bobby Keys, Moon – all the usual shower – providing accompaniment that was sometimes audibly half–seas over, he and Lennon wrapped up *Pussycats* in New York after the sessions in Los Angeles had collapsed in a blur of stimulant abuse that was discernable on a disc veering fitfully from long, dreary sub–'Without You' *lieder* to unfunny gabblings on such as 'Good For God' to strident but oddly flat revivals of such as Bob Dylan's 'Subterranean Homesick Blues,' a mickey–taking 'Loop–De–Loop' – a US smash in 1963 for someone named Johnny Thunder – and a 'Rock Around The Clock' which was 'speedy' in every sense of the word.

Using the *Pussycats* shipwreck as a landmark, Ringo began work on a more focussed effort, *Goodnight Vienna*. The affable Lennon stuck around in Los Angeles long enough to strum guitar on one of the tracks, but was soon to head east again to reunite eventually with Yoko in New York's snooty Dakota block, and achieve a satisfactory resolution of his immigration woes. Though nearing the end of his life, his happiness would be completed with the arrival in 1975 of his and Ono's only surviving child.

Back at Stone Canyon Road there was a *fin de siecle* mood. As a bee-hive can function for a while without its progenitive queen, so the fun continued. Nevertheless, after a matter of weeks rather than months, the gang was breaking up. Having gained no contentment from hanging onto Ringo and John – and Keith's – coat–tails, Mal Evans' slaughter in January 1976 by gun–toting LA police was said by some to have been a form of suicide.

However, with remarriage and the birth of his first child, Harry Nilsson was perhaps the first to pull back from the abyss. Artistically, he proved capable still of startling moments, among them the composition 'Easy For Me', the strongest track on Ringo's *Goodnight Vienna*, but his living rested mostly on earlier achievements, exemplified by a 1978 stage adaptation of *The Point* in London's West End, and headlined by former Monkees Mickey Dolenz and Davy Jones.

While making the most of whatever new opportunities came his way, Nilsson continued to issue a treadmill LP every year until his RCA contract expired. On 1980's *Flash Harry*, he was to mobilise illustrious contemporaries again, among them John Lennon – though their friendship had cooled because he was regarded by then – with sound reason – as the proverbial 'bad influence' by Yoko. Indeed, he passed much of the next decade jet–setting whilst nursing debilities – notably alcoholism – not unrelated to the artificially–energized roisterings during his old pal's 'lost weekend'.

These came home to roost for Ringo too, and his glassy–eyed musings and vocational turbulence slopped over onto albums during and after a period wandering a rootless Earth as a result of both his *decree absolute* and the depredations of Britain's Inland Revenue.

The further loosening of family ties and, according to the *New Musical Express*, 'tax reasons' caused the unleashing of the gypsy in Keith Moon's soul too. Nevertheless, despite misgivings shared with other expatriate Britons like David Bowie – who called it 'the most vile piss–pot in the whole world' [11] – all signposts pointed back to Los Angeles and thereabouts where Keith burnt bridges via the purchase in 1976 of a revenue–draining pile in Malibu with a spellbinding view of a bay in which dolphins gambolled.

A lackadaisical assumption that he had wealth beyond calculation was to defer to circular and half–understood discussions filled with phrases like 'convertible debenture' and 'tax concession', and much probing about how this figure had been calculated and why so–and–so had been granted that franchise. Yet Keith Moon did not master his inner chaos and take professional and personal stock. His head thrown back with laughter at some vulgar joke shared in the liquor–sodden jollity of the Whisky–A–Go–Go, how could he have known that he had only two years left?

Notes

1. *Loose Talk* ed. L. Botts (Omnibus, 1980).

2. *Disc*, 22 December 1969.

3. Whose drug–related problems would lead to his departure from Traffic in 1971. Later, he was to be incarcerated in an asylum for the criminally insane after murdering his mother.

4. *Rolling Stone*, 16 May 1970.

5. Though the Lyceum recital filled side three of this double–album (as a performance with The Mothers Of Invention does side four)

6. *Rolling Stone*, 6 November 1972.

7. *The Sun*, 23 September 1982.

8. The World's Greatest Cranks And Crackpots by M. Nicholas (Octopus, 1982).

9. *Melody Maker*, 12 April 1975.

10. *Melody Maker*, 6 December 1975.

11. *Alias David Bowie* by P. and L. Gillman (Hodder and Stoughton, 1986.

"Legs" Larry Smith remembers Keith Moon (The Bonzo Dog Doo–Dah Band): *Screaming Lord Sutch had dropped us off – swinging his Union Jack Roller from a groggy breakfast taken 'somewhere or other' – up through the twists and turns and the one night stands of Laurel Canyon, LA. It was a bakingly hot day and immediately, stepping from the air–conditioned car and thrust into the blinding heat, Keith and I decided that we needed refreshment – without delay. We found a tiny bar that was quietly sweeping up last night's debris, found a booth and ordered a couple of ice–cold beers.*

If truth be known, we were still high from yesterday's 'something or other' and alcohol was most definitely required – it would smooth and sooth the morning jitters and make us both likable again. A pick–me–up. We found a quarter and called our dear friend Miss Pamela – (Pamela Des Barres) thinking that she might like to join us for the coming day's activities – alas, she was booked in for a lengthy 'panty fitting' and sadly had to decline. She would of course be punished for failure to attend a board meeting.

Keith shuffled about, grabbed more beer and looking a bit nervous – shifty almost – said that today he wanted moral support. "Why?" said I – giving him a reassuring – stifled almost – belch , "where are we going?"

"Peter Tork's place".
"My God – isn't he a damned Monkee?"
"He's a good bloke".
"Fine".

We left the bar feeling flushed and human again. Mr Moon kindly informed me that David Sutch had deposited us as close as the scrawled address (now appearing from his pocket) would allow, and blinking at the scrap of paper in the bright sunlight and glancing about (as explorers surely do) we thought that we'd be dashing and brave and make the rest of the journey on foot.

We would walk there – with feet playing an important part. Mr Tork's house couldn't be that far away, could it?

Well, dear reader, we turned into one of the Canyons. It went up and up – and on and on – and the road seemed to be covered in a thick layer of yellow dust – naturally we tried snorting it, but to little effect.

Tiny Log Cabin dwellings – shacks – poked out from behind thick cactus scrubland and were adorned with hanging vines, bushes, palm tress and pretty flowers. Bamboo wind chimes and porch mobiles made of coloured glass clunked and flashed at us as we gently strolled by. Sweet smelling music and soft country rock floated towards us – every home was grooving. We hummed along as happy as could be.

Alas, we soon started puffing and blowing – for offstage we weren't as fit as we thought we were. We sat down in the middle of the road. We stared at our shoes – Keith's scuffed pointed boots and my – (sorry, can't remember) – oh, damn it – let's say I was in 5 inch court shoes. We were madly exhausted and we'd only just started out! We fell back on our elbows, dazed and confused, still puffing and breathing hard. There was no shade, no bar. We'll fry – we'll die.

Keith's hand slipped inside his Brocade waistcoat – just the thing for the tropics – and he pulled out a couple of pills. "Lets pop these little devils, dear boy. " They slipped down with a swig of warm, wet beer. "Oh, that's better" – said I – "You know where you are with a pill". Which of course was complete madness, entire nonsense. How on earth does anyone know what's inside a bloody pill? But we didn't care, we didn't grumble.

We were quickly regaining our strength and our spirit, looking down over smoggy LA, peering towards the dot people and the dot cars. Then a weird thing happened. A trickle of a stream said: "Hello". It was lazily making its way downhill (behind us) and made straight for the two 'strangers' that were sitting in the middle of the road. Aagh! we leapt up (in more ways than one) and patted our damp, wet arses in complete surprise. Where did it come from? An irate fan? A drug crazed official from the water board? What a cheeky little stream. Rock Stars don't have wet bums, they don't get them, it ain't cool. Well, they might well pee themselves or poo themselves, but that's generally done in private. In a hotel room – and generally in front of consenting adults.

As it happens, Peter Tork's house was up a bit and round the corner – we journeyed on, we were almost there. Our host was pleased to see us – at least, he said he was. Catching a quick glint of sheer terror in his one good eye (for we must have looked a bit of a mess) Keith and I strolled in and promised to behave.

Peter was a quiet, gentle, mellow man. Always doing things, engrossed in something – solving a problem, a bit of DIY. The house was huge and wonderful, homely – and even higher than the stream. We took our drinks out to the pool. Keith whispered that the house was about all Peter had managed to acquire from his marathon slog as a Monkee. I knew the feeling.

Out on the patio, bamboo wind chimes and porch mobiles made of coloured glass clunked and flashed at us as we gently – wait a minute, we've been here before. I needed a pee, I excused myself and found a Loo – I pushed open the door – bamboo wind chimes and mobiles made of coloured glass clunked and flashed at me as I – wait a minute – stop this.

And then the source of Keith's concern – appearing like a vision from Mothercare: the hugely wonderful Mama Cass – she swept past the bamboo chimes – her floor length print ballooning out like a giant kite – and rushed over to where we were sitting: "KEITH! – DARLING! – KEITH"– he tried to leap sideways but it was too late. She flung herself at him, knocked him out of his poolside lounger and flattened him. Forty rows of beads and pearls and bells and tie–dyed nonsense held him there. Accompanied by 22 stone of heavenly Melody Burger. He managed to save his drink as they both crashed backwards – for he was a true gentleman, a true professional. However, it was the first time that I'd ever seen my dear friend speechless – embarrassed. (Which I guess is why I'm recalling this particular day's adventure). He just couldn't handle her – or the devastating 'crush' that she had on him. She terrified him. Oops! Peter had said earlier that she might 'pop by' – and I saw Keith go cold. He adored her but she wouldn't let go of this fantasy, her dream that they might both end up together. In love. The Mama Moon Band – appearing at your local 'Drive–Thru'. However,

241

things settled down – Mama Cass groaned pleasantly, whispered something in his one good ear and rolled over. Freedom. Keith blinked and sat back up again, someone 'freshened our drinks' and we spent a glorious day, chatting and boozing and talking about the dot people – the cars they drive and the things they do.

The strangely tragic thing is – I understand that Keith Moon and Mama Cass Elliot both died in the same flat in Park Lane, London – albeit several years apart – but I still find it a touch sad, a touch creepy.

Move Over Mr. M: A Reassessment Of Keith's Solo Album

You will tell me, no doubt, that Mrs. Patrick Campbell cannot act. Who said that she could – and who wants her to act? Who cares two pence whether she possesses that or any other second–rate accomplishment? On the highest plane, one does not act, one is' – George Bernard Shaw

1973's 'Giving It All Away', Roger Daltrey's biggest smash under his own name, and *Daltrey*, the LP from which it came, were the most conspicuous indications that the post–Woodstock Who were growing apart. That same year, John Entwistle issued *Rigor Mortis Sets In*, his third album without the others, and all hot on the heels of Pete's first solo set *Who Came First*.

Soon to dwell in a different continent to John, Pete and Roger, Keith dismissed the suggestion of a collection centred on drum solos. These had always been tedious to him anyway. Besides, Cozy Powell, fresh from The Jeff Beck Group, was already filling what he'd deduced to be a market void for a Sandy Nelson of the 1970s with 'Dance With The Devil', close to topping the British charts over 1973's Christmas sell–in. Smaller hits were to follow – as was similar fare from Manfred Mann's Mike Vickers and Clem Cattini's current paymasters Spaghettihead.

Instead of trying to compete against Cattini, Powell *et al* therefore, Moon placed himself at the central microphone as lead vocalist throughout his 'first – and possibly last – solo album'. Thus he shrugged off *Two Sides Of The Moon* in a US radio commercial featuring excerpts – a 'collage of crap', he called them.

He was being too modest. While *Two Sides Of The Moon* wasn't up to the fighting weight of Entwistle and Daltrey's albums, it was at least enjoyable – and far less objectionable than efforts by Jesse Ed Davis, Jim Gordon, Bobby Keys, Leon Russell and other of those interchangable and self–styled 'supersidemen' with whom Moon rubbed shoulders both in The Plastic Ono Supergroup and during his stay in California.

Tinged with a complacent snobbery about who was or wasn't worthy of their highly–waged attention, big–name approbation had been a springboard to solo recording contracts for Leon, Jesse Ed, Bobby *ad nauseum*. You didn't need to hear any given example of any given

– and usually eponymous – album to know what it was like: maybe four flabby tracks a side, all 'laid–back' and incredibly boring. The self–written songs, delivered in a 'raunchy' caw and post–hippie slang might be about 'toking' cocaine, 'balling chicks', loving the one you're with and other overworked myths of the rock band lifestyle. All these guys were, needless to say, hung like horses.

Because of their profession's peculiar exhilarations, miseries and Dracula hours, the Hollywood studio ubiquaries tended to stick together off–stage as well as on. Every pop generation, even pub–rock and punk, has, by its very nature thrown up an assortment of self–contained, privileged cliques. None, however, was so insufferably smug as that of the early to mid–1970s, which 'traded licks' and exchanged opportunist smirks across the console with financially negotiable Englishmen like George Harrison, Ringo Starr, Traffic and Eric Clapton. They augmented The Rolling Stones on the boards; joined 1971's *Concerts For Bangladesh* rank–and–file – and entered the ranks of Joe Cocker's cumbersome big band, Mad Dogs And Englishmen, overwhelming it with their up–front encroachment; Leon Russell's perpetual top–hat and apparent pride in his lips as he took over as *de facto* leader; an aggressive friendliness – and the rhythm section's squeaky–clean and relentlessly snappy jitter, described as 'economic', 'tight' and by that faintly nauseating adjective, 'funky'.

While none of them could accomplish what the old beat groups, for all their naivety and errors, had committed to tape instinctively, it was as if rock 'n' roll couldn't be done in any other way or with any other people than that self–absorbed elite whose only contact with life out in Dullsville was through narcotics dealers, gofers, managers and bodyguards.

Sometimes an inkling of some fad that the Anglo–American 'superstars' and their hangers–on were 'into' would leak to Average Joe via *Rolling Stone* or some such magazine. There was nothing too outrageous or ground–breaking. They'd lay down a groove with the Memphis Horns at the trendy Muscle Shoals complex in rural Alabama – 'very laid–back and relaxed,' reckoned Leon Russell [1] – or flirt with Jesus, heroin, Buddy Holly B–sides, buckskins, coke–spoon earrings and stars–and–stripes singlets revealing underarm hair – and so would all those who bought their records. Then they'd truck on down to the Whisky on Sunset Strip to dig the backstage vibes, and rap with

Stoneground – who were due on stage an hour ago, but that was cool. Let 'em wait.

Keith Moon could be just as unperturbed by the discomfort and scorn of real people. Nevertheless, beneath the trappings of the limousines, the champagne and the fancy clothes, he – in common with his Who colleagues – wasn't especially comfortable with the distancing of the humble pop group from its essentially teenage audience. While a fully–integrated mainstay and wanted party guest of the Hollywood Raj's ruling class, Keith – unlike Ringo – chose not to earn legion sleeve credits for assisting on albums of what was to become 'adult–orientated rock' by this or that 'supersideman' or by any of the other familiar faces that had greeted him from among the many British musicians also seeking their fortunes in southern California.

Yet he couldn't help but go beyond merely stringing along with Ringo, Harry Nilsson and Mal Evans when they went out on the town or extended a glad welcome to callers whose freewheeling ebullience and detailing of the previous night's carnal shenanighans and drug intake could prove monotonous. Otherwise, they were good company to one who found it laughably easy to checkmate any one of the sidemen in the wildest, foulest and most peculiar recreational activities they could propose.

Among the mildest of these was the making of a solo immortalisation of his own cultural arrogance with stellar assistance from a small army of famous pals. Starr had led the way with 1973's *Ringo*, coloured as a bastardised Beatles collection because all four ex–members were together, theoretically, on the same lump of plastic. It was freighted too with restricted code, aural hints of giggling intemperance and a lengthy closing monologue that thanked everyone who'd taken part.

The notion of Moon having a go too had been fermenting since the release of *Ringo*, and, with The Who in relative abeyance, time hung heavy. Crucially, like the man who paid to conduct the London Symphony Orchestra at the Albert Hall for just one night, Keith too had the financial means to fulfil a dream.

Two Sides Of The Moon was as intrinsically vainglorious in its manner as not only *Jesse Ed Davis*, 1972's *Bobby Keys* or the *Leon Live* triple album, but also John and the second Mrs. Lennon's *Two Virgins* with its shy–making nude sleeve photographs and messings–about with tape recorders. Yet, even if he too showed off his naked buttocks on the back cover, at least Keith was taking on 'decent' music instead of any John–and–Yoko rubbish. Retailers' attention could also be directed to the presence of all manner of Moon's musical cronies and his hiring of fashionable producers in Mal Evans – still breathing the air round three of the ex–Beatles – and, after Mal was relieved of his duties by Moon's anxious record company, MCA [2], by high–flying Skip Taylor, who was amassing a reputation for re–igniting waning stars such as Arthur Lee, Canned Heat and Flo–and–Eddie (alias Howard Kaylan and Mark Volman, sometime vocalists with The Turtles and then The Mothers Of Invention).

Among the hurdles Evans and then Taylor had to jump was Keith's singing. Neither was so deluded as to think Moon a 'quality' vocalist any more than frail, straining Johnnie Ray – an entertainer, incidentally, that I am perverse enough to admire. Indeed, so lacking in conviction – and accurate pitching – was Moon that another was instructed where necessary to sing along in unison out of microphone range or over the headphones, and the more suspect high notes were veiled in reverberation.

On the initially unpromising beginning – and, as it turned out, ending – that was *Two Sides Of The Moon*, it could have been a faceless anybody on 'Back Door Sally', the raucous 'Move Over Mrs. L' and 'One Night Stand' (with Rick(y) Nelson as prominent as Moon in a virtual duet), and much of Keith's style was borrowed. 'Crazy Like A Fox' could have been from David Bowie's *Aladdin Sane*, and Moon overplayed his hand as the effete Englishman completely in the mannered monologue of 'Solid Gold', though, towards the fade, it mutated into a vague hybrid of 'Grandpa Munster' and Long John Robert Newton. He bordered the same area for 'Teenage Idol' – in like lyrical vein to Gene Pitney's 'Backstage' from 1966 – by coming on, perhaps appositely, as the polite, inhibited and too gentle pre–Merseybeat British rock 'n' roller, much as you'd imagine Piers Fletcher–Dervish of ITV comedy series, *The New Statesman* sounding if re–cast as a pop idol.

However, Moon was effective enough as the funnyman–being–serious on wracked 'I Don't Suppose', taped but not selected for *Two Sides Of The Moon* [3]. Moon also made a fair if console–aided fist of The Beach Boys' hot–rod melodrama, 'Don't Worry Baby'. On this, one of his eternal favourites, he stuck to a natural baritone on the album, but managed a *falsetto* on the take earmarked as *Two Sides Of*

The Moon's first spin–off single, though it was less Brian Wilson than Frankie Valli – or the Frankie Valli heard on his Four Seasons' curious joke adaptation in 1965 of Bob Dylan's 'Don't Think Twice It's All Right' – under the *nom de turntable* 'Wonder Who?'. The song itself mattered less than Valli's controlled 'baby' screech – supposedly his impersonation of jazz singer Rose Murphy.

Yet Keith decided not to try – and, most likely, fail – to hit that high G coda of 'In My Life', a number more in the air than actually popular in 1975. George Harrison's vocal cords were weakened to a tortured rasp on in–concert renderings during the previous winter's North American solo tour when 'in myyyyyyyyy life', he loved *God* more. As well as not fracturing with one word the emotive intent of arguably the most nostalgic songs The Beatles ever recorded, Keith elected to half–recite it in the manner of Serge Gainsbourg, following the longest silence on the LP.

A Caruso–loving fly on the studio wall may have blocked its ears when Keith strayed outside his central two octaves but, in context, his humble vocal endowment was not unattractive, even gruffly charming – as it had been when employed as an infrequent novelty by The Who. In any case, who wanted Keith Moon to be a Pavarotti or Scott Walker when he stood a better chance of carving as deep a niche of true in-dividuality as not so much Johnnie Ray, as such disparate so–called vocalists as Jimmy 'Schnozzle' Durante – luminary of 1940s musical comedy, despite a half–spoken nasal twang – and Mick Farren, main-stay of The Social Deviants, forever on Britain's 'alternative' circuit of one–nighters in the late 1960s? Farren may have regarded himself as 'probably the worst singer in the history of rock 'n' roll ever to record more than a dozen albums' [4], but he was still to give 'The Man Who Shot Liberty Valance' what it deserved on 2002's *He's A Rebel*, a Gene Pitney tribute album.

As a pitch–conscious exponent of what the Germans would call *Sprechstimme* (speech–song), Moon's streets–of–Wembley intonation and untutored phrasing was potentially just as capable of compound-ing a mesmerically hideous allure common to certain singers who superimpose a disjointed range and eccentric delivery onto a given song's melodic and lyrical grid. As well as Durante and Farren, oth-ers in this idiosyncratic oligarchy are wobbly Ray Davies, weedily an-drogenous Adam Faith, swollen–vowelled Mrs. Miller, semi–hysterical Wild Man Fischer, Eilert Pilarm – the un–Presley–like 'Swedish Elvis' – and, probably most germain to this discussion, the glottal, pseudo–Cockney daredevilry of Anthony Newley, who turned his back on pop to concentrate on acting.

Moreover, from a purely commercial perspective, however unmelodious the voices of further celebrities, a combination of personal vanity and commercial expediency has led to all manner of unlikely names appearing not only on record labels, but, occasionally, in the charts.

Notoriety for his crimes, rather than any specific felony, was to pay for Ronald Biggs when he joined the remnants of the Sex Pistols for the Top Ten A–side, 'No–One Is Innocent'. Janie Jones, another ex–convict and 1960s Top Fifty contender, was the subject of the opening track of The Clash's debut LP, and self–penned items by Charles Manson, mastermind of the Sharon Tate bloodbath, proved useful demos when covered by both The Beach Boys and Guns N' Roses.

In 1965, Michael Chaplin, son of Charlie, had galloped into the arena with a one–shot single, 'I Am What I Am' – and thirty years later, Cynthia Lennon, John's first significant other, revived Mary Hopkin's 'Those Were The Days' as a single for a German independant. If not exactly related to pop stars, particular (or not so particular) groupies sometimes had their tenacity rewarded with relationships with the objects of their desire that were more enduring than backstage knee–tremblers. Indeed, produced by Frank Zappa and containing Keith's old flame, Pamela Miller, the GTOs's album, *Permanent Damage*, proved that they had everything it took to be rock stars themselves – except the raw talent.

Permanent Damage was bought principally by curiosity seekers, but *Two Sides Of The Moon* was the stuff of those for whom the concept of collecting–every–record–The–Who (or its members) –ever–made was not yet economically unsound. Quite a few had only the vaguest notion about what they were parting with hard cash for, convincing themselves perhaps that some of that Who magic was going to radiate from the grooves. Instead of magic, however, there was mere music played for the benefit of the musicians almost as much as the customers.

As well as Starr and Nilsson, in attendance too were Jesse Ed, Bobby Keyes and blah blah blah – including Jim Keltner, now Clem Cattini's US opposite number, with first refusal on all LA studio dates. Then there was Klaus Voorman, an old crony of Ringo's, plus four other bass guitarists; Jay Ferguson (formerly of Spirit), one of five keyboard players, on Jerry Lee Lewis–esque eighty–eights for 'Back Door Sally', which featured too some ascending *aaaaaah*s from Volman and Kaylan that were purposely reminiscent of those in their 'She'd Rather Be With Me' smash from their days as The Turtles.[5] More illustrious a pop icon than Flo and Eddie then, Jim Gilstrap. a hit–maker from Philadelphia – then as crucial a pop Mecca as San Francisco had been in the previous decade – was in what amounted to a backing choir, most conspicuously with the lone piano tinklings on 'In My Life'.

From out of the sub–cultural woodwork, Keith had drawn Spencer Davis, who, with his very name a millstone round his neck in Europe, had emigrated and accepted a post at Island Records' West Coast office. For those who remembered his Group with Steve Winwood, 'Spencer Davis' on acoustic guitar looked well in the credits for 'Crazy Like A Fox', *Two Sides'* opening salvo. Elsewhere, so did those of Dick Dale and John Sebastian. Guitarist Joe Walsh – a New Yorker who was soon to join mid–1970s men–of–the–moment, The Eagles [6] – gave the record a heavy–metal touch–up, and the entire personnel of the all–female Fanny helped out on 'Solid Gold', penned by their Nicole Barclay. [7]

Though some of the supporting cast – including, reportedly, Brian Wilson – requested not to be mentioned in the credits, the presence of up–and–coming acts as well as some of pop's elder statesmen was among trace elements that helped forestall an immediate tumble into the bargain bins when *Two Sides Of The Moon* was unleashed in December 1975 – and, in retrospect, there is much to praise about the album. Witness Dick Dale's cameo on 'Teenage Idol': biting, heavy–gauge *arpeggios* and his old *stacatto* fretboard dive–bombing, emulated by a string section later in the song.

In a Tony Curtis accent, the now–sexagenarian 'King Of The Surf Guitar' has a tendency to refer to himself in the third person. Among his most telling statements in a 1996 interview was 'Dick Dale is not a musician; he's a manipulator of instruments. The average person can't tell you what an augmented ninth is – and neither can Dick Dale. Yet no critics can say Dick Dale sucks – because he doesn't pretend to be something he's not. He plays from the anger, pain, frustration, warmth and happiness that is generated by playing to those who can only understand a count–in. Dick Dale has always been a product of the people because he's grassroots.'

He was also a man of Moon's 'the show must go on' persuasion. After cancer was diagnosed in 1966, fourteen inches had to be removed from his rectal tract. 'Six tumours and seven cysts,' he enumerated, 'Dick Dale went down to ninety–eight pounds. Dick Dale had never missed a show in his life, no matter how ill he was – and then he missed one because of the beginnings of cancer.'

When he arrived for the 'Teenage Idol' session, Dale – who used to throw away up to four empty cigarette packets a day – was reinventing himself as a naturalist: 'Dick Dale found peace only with animals. The white man is the filthiest, deadliest, most dangerous creature on this planet because of the way he is raised'. Putting action over debate, Dick used occupants of an expanding menagerie – that included lions, tigers and birds of prey – as visual aids when he functioned as an itinerant lecturer on music and metaphysical spin–offs in educational establishments across the nation.

He did not, however, turn his back altogether on the sordid holocaust of pop. Indeed, still a total 'Dick Head', Keith had stumbled upon his hero at the Whisky–A–Go–Go in 1974. 'I was in the middle of a song,' related Dick, 'when he walked up on stage with Mal Evans. Keith was stoned, and he grabbed the mike right out of my face and said, "Dick Dale, I'm Keith Moon of the Who!" Who? Dick Dale had never heard of The Who, but he told me – and everyone else – that he'd got John Lennon and Ringo on his solo album (*sic*), and if Dick Dale didn't play on it, he'd junk the whole project.'

Dale was to remember his hand in *Both Sides Of The Moon* as 'a whole lot of fun' – and it was pleasant enough for others too as long as they overlooked the cancellation and curtailment of many sessions through the principal's intoxication. Often roaring drunk in the vocal isolation booth, Moon was the fount of numerous otherwise needless re–takes and drop–ins. There was plenty of further scope for squiffy errors from all the dissipated old mates, united by a taste for liquor, who hovered round the mixing desk, distracting engineers who, themselves, may have wanted to collapse, screaming with laughter onto the carpet as Keith, tottering dangerously in front of a uni–directional microphone, tarnished 'In My Life' – The Beatles' introspective meditation from *Rubber Soul* – and 'Don't Worry Baby' – which co–writer Brian Wilson once considered 'the most perfect pop record of all time'. [8]

It had been beyond Keith to come up with a solitary composition of his own to break up a selection of wall–to–wall non–originals. It had been a long time since 'I Need You', but, bathed in tedium, he might have put down his schooner of white wine, or dram of brandy, depending on the hour, to mess about with the rudimentary chords he'd picked up somewhere or other on piano or guitar, but hours would trudge by without a glimmer of a tune or lyric – or else everything he attempted sounded the same. Then it would seem too much like hard work.

Yet he found time to figure out a new arrangement of 'The Kids Are Alright' from The Who's early portfolio (of which he knew most marginal US fans of The Who wouldn't be aware). Such a strategy was becoming common. Old hits had been revisited – or were soon to be so – by The Nashville Teens, Downliners Sect, The Dave Clark Five's Mike Smith, Denny Laine of The Moody Blues, Brian Poole *sans* Tremeloes, The Tornados, Colin Blunstone (with a *third* crack at his Zombies' 'She's Not There'), Dave Berry, The Troggs, Alan Price, The Hollies – and Ringo Starr and John Lennon [9]. Occasionally, if an indefinable something was missing, it wasn't always obvious, but rarely were the results of the retreads superior to the original. Suffice to say Moon's 'Kids' revamp, while likeable enough, didn't come close to the version on *My Generation*. But his heart was in the right place and its succinct Sandy Nelson–tinged drum solo – the only one on the album – was terrific, while the isolated minor chord was as potent as ever on the 'but I know' phrase, bestowing an endearing *soupcon* of doubt about a moral generosity that had been at odds with Keith's own character.

Inescapably perhaps, fashionable country–rock entered the proceedings and dominated 'One Night Stand', an opus penned by one of Rick Nelson's Stone Canyon Band [10], but remaindered from John Lennon's *Walls And Bridges* album in 1974, 'Move Over Mrs L' was sub–standard rock n roll. Perceived as a lyrical dig at his estranged spouse beneath a saxophone riff lifted from a 45 by Lord Rockingham's XI – resident house band on *Oh Boy!*, an ITV pop showcase in the late 1950s – the song was a million miles from his earlier paeans of love – 'Jealous Guy', 'Oh Yoko', 'Oh My Love' *et al* – but as Lennon was still carrying a torch for the volcanic Yoko and thus fearing it would upset her, he tossed what was not his finest hour as a composer to Moon [11]. While such a gift, however trite, was no longer the licence to print money that it had been in the dear, dead Swinging Sixties, it was all grist to MCA's publicity mill as the label pondered the mounting costs of *Two Sides Of The Moon*, and derived what gain it could from the a mere ten tracks, all around the two to three minute mark, that gave short weight, even by the needle–time that was the norm of US album pressings.

Nevertheless, during 1975's Christmas sell–in, MCA's press office maximised its similarities, superficial and otherwise, with million–selling *Ringo* and, snapping at it heels, *Goodnight Vienna*. Like Starr's efforts, English humour – as opposed to North American *humor* – or at least a sense of fun, effused from the stereo speakers, even if, say, the inane 'Did you always want to be a pop star?' comment that kicked off 'Don't Worry Baby', and Keith and Ringo's 'crossover' routine – a centre–stage comedian constantly interrupted by another – over ersatz–reggae in the 'Together' finale, a Nilsson composition, palled on replay as recorded comedy often does. This is particularly true if it revolves around weak music hall gags [12] – such as Starr's 'I don't drink any more. I don't drink any less' – the usual in–joking, and a sequence that was in overt imitation of Viv Stanshall's 'The Intro And The Outro' for the Bonzo Dog Band.

Even on an opus as funny as this 1967 roll–call of increasingly unlikely participants in a fictitious jam session – General de Gaulle on accordeon, Adolf Hitler on vibraphone... – you can never quite re-capture that initial sensation of first hearing it. Often, something that once raised a laugh either doesn't bear periodic repetition, leaves a funny–peculiar aftertaste when divorced from any visuals, or relies on affection for the artist to blind fans to sub–standard dialogue.

In Keith's case, it was roughly the opposite. On *Two Sides Of The Moon*, he was Keith Moon – neither a great singer or even an espcially hilarious comedian – being what the public expected Keith Moon to be like, even when smothered in excessively grandiloquent orchestra-tion like that washing over 'Don't Worry Baby' – though, give him credit, Keith didn't remove The Beach Boys' hot–rod references as most other covers did. [13] Neither was his 'One Night Stand' as soporific as the conveniently trendy country–rock that wafted from Californian brand–leaders The Eagles, whose *Greatest Hits* would be ensconced in the US album lists for most of 1976.

Two Sides Of The Moon, however, struggled in the lower reaches of even regional charts, and 'I don't know. What do you think?' was the spirit that prevaded MCA's customary weekly board meetings after Keith thought aloud about a second album. As always, the record industry was voracious for new faces to exploit and discard for a fickle public, and the danger of Keith Moon being left behind in this soul–rotting race was perceptible even in the States because, unlike *The Eagles' Greatest Hits, Fleetwood Mac, Songs In The Key Of Life* by Stevie Wonder, *Frampton Comes Alive, Wings At The Speed Of Sound* and other massive sellers from artists whose marketing budgets were assured for futrure releases, *Two Sides Of The Moon* washed up on the wrong beach of the vinyl ocean as punk built from a tiny black cloud on the horizon to a heaven–darkening thunderstorm.

Yet studio time was allocated, and Steve Cropper of Booker T and the MGs, who picked guitar on both *Ringo* and *Goodnight Vienna*, was appointed to organise a small, hand–picked crew to back Moon, and anchor the antics of special guests such as English comedian Peter Cook – who had pop star aspirations – and, as always, the faithful Ringo.

Among extant items from these sessions are Randy Newman's sardonic 'Naked Man', and Cropper's maddeningly catchy 'Do Me Good' – which would have been more suitable for Starr, along with 'Real Emotion' in which a jogalong and in–one–ear–and–out–the–other melody is layered with a wah–wahed fretboard *obligato* and verses about a couch potato slumped in front of afternoon television. Yet, for reasons connected to his Who committments and Moon's worsening alcoholism, the project was abandoned. The master tapes, such as they were, were not erased however, but stored unforgotten until put to monetary use as bonus tracks on a turn–of–the–millenium CD reissue of *Two Sides Of The Moon*.

As late as 1978, there was discussion about a second Moon album to be produced by British music business jack–of–all–trades Kenny Lynch. A deal was negotiated with a Japanese outlet – possibly because worthwhile interest could not be kindled in any UK or USA companies – but Keith's death intervened in furtherance of this project, and *Two Sides Of The Moon* remained his only solo testament [14], an album that most consumers of today's cultured 'contemporary' rock have brought their children up to consider as a mistake, a *faux pas* and, at best, a product that was almost *meant* to be expedient crap.

In absolute terms, *Two Sides Of The Moon* was like that in places, but if a second–hand copy of the original vinyl surfaces at a car boot sale, I'd recommend a purchase as both an investment and to spin on occasion for the flawed charm and sense of time and place it evokes.

Notes

1. *Back In The High Life* by A. Clayson (Sidgwick and Jackson, 1988)
2. Evans spent the rest of 1975 working with a group called Natural Gas, formed by former Badfinger member, Joey Molland.
3. And without even a composing credit (but possibly the work of either Nilsson or Randy Newman).
4. *Ugly Things*, autumn 2002.
5. As the whole song was of 'I Want Your Love', a 1950s jump–blues obscurity by The Mellow Drops.
6. Not – of course – the British beat group whose adaptation of 'The Cornish Floral Dance' – as 'Come On Baby (To The Floral Dance)' – was issued on 45 by Pye in 1963.
7. Fanny's singing bass guitarist was Patti Quatro, sister of Suzi, then concluding a three–year chart run in Britain.
8. *Inside Classic Rock Tracks* by R. Rooksby (Backbeat, 2001)
9. Whose in–concert 'I Saw Her Standing There' was to B–side Elton John's 'Philadelphia Freedom' in 1975.
10. After flowering in the wake of Elvis Presley in the late 1950s, the late Ricky Nelson – and Bobby Darin – attempted rebirths as singer–songwriters *a la* Bob Dylan, and dropping the compromisingly twee diminutives from their respective names – a strategy as disturbing in its way as, say, *Mick* Mouse, *Tone* Hancock *Frank* Valli, *Rob* Williams or *Kyle* Minogue.
11. Though a new Lennon recording of 'Move Over Mrs. L' was to be the flip–side of his 'Stand By Me' later in 1975.
12. Which were also to be a salient point of 1987's 'Wig' by The B52's.
13. The Tokens, The Ivy League and Bryan Ferry were among those who also released versions of 'Don't Worry Baby'.
14. Unless you count his 'When I'm Sixty Four' on the film soundtrack of 1977's *All This And World War Two*.

Steve Gibbons remembers Keith Moon: *'He was very interested in me writing songs for his intended solo album. It was a tall order, but I came up with two possibilities, "Long Live The Moon" – which was sort of half–finished – and "Bye Bye Blues" – nothing to do with the Bert Kaempfert number – which I taped and played to Keith in a hotel room somewhere in the States. He liked it enough to ask me to come to his flat in London to play it to his girlfriend as soon as we landed in Heathrow when the tour was over.*
We arrived back on a Saturday afternoon, and set off in his chauffeured Rolls. En route, we pulled over at a pub. Keith made a Grand Entrance in the lounge, and faces peered in from the other bar – where we then went to use the juke–box.
There was a little hostility from some heavy–duty regulars, but the mood changed when Keith stood drinks for the whole pub.
When we finally arrived at his place in Belgravia, I sang "Bye Bye Blues" to a guitar that was to hand. Then champagne was served, and we chatted for a while. I think he just wanted a bit of company, but I had to get a train to Birmingham that evening, and asked if I could ring for a taxi, Keith said, "Nonsense, dear boy, my chauffeur will take you." So it was that I was driven not to the station, but all the way home in the back of a limousine which braked outside my front door, where the chauffeur leapt out to carry my luggage in. God knows how much that journey might have cost under less extraordinary circumstances.'

"Beautiful magic that lights up the night,
Shines on the darkest places.
Lunacy lurks in his countenance bright.
Long live the Moon!"
(S.Gibbons, unpublished)

The Punks And The Godfather

Pete Townshend talks about it like religion, and then there are others like me who think it's really a lot of overblown nonsense' – Mick Jagger [1]

Whether under the aegis of Gorden and Meadon or Lambert and Stamp, not much of an attempt was ever made to reshape The Who into what a respectable – and, possibly, slightly naive – record company executive in the mid–1960s presumed a decent pop group to be: dependable in the studio; garbed in uniform but not too way–out suits, and given to stage patter that didn't include swearing or over attempts to pull front–row 'chicks'.

For all Lambert's admiration of Larry Parnes, the grooming process would not embrace any tempering of The Who – especially Keith – displaying a take–it–or–leave–it attitude towards important figures in the music industry who, despite finding the group personally objectionable, would be obliged to promote their continued chart success in order to cater for a considerable and, in many cases, equally repulsive teenage following. In this resolve, The Who – if to a lesser degree than The Kinks, The Pretty Things, The Small Faces and others – anticipated by more than ten years the prevalent attitude of The Sex Pistols and their disciples.

By the time the 1970s pop came to be dated either pre– or post–Sex Pistols however, not a solitary note had been heard from The Who for an entire year. Yet, if they'd abandoned the world, the world hadn't abandoned them, not while their work was being kept before the public .The most vital nod to them within punk was a high velocity 'Substitute' smashed out among other Swinging Sixties items during the Pistols' speculative stumblings,[2] and still in the set in 1977. Rat Scabies, Rick Buckler and Mark Laff, drummers respectively with The Damned, The Jam and Generation X, acknowledged Keith Moon's influence, and Paul Weller, The Jam's mainstay, went so far as to sport a Rickenbacker model just like the ones Townshend had used – and abused – in the 1960s. As the most heavily influenced of the new breed, Woking's finest also covered 'So Sad About Us' as the B–side to their 1978 single 'Down In The Tube Station At Midnight' and pasted a photo of Keith on the picture cover's back side as a tribute to the man who had died a few weeks before its release.

Collectively, The Who, albeit hottish property still in the laid–back States, were one of few old acts, therefore, that were rated in the punk explosion, even though not as highly as Lou Reed, Iggy Pop, Alice Cooper and The New York Dolls – all blips on the test–card of a post–Woodstock era as devoid as it could be of whatever makes pop 'fun'.

Nevertheless, the party–line on Keith Moon was that his machine–gun drumming with The Who, the TV–sets–out–the–window behaviour that had precipitated bans by hotel chains across the globe, and his stirling acting – if it *was* acting – in *That'll Be The Day* and *Stardust* could barely erase his compromising connections – however remote, indirect or long ago – with such as Melanie, Elton John, the overblown *Tommy* rehashes, *Pussycats* and, before he 'went punk', John Peel, in his capacity as reviewer of singles in *Disc* back in 1972, chortling that Ringo Starr's was 'one "superstar" family that still makes it' [3] in 'Back Off Boogaloo'. Keith could beat drum kits into the ground and be 'J.D. Clover' for the next hundred years and yet never wipe out the memory of his standing as one of 'contemporary' rock's nobility, providers of elitist music for all those over–thirties swollen with 'what's–the–matter–with–kids–today?' venom .

Once a real cool cat, he was damned with faint praise by Julie Burchill and Tony Parsons, the Elizabeth Barrett and Robert Browning of punk, who dismissed him in a few sentences as' Quite Amusing But Ultimately Rather Shallow' in their book–length critique, *The Boy Looked At Johnny: The Obituary Of Rock 'N' Roll*. He was also derided by punks and hippies alike as one more bourgeois liberal with inert conservative tendencies, a fully paid–up member of what 'neil', a hippy–drippy anachronism from the 1984 BBC series *The Young Ones*, would call 'the Breadhead Conspiracy'. What was escapism for most was the world in which Moon lived – which was mostly in his spread next to that of a nervous Steve McQueen in Malibu – and, when in Paris, say, no waiter's eyebrows would rise if he ordered sausages and chips to go with a minor Beaujolais in Montparnasse restaurants where only such as Jackie Kennedy, Sartre, de Beauvoir, Dali, Fellini, Warhol, Hemingway and Bardot could afford to dine.

He had the funds too to go on more holidays than the future Duchess of York would in the decade that followed. During the two month interval between the end of a string of stadium shows in Europe and the start of The Who's second North American tour of 1976, he booked into one of Tahiti's tortured patchwork of high–rise hotels – in which he was thinking half–seriously of investing – and spent the days fishing or lying on a beach where his lilo might be adjacent to that of, perhaps, Marlon Brando or Jacques Brel. In common with the dolphins he might have sighted there, Moon seemed to be devoting the rest of his life to the pursuit of pleasure.

When he returned to England, seemingly for good, in 1977, he would miss the West Coast sunshine, but, in regaining a little lost native popularity, he'd understand how homesick he'd become during his years of globe–trotting. Who could fail to adore the cold and rain, and only three TV channels in a homeland where female traffic wardens called you 'love', cigarettes could be bought in ten–packs, pubs were more than places where men got drunk and *Monty Python's Flying Circus* repeats had cleared the ground for such as *Ripping Yarns* and *Fawlty Towers*, heaving British television from the mire of 'more tea, Vicar?' sit–coms or half–hours freighted with innuendo about wogs, poofs and tits?

Though resident in the bluster of central London, Keith was perusing the property pages of *Country Life* for somewhere like 'Tara', his long–abandoned place in Chertsey that, while it hadn't been exactly an arcadian shangri–la, had combined privacy without imprisonment. As important as the dwelling *per se* was the space between it and the nearest neighbours. With rapidly accelerating advances in communication technology, close proximity to both epicentres of the record business and the other Who personnel wasn't as vital as it might have been before his evacuation to California.

That, however, needn't have been a prime consideration. If there were any gathering conspiracies, he'd be glad to be distanced from them. As in the 'happy ending' of a Victorian novel with all the villains bested and the inheritance claimed, Keith may have imagined that, as long as he remained in a fool's paradise about his bank balance, he was well–placed to 'settle down' to a prosperous lassitude where nothing much was calculated to happen as the seasons of pop changed without him.

Spoken of sometimes as if an old nag out to grass, the fellow was seen to do hardly a stroke of work. Yet a rising of sorts from vocational slumber became perceptible when, very publicly, Keith took the trouble to sample for himself this new sub–culture that was being acclaimed by a fairweather music press.

After he'd dressed as if for a regimental dinner and donned a fur coat against the evening chill, he'd be bowed out of a white Rolls–Royce by his door–opening, cap–tipping chauffeur outside this or that punk dungeon in the middle of London. Then he'd saunter to the head of a gaping queue that didn't know whether to laugh, applaud or shout abuse as he swanned on past the similarly consternated bouncers, confronted by a personification of rock aristocracy. Though Keith Moon was at their mercy, they couldn't describe how courage oozed out of them when mesmerised by over a decade of hero–worship. Who'd have thought that the old boy could still have it in him?

Within minutes of entry, a feeling of *deja vu* crept up on Keith during the bursts of aural debris – with guitars being thrashed *allegro con fuoco* to relentless drumming behind some ranting johnny–one–note who behaved as if he couldn't care less whether you liked it or not. Not a week went by without the *NME* or *Sounds* howling about another fresh sensation ringing some changes. Somehow, most of them owed as much to The Sex Pistols as The Sex Pistols did to, well, The Who. The only difference was that some sounded like The Who would have done, had Roger been moved to the drums and Keith been installed as permanent lead singer.

Superficially rivetting, but lacking the musical strength of both the 1960s beat boom and psychedelia, punk, he concluded, had always been doomed to be ineffectual. As he might have predicted, the Pistols disbanded after a US tour, their separate parts never equalling the whole. With their departure came a mopping–up operation as the grubbing music industry stole punk's most viable ideas and got its most palatable entertainers to ease up, grow their hair and get ready to rake in the dollars. Generation X's aptly–named Billy Idol was re–invented as an updated Ricky Nelson, and would one day be among featured pop celebrities performing *Quadrophenia* with a latter–day Who.

As early as the second half of 1973, The Who had been happy too for Kilburn and the High Roads to support them on eight dates up and down England, though they contained one who spat out in 'oi–oi!' cockney his perspectives on London low life. Crippled and pugnacious, Ian Dury was to be described four years later with vague accuracy as 'a sort of dirty old man of punk' by the *Daily Express*'s William Hickey [4]

'It was a hectic fortnight,' Dury would recall, 'at the Lyceum this flunky came down with the plates of food, and Keith Moon smashed the lot. It was the same the next night. The third night, they came down with paper plates, and he tore them all up. He lived by his convictions, that man. Humphrey Ocean, our bass player, witnessed a load of dodgy reporters telling Roger Daltrey and Keith Moon to throw things and kick the walls down: winding them up so they could get some shots.' [5]

Like anyone else would, Dury was to be more astounded when The Sex Pistols gained national notoriety by cursing on an early evening TV magazine, beer–induced vomiting in an airport's departure lounge, and a drunken invasion of a major record company's offices. Well, The Who had been there and done that since what was time immemorial by pop standards. Back in January 1968, they'd been escorted from an aeroplane in Australia for 'making the hostesses cry' and general misbehaviour. The following May, Townshend spent a night in gaol after he'd kicked a policeman offstage at New York's Fillmore East, mistaking him for a fan. As for Moon..............

Notes

1. *Rolling Stone*, 21 August 1980.
2. These also included the Dave Dee, Dozy, Beaky, Mick and Tich B–side 'He's A Raver', Love Affair's 'A Day Without Love' and The Small Faces' 'Whatcha Gonna Do About It (with the rewritten opening couplet, 'I want you to know that I *hate* you, baby/I want you to know I don't care').
3. *Disc*, 17 March 1972.
4. *Daily Express*, 12 May 1977.
5. *No Sleep Till Canvey Island* by W. Birch (Virgin, 2000).

Waspman And The LS Bumble Bee

'Keith Moon had a look on his face like he was suffering the ultimate torture' – Richard Green on The Who's performance at 1969's Isle of Wight Festival [1]

In the beginning, Keith Moon didn't drink much – though, traditionally, booze has always been the most common stimulant in popular music and – as exemplified by the old English air, 'John Barleycorn' and the 'What Shall We Do With The Drunken Sailor' sea shanty – the earliest to be celebrated in song. Random instances from the past half–century include 'Cigarettes, Whiskey and Wild, Wild Women', 'A Pub With No Beer', 'White Lightning', 'Mama Weer All Crazee Now', 'Red Red Wine' and any number of gutbucket Mississippi and Chicago blues items.

However, though I know it's distasteful to mention such things, alas it's true, pop musicians have also partaken of forbidden drugs. Cocaine was mentioned in Cole Porter's 'I Get A Kick Out Of You' way back, and amphetamine was the subject of Bo Diddley's 'Pills' long before pop stars and drugs became hand–in–glove in mid–1960s newspaper headlines, and 'getting high' a way of sharing something with such disparate and often doomed heroes from a long list that includes Charlie Parker, Johnny Cash, Keith Richards, Eric Clapton, Jimi Hendrix, Janis Joplin, Peter Green, Lou Reed, Syd Barrett, Gram Parsons, Phil Lynott and Boy George – whose credibility was enhanced by promoting a drug habit necessary to keep the Dracula hours of their profession rather than fight domestic exhaustion like the tablet–swallowing housewife in The Rolling Stones' 'Mother's Little Helper'.

Perhaps not at Ultra Electronics, but probably at the job he was doing when he joined The Who – as a very junior clerk at British Gypsum– Keith too would dip into a surreptitious pocket every now and then for a black or blueish capsule. How else could he cope? In the first weeks of being a Beachcomber, he'd managed on Pro–Plus, the caffeine–based tablets that students could buy over the counter in readiness for all–night exam revision. However, when the double life of the day job and moonlighting with the group started to burn the candle to the middle, Keith had become all too aware of the more dazzling effects of amphetamine sulphate – 'speed' – and, when necessary, the counterbalancing barbiturates. These were the active constituents in 'Purple Hearts', 'Black Bombers', 'Mandies'. 'French Blues' and the like. Soon, Keith was taking them compulsively – and would continue to do so for as long as he lived – to stay awake, to fall asleep, to calm nerves, to lift a blue mood – or by way of simple experiment, regardless of the repercussions.

A supply could be obtained with ease near work, what with the Government's net–closing Bill 'to penalise the possession and restrict the import of drugs of certain kinds' over a year away. It would be no hanging matter then if you were caught anyway. As late as October 1964, the *Hampstead And Highgate Express* reported that a Robert James Moir got away with a conditional discharge for being found with thirty grams each of cocaine and heroin. [2]

With more readily–available and, theoretically, less dangerous chemicals inside him, Keith could go the distance of work and play. Free from British Gypsum for the day, he'd hurry home and dive into a bath. Afterwards, with Sellotape, back–combing and his sisters' drier, he'd restyle his hair from the combed–back flatness required to escape persecution in the office, to Beatle–like moptop. Because amphetamines are appetite suppressants, he would often forgo an evening meal when waiting for an overloaded van an hour late to transport him to the venue where the encore would be as energetic as the opening number. When the show was over, Keith, with eyes like catherine–wheels, would be ripe for mischief.

There was, of course, a price for burning up months of youthful energy in a few hours of metabolic chaos. Though inconsistent, the more common – and more gentle – after–effects of consuming speed embrace diarrhea, ringing headaches, hyperactivity, facial tics, indigestion, rashes, nausea, panic attacks, raging thirst, irritability, and long wakeful periods in bed. More sinister are muttered trepidation building to Hitlerian screech; the bawling of purgative obscenities in public (on stage, for example); muzzy eyesight as a harbinger of temporary loss of vision; uncontrollable shivering, dizziness, swaying and staring vacantly as preludes to a convulsive fit; nightmare hallucinations ('the horrors'); suicidal depression, and other disturbances that would reduce a group's live wire to a pathetic isolate.

As Moon grew older, most of the worst symptoms of his amphetamine habit would manifest themselves – especially when combined with increasing alcohol intake – but, when he was incapable of thinking about tomorrow, Keith suffered only a general drowsy malaise when snatched sleep and the lingering buzz of 'leapers' that 'downers' might not have quelled, could render him unable to think straight at British Gypsum. He'd muddle from nine 'til five on automatic, making illicit use of the telephone for group business, while glancing over his shoulder for the nosier members of staff, and staying just a few degrees short of open insolence towards any of his immediate superiors who paused at his desk. Otherwise, Keith let his body relax and mind go numb with accumulated fatigue and the spirit–crushing listlessness of someone who wasn't permitted to take off his suit jacket, even in summer.

Yet, when out of workaday apparel, it would be flattery of a kind that, on first acquaintance, Pete Townshend judged that Moon looked disreputable enough to know what 'pot' was. Would he care to sample some? It was packed into a large cigarette called a reefer, and smoked communally in a hidey–hole like, say, The Who's van. It sounded a bit too cloak–and–dagger for Keith until no less than The Beatles giggled through the shooting of *Help!* in the haze of its short–lived magic. Therefore, as well as maybe drinking from the few cans of lager and a bottle of harder stuff in the dressing room, Keith became quite accustomed to not only gulping down some speed to wire him up for the show, but drawing on 'spliff' to unwind tense coils within afterwards. [3]

By post–Mod 1967, however, extremes of drug experience beyond mere pep pills and reefers were implied in the self–consciously 'weird' debut singles by chart newcomers like The Move and The Pink Floyd as well as the transition of The Pretty Things, Small Faces and other established groups from boy–meets–girl songs to musical insights that were not as instantly comprehensible. Not yet versed in hip jargon, the BBC passed The Small Faces 'Here Comes The Nice' single – dealing with the rush of speed – as it did Bob Dylan's mind–expanding 'Rainy Day Women Nos. 12 & 35' and its 'everybody must get stoned!' chorus. 'My Friend Jack' by The Smoke and just plain 'Heroin' from The Velvet Underground, however, hadn't a hope of a solitary Light Programme spin, and the Corporation frowned on The Byrds' 'Eight Miles High', and, later, even Beatles tracks like 'Tomorrow Never Knows', 'A Day In The Life', 'Lucy In The Sky With Diamonds' and 'I Am The Walrus' as the 'us and them' divide intensified with the

Fab Four among celebrities advocating the legalization of marijuana, and assisting on 'We Love You', The Rolling Stones 45 issued in the aftershock of the famous drug bust in 1967 at Keith Richards' Sussex cottage.

Out of sympathy too, Kit Lambert paid for a space in a national daily to object to Richards and Jagger being 'treated as scapegoats for the drug problem' [4], and royalties from the three weeks in the lower reaches of the Top Fifty for The Who's dashed off revivals of two recent Stones numbers were to be donated towards their legal costs.

Another release that year, the spoof 'LS Bumble Bee' by Peter Cook and Dudley Moore, was indicative of a general knowledge if not use of lysergic acid diethylamide – LSD – which had been 'turning on' factions within London's In Crowd for almost a year before it was outlawed for recreational purposes in 1966. Nevertheless, the pop industry's association with 'acid' had led The Troggs' manager to confine his clean–minded lads to provincial bookings in Britain to minimalize the chances of illegal drug publicity sticking to them while Dave Dee, Dozy, Beaky, Mick and Tich announced in print that, to them, all LSD meant was pounds, shillings and pence.

Keith's cavalier decision to turn on – or 'take a trip' – was for reasons much the same as those of fellow raver, Eric Burdon of The Animals: 'I want to take a piece from every book. I want to learn from everything. That was why I originally took LSD. No, that's not right. I took it just to get stoned.' [5] Moon – and Pete Townshend – may have quizzed Burdon and others about LSD prior to trying it themselves, but they were advised in only the broadest terms.

The effects, see, varied from person to person, from trip to trip. On an aeroplane flight back to London after a US tour, both Keith and Pete chose to while away the long haul with a trip. For the guitarist, the mental distortions on this occasion were akin to a mystical reverie, an incredible journey to unknown – and upsetting – realms of inspiration. Yet LSD had never been all it was cracked up to be for Keith, who blamed The Beach Boys' estrangement from the surf in *Pet Sounds* and the jettisoned *Smile* on leader Brian Wilson's acid–drenched bleariness and associated artistic decline. Moon understood too that, by the later 1960s, it tended to be mixed with speed. Some more unscrupulous pushers even adulterated it with Ajax or Vim scourer.

If LSD, pure or not, was contributory to Moon's condensing inner turmoil, it made no obviously appreciable difference to him beyond hallucinations and surreal sensations that lasted only until he 'came down'. While Townshend spoke openly about their psychedelic escapades, he hadn't much to add – except that, wherever The Who went these days, local narcotics dealers were welcome to contrive a network from the outside to sell their goods to him.

Yet drugs did not always make the duller aspects of touring any more bearable. Nevertheless, by the 1970s, a sense of longing rather than self–loathing propelled Keith's propensity for the snorts of cocaine – and some quaaludes to even them out when it was time to hit the sack – that he was imbibing as carelessly as drams of brandy–and–ginger. While 'coke' took gradual if unknowing possession of him, he imagined – possibly correctly – that he could give it up any time he liked. There was, however, only a solitary – and stomach–pumpingly disasterous – flirtation with cocaine's sister narcotic, heroin – which, when taken with a cocktail of speed, spirits, angel dust and, allegedly, horse tranquilisers – a new one on Keith – was behind the headline–making episode whereby he collapsed over his kit at San Francisco's Cow Palace on 20 November 1973, forcing Pete Townsend to request an amateur drummer come forth from the crowd to get The Who through the rest of the show.

During Keith's final year, an overdose of valium in Los Angeles brought him to the brink although, back in London, while amphetamines and even LSD were helping to fuel punk, lager – as recognized in the 'get pissed, destroy!' finale of The Sex Pistols' 'Anarchy In The UK' – was more likely to sustain its exponents.

Moon, however, was attempting to kick booze by then, but it would be chlormethiazole – filling the most important bottle in a bathroom cabinet's worth of prescribed medications to battle his alcoholism – that would finish him just as outward signs of remission were correlated with a renewal of professional activity. Death seemed to be allowing him to purchase from his plight a few months – maybe years – of respite. At last, he was listening to what his body was telling him – and perhaps he'd been warned too by the vehement hostility to drug culture from other musicians, both in interview and record grooves.

'The general consensus of opinion is that it's impossible to do anything creative unless you use chemicals,' snarled Frank Zappa [6], whose

'Cocaine Decisions' swiped at the drug most prevalent in the music industry in the 1970s and 1980s, while John Mayall's 'Accidental Suicide' was less a tribute to the late Jimi Hendrix than a caution of the same kidney as Steppenwolf's 'The Pusher' (whose trade catered for addicts 'with tombstones in their eyes'), Eric Clapton's 'Cocaine' – and 1971's 'Behind Blue Eyes' by The Who. Even The Grateful Dead had wagged a rebuking finger in 'Casey Jones' with its 'you'd better watch you speed' hookline, and Godfather of Soul James Brown exerted his quasi–monarchial influence to block trafficking with 1972's admonitory 'King Heroin'.

That artificial energy continued, however, to drive many of pop's foremost icons might be demonstrated in the in–concert 'laughing' version of 'Are You Lonesome Tonight' by an addled and bloated Elvis Presley, prey in the end to obesity, hypochondria and paranoia. His bathroom death on 16 August 1977 reached a basement club frequented by London punks, some of whom raised a gleeful cheer. Someone telephoned the news to an appalled Keith. He had never met Presley, but, while death is supposed to diminish us, the King's 'diminished' him a damn sight more than others he had known well, even that of Vinnie Taylor, twenty–five–year–old guitarist with Sha Na Na, taken by an overdose three years before.

Over the next few weeks, Keith poured a huge and frenzied quantity – even by his standards – of pills and drink into himself during what amounted to an unspoken wake and a tacit acknowledgment that his own time wouldn't be long either.

Notes

1. *New Musical Express*, 6 September 1969.
2. *Hampstead And Highgate Express*, 30 October 1964.
3. In *That'll Be The Day*, one scene depicts Keith and other members of The Stray Cats sharing a spliff (or 'joint') when relaxing in a New York hotel suite.
4. *The Lamberts* by A. Motion (Chatto and Windus, 1986).
5. *Don't Let Me Be Misunderstood* by E. Burdon and J. Marshall Craig (Thunder Mouth, 2001).
6. *Loose Talk* ed. L. Botts (Rolling Stone Press, 1980).

Jim McCarty remembers Keith Moon (drummer with The Yardbirds): On both of the two occasions I experienced The Who – at the Marquee and in the Goldhawk Social Club, I was very impressed by Keith's drumming – as I was when The Yardbirds and The Who appeared on a Ready Steady Go outside broadcast at La Locomotive in Paris. Keith let me borrow his kit, and I noticed that there was a lot of his congealed blood on it. The show was memorable too for his confession to me that he'd swallowed about a dozen Purple Hearts just before their opening number, and for afterwards when The Who lined up before the cameras to piss in an alleyway at the back of the club. It was some sort of send–up of the French.

Keith was always up for a laugh, forever larking about. At the Cromwellian one night, he was very taken by this bald wig I was wearing, and wanted to get in on the joke.

'Had Enough': The Last Show On Earth

Drugs, booze... everything was being done to excess. It was becoming a pantomime. Then, in 1978 when Keith Moon, who was a good mate, died, I thought that if I continued, I'd be next – so I quit the music scene' – Steve Ellis (Love Affair) [1]

In the mid–1970s music press, the smart money was on Keith Richards – nominated by the *NME* as 'The World's Most Elegantly Wasted Human Being'[2] – but Keith Moon ranked too in a morbid sweepstake about the next live–fast–die–young pop idol to follow Brian Jones, Jimi Hendrix, Janis Joplin, Jim Morrison and like unfortunates to the grave. Furthermore, the lyricist of The Righteous Brothers' 1974 US smash, 'Rock 'N' Roll Heaven' – where 'they got one hell of a band' – may have been searching for rhymes for 'Moon' and 'Keith' for the periodically updated concert rendition. The number was already glutinous with both orchestration and declamations with buoyant pride of the names of 'Janis', 'Jimi', 'Jim' and suchlike. Neither of the two unrelated siblings admitted in song that it was the sex–and–drugs–and–rock 'n' roll lifestyle that had led to many of the mentioned individuals' wretched ends. [3]

Like all of them, Keith was living evidence that the majority of the sick are not in bed. Another shared characteristic was that he was trying to cope with sufficient personal desolations to start World War III, and a debilitating affliction – by then the only suitable expression to that was losing him a race against death.

Yet, on the face of it, while every day that Moon still lived was a bonus, whatever had been wrong seemed to be righting itself as he approached his thirty–second birthday, even if he continued to play up to the old expectations by, say, playing as the life and soul of the backstage party after a recent Wings show, albeit with the grooved cheeks of a man maybe a decade older, and the coldly professional expression of a conjuror repeating a popular trick to amuse children.

At some music industry festivity or other, of the many he attended nowadays, he'd appear to be relatively sober and coherent at his table, but like bosom–buddy Oliver Reed, his opposite number in the world of drama, he'd become real, real gone if called to a podium or if required to climb a stage, heaving with stars and starlets, for an 'impromptu' valedictory jam: dear, old Keith, drunk before breakfast, stoned before lunch time.

As the 1980s loomed, Moon was endeavouring to give the outward impression of a person completely in command of his faculties. If his financial credit wasn't what it was, for instance, there was another Who album on the way, not to mention income from the forthcoming film portrait of the group, *The Kids Are Alright*, as well as compilations like 1976's *The Story Of The Who* and the Germany–only, *The Who: Best Of The Sixties*.

With a character all but unblemished by a criminal record, despite everything, he was settling comfortably if strangely into his thirties on the consolidated fruits of his success. The adulation, the smash hits, the money down the drain could be transformed to matters of minor importance compared to the cosseted life of leisure he felt he deserved and, as an after–thought, providing his neglected daughter with the best of everything, especially as his divorce from Kim had been rela-tively painless. She was now being 'talked of' with Ian MacLagan, a highly–waged jobbing keyboard–player since the sundering of The Faces – the group that followed The Small Faces – and, in 1978, they were to wed and move to the USA.

Keith had been thinking aloud about marrying again too. He seemed as besotted and as full of jaunty vitality as a bloke with a prematurely middle–aged physique could be, with his stunning Annette Walter–Lax. In reciprocation, Annette looked forward to the rattle of his keys at the front door that heralded one more deliverance from the treadmill of the road. Too soon for both of them would come another departure for a stage in another continent or weeks of work on the next Who album.

Nonetheless, he wouldn't have been the Keith Moon of bed–hopping legend if he hadn't been the focus of media gossip about exploits on tour with girls who were proud of their celebrity–inflicted love–bites. This was more than a trifle mortifying for Annette. Adding insult to injury, the *Daily Express* quoted Keith as confiding that she was mere-ly his favourite in a seraglio dotted around London and beyond. Yet Annette was prepared to be understanding about both his amorous infamies and her own position as his 'constant companion' during an erosion of her vocational prospects as a model of similar natural radi-ance to Jerry Hall, Mick Jagger's latest flame. More like an orderly in a psychiatric unit than passionate inamorata these days, Annette let Keith fulminate and bluster without reproach, and talked him through his neurosis.

Their blossoming romance was assumed to be stormy by those who witnessed an irate and inebriated Keith being prised from a plane at Victoria airport in the Seychelles and driven to a hospital's accidents–and–emergency department for a sedative and an overnight stay – and Annette flying back to Heathrow alone to be met by scribbling news-hounds, who saw no reason why the incident could not be portrayed as a regular occurrence.

The subject of their speculation boarded a flight back to London. Staring vacantly back at him from the mirror of the business class compartment's lavatory was the worn–out, parchment–like counte-nance of a persistently poorly old–young creature. Back in his seat, as he slumped into the uneasiest of slumbers, melancholy penetrated his disjointed thoughts during this final sanctuary before touchdown and the dazzling constellation of flashbulbs after he disembarked.

Moon was able to stifle the image of all the doctors he'd consulted shaking their heads at his way of life. The latest one had prodded his bloated body gingerly as if it was some dead mammal, and spoken to him as if he was a retard. After some unpleasant procedures had winkled out high blood pressure, organic deterioration and arterial blockage, he'd been prescribed a course of various medications and the avoidance of stressful situations. The tallest order of all, of course, had been to cut back on and, eventually, give up the booze. Anticipating the worst, Keith couldn't prevent the stomach–knotting that afflicted itself on him as he built up a damning picture of his state of health before placid denial that there was anything to worry about. Maybe he was panicking unduly.

At Heathrow, an overweight figure walked stiffly with his hand–lug-gage through the customs area, budgerigar eyes bloodshot with alco-holic and emotional fatigue. Once, it had been a lucky taxi–driver that picked up Keith Moon – for, regardless of his oscillating fortunes, he'd always been known as a generous tipper of not only cabbies, but por-ters, chambermaids, bell–boys *et al.* Now only a personal chauffeur was privy to the shared joke as Keith still laughed his maniacal laugh and grinned askance at the occasional surrealities of life on the pave-ment. Yet, now and then, he seemed faraway. A shadow of unspeakable misery would cross his face. Others in close contact like Annette and his Who associates were as uneasily aware too that there might be less than two years left. There were more subjective worries that he would attempt suicide – again – out of spiteful bravado.

Yet it was realised too that – however much he trivialised it – unless he himself took the initiative, the distasteful topic wasn't to be mentioned outright. A major reason why talk of death was *verboten* was that, in this respect, it had been a harrowing season for pop. Over in France, a domestic accident involving electricity had just snuffed out Claude Francois, a sort of Gallic Cliff Richard. Closer to home, if not so worthy of media attention, poverty–stricken and mentally ill Pete Meadon, The Who's first manager, would depart for that bourne from which no traveller returns on 13 July 1978. Depending on which tale you believed, it was via either a deliberate or accidental, but nevertheles excessive, quantity of drink to wash down barbituates, or a brain haemorrhage from falling down the stairs of his parents' house in Edmonton, where he'd been dwelling since co–ordinating a 1972 tour – riven with administrative incompetence – for Captain Beefheart and his Magic Band. [4]

The previous summer, Marc Bolan had perished in a car crash shortly after the Grim Reaper had come for forty–two–year–old Elvis. After Moon could no longer not believe it, there'd come a kind of despairing triumph in the realisation that Presley's passing had been the finish too of so much more. It was the final gasp of Keith Moon's own dangerously extended adolescence, the last mile of a journey that had taken him too from humble foothills to the highest range of pop's purple–headed crags. Yet, as his distant friend, John Lennon, could have told him: don't bother trying to Make it because when you do, there's nothing to Make.

Look at where it had landed Ringo, so frequently and obnoxiously drunk that, during one US chat–show sofaing, he'd fiddle with a Polaroid on his lap, and reiterate his perplexed and then outraged host's questions as well as his own answers, raising his voice almost to a shout, then dropping to near inaudibility. Footballer *manqué* George Best would likewise make a clown of himself before millions on British television.

Less publicized was P.J. Proby who, outstaying his welcome on an early evening magazine on an UK provincial station, had staggered from the Plymouth studio to busk on a carelessly–strummed guitar in the foyer of the nearby Drake Cinema. He'd been getting sloshed on a daily basis for years more than Moon. Indeed, the studio date that had resulted in Proby's idiosyncratic mannered 1964 reading of *West Side Story*'s 'Somewhere' – in a deep, swollen and affected baritone that became the blueprint for a Tom Waits version a decade and a half later – was, according to Clem Cattini, 'hilarious. He sang laying on the floor, absolutely blotto. That's how "Somewhere" came out the way it did. He had a terrific voice, mind.'

Even Kenny Slade, with his down–to–earth *Coronation Street* accent, was a booker's risk too. 'He was way in front of all the other drummers,' sighed Frank White, 'but he lost it through putting too much stuff down his throat.' [5]

Ronnie Bond too was closing the door, however involuntarily, on his musical conferes. Some nights, he'd look as if he'd never totter on stage. He always did, but it might have been better sometimes if he hadn't. One day, the other Troggs would be unable to grope for more excuses for poor Ronnie's conduct, and would disguise an ultimatum as a gentle suggestion that he ought to take time off to sort himself out. In his heart–of–hearts, however, Bond understood that this was the finish, and cried into his beer.

Keith knew them all: chronic and apparently unsalvagable alcoholics who, specialist doctors would suggest, should avoid even *coq au vin*. Chewed up and spat out by the Swinging Sixties too, the likes of John Bonham [6], Wayne Fontana, Vivian Stanshall, Kit Lambert and, of course, Keith Richards were bobbing like corks on seas as shoreless. Heroin, tranquillizers, Scotch, beer – whatever the drug of choice, it was but a temporary analgesic, an alleviation of the pangs of despair, and became so immoderate that stray newspaper paragraphs would hint at sojourns in 'homes' where they were helped to confront and wrestle with unknowable conflicts.

Killing a lot of time in the saloon bar vicinity of Messrs. Pimms and Johnny Walker, Fontana lamented that that Great Leveller alopaecia had attacked his hairline as it had his elder brothers before him. No longer able to get a hit to save his life, he had descended into a cabaret netherworld where current chart status had no meaning, his very name a hindrance to any opportunity of escape. 'I can't tell you the point where I realised I was an alcoholic, that life was hell without booze,' he'd confess when it wasn't any more, 'Though maybe it wasn't me that was going through hell, but the people around me. The next day was hell for me, mind, but I soon cured that by getting tanked up again. I wasn't too well as a result, couldn't sleep, so the doctor prescribed tranquillizers. I was on Valium – a tablet every six hours – for twenty-four years. Even without the drink, I was in a stupor, anaethetized.'

As it was with Keith Moon, Wayne imagined falsely that he was over the worst, 'therefore, I could have just one little drink – and I was off again, just as if I'd never stopped'. With terrifying sureness, Wayne checked in at a hostel for alcoholics in his native Manchester, a stay blighted by a 'creative' tabloid scribe – rebuked later by the Press Council – gaining a sordid scoop by deceit and theft of family photographs.

Though not a Latin scholar, Keith Moon, however effectually, started practicing Seneca's maxim, *pars sanitatis velle sanari fruit* [7] too. He endeavoured not to keep the company of others who liked their booze, and replaced spirits – except for his regular afternoon brandies – briefly with the less toxic wine – rather like someone embracing vegetarianism apart from bacon sandwiches. He was persuaded also to contact Alcoholics Anonymous, but mocked the intelligence of concerned parties by firstly imbibing in secret and then hurrying, quite openly, to the nearest licenced premises the minute each AA session was over.

Keith made no long–term plans. How could he when, denying that his alcoholism was all that critical, he'd wake up thick–tongued and with a blinding headache after another bender? If swearing not to touch another drop, he'd be sinking three fingers of hair–of–the–dog brandy within half–an–hour of getting dressed.

Away from home, Keith played a major part in not only the sex, but also the harder drugs – though not as hard as the heroin that had come close to killing Eric Clapton – and, in 1975, had rendered Free guitarist Paul Kossoff 'technically dead' for half a minute, and, a few months later, 'technically dead' to this day. A combination punch of heroin and alcohol plus his trademark corpulence was to knock Canned Heat's Bob 'The Bear' Hite into eternity too.

Yet Viv Stanshall, Harry Nilsson and Alice Cooper had or were sweating away the blue devils; Cooper using his experiences as the theme for a 'comeback' album. When obliged by law, Keith Richards was conquering heroin by acupuncture while, through the love of a good woman and his spell in the nursing home, Wayne Fontana had overcome his dependence on both drink and Valium, and would be back in business with a new Mindbenders.

Keith wondered too about residential care where, when jerked from sleep by phantoms threatening to engulf him, help would be always at hand at the press of a buzzer. After all, Wayne responded well within the orderliness of the regime – too well perhaps as 'I was getting institutionalised because I was so content in that place. After two–and–a–half years, they said I was ready to move on, and I didn't want to face it because I'd been cocooned: looked after, clothed and fed.' More off–putting for Moon was that, as well as counselling – much of it by recovering sufferers – treatment included compulsory exercise, group therapy, confinement to the premises and no sex. In cold print, it read like prison.

Why should he bother? So far, he hadn't died in Hades like Elvis – and it wasn't as if he was in the same endless highway dilemna as an olde tyme rocker or black bluesman of a pre–Beatle epoch, with singing and playing an instrument his only saleable trade. Nevertheless, inactivity was Keith's worst enemy, and to combat this, he telephoned journalist and BBC Radio One presenter Anne Nightingale late in August 1978, to ask her to attend to the literary donkey–work in the writing of his autobiography. He'd come up, he told her, with a working title, *The Moon Papers*, and proposed continued discussion at her home in Brighton.

The following Wednesday – 6 September – Nightingale noticed Moon in animated conversation with Paul McCartney at a table in the Peppermint Park restaurant off Covent Garden. She was among celebrity guests at a finger–food celebration to climax the third of the annual Buddy Holly Weeks inaugurated by the ex–Beatle. This time round, it embraced a concert by what was left of the bespectacled Texan's accompanying Crickets; rock 'n' roll dance exhibitions; poetry and song-writing competitions, and, after the Peppermint Park party, a midnight premiere of *The Buddy Holly Story* feature film at the Leicester Square Odeon.

Twenty years earlier, Holly and his Crickets' only British tour had been one of the principal elements that coalesced to produce the British beat boom. Among schoolboys who found the two guitars–bass–drums stage act and compact sound instructive were Mick Jagger, Dave Clark and Brian Poole who, from Kent, North London and Essex respectively, caught a performance in London. At the Manchester stop were future Hollies Allan Clarke and Graham Nash, and a spindly youth named Garrity, lately parted from a girlfriend who'd disapproved of him singing in a new group called Freddie and the Dreamers in which he wore black horn–rimmed spectacles just like Buddy's – as would Brian Poole after he'd approached lads at his Barking secondary school about forming his own Crickets with himself as Buddy Holly.

Moreover, one London Teddy Boy was to merit the nickname 'Sunglasses Ron' as he was never to remove the said shades after reading of Buddy's death not quite a year later. Hearing of it, Wiltshire guitarist Trevor Davies – later the 'Dozy' in Dave Dee, Dozy, Beaky, Mick and Tich – 'cried all the way home. Yes, he was a big hero.'

Most decisively, The Crickets and Holly had demonstrated how rock 'n' roll could be self–composed, simultaneously forceful and romantic, and could progress without getting too complex. Upon discovering this, Paul McCartney suggested to a younger friend George Harrison that they too pen their own songs before Paul found a keener collaborator in John Lennon, leader of the skiffle group that was to mutate into The Beatles.

Keith too acknowledged Buddy Holly's influence, having logged, for instance, the steady and unbroken paradiddle pounding that alternated between floor and small tom–toms on 'Peggy Sue', Buddy's first solo million–seller, and the pitter–pattering of hands on trousered knees serving as the simple but effective percussive drive on 'Everyday', one of the posthumous B–sides.

Neither Moon nor McCartney, however, were impressed with *The Buddy Holly Story*; Keith – with Annette – going so far as to shuffle out before the end. Following an ill–humoured meal, they went to bed. In the grey of morning, his sticky eyelids parted as if slit with a knife, and he demanded breakfast, which a resentful Annette cooked for him to eat propped up on the pillows. With a sated grunt, he drifted off to sleep again on the tide of twice the recognised lethal intake of a potion to combat his alcoholism. His last coherent utterance had been a foul–mouthed directive to Annette.

The flame was flickering lower as a pneumatic drill commenced its raucous stutter a few streets away. His breathing slackened, and the spark went out. Death had taken Keith John Moon without effort when the clang of the ambulance bell impinged upon the churn of afternoon traffic. The paramedics applied cardiopulmonary resuscitation and further procedures for a full half–hour. As they lifted the corpse onto a stretcher, one of them remarked that it looked at least sixty years old.

To that whey–faced girl at a bus stop the next day with a newly–purchased *Story Of The Who* under her arm, the whole business would beggar belief, but few who knew 'The Madman' were caught completely unawares by his body's final rebellion after a lifetime of violation. It crossed the minds of some to say as much when approached to contribute sound–bites for that creepy Thursday's evening news bulletins.

As twilight thickened, the black carnival was well underway. Keith had bade farewell too late for headlines to be chalked on newspaper stands, but during stop–starting overground journeys through rush–hour London, commuters would look without instant comprehension in the windows of electrical goods shops where silent televisions showed Keith drumming with The Who. Car radios elaborated raw information; estate agents wondered who was doing the probate assessments, and sick jokes circulated among journalists shoving together hurried obituaries for the next morning, distorting the old, old stories even more.

Hardly any media or fans had divined any information about a send–off that was as private as it could be a week later, but a handful converged on Golders Green Crematorium where Roger Daltrey – who cried and cried – and Charlie Watts were among the famous who prompted speculation about who could not be observed even opaquely behind the smoked windows in the procession of Mercedes, Bentleys, Porches and Rolls–Royces that crunched up to the chapel for the prayers and eulogies.

Of more conspicuous respects paid, Keith Moon's demise at the beginning of the puny 'Mod Revival' was seen by one or two cynics as an excuse for The Jam to buttress their standing with a credible influence by cranking out 'So Sad About Us' as a B–side with slightly more guts than the Who template on *A Quick One*.

Yet there were no reported deed–poll Keith Moons, bedroom seances and letters written to him years after 7 September 1978. Moreover, the death had been too public for anyone to manufacture a survival story.

Keith was never to be spotted behind the counter of an Uxbridge fish–and–chip shop, clipped–bearded and crewcut in a borough of Toronto or opening a bank account in Hong Kong. Neither did any significant conspiracy theories fly up and down, other than Roger Daltrey's vague meditation that his colleague's passing was a rite, a sacrifice if you will, through which The Who would be rejuvenated.

This was a bit too aerie–faerie for the *nouveau* Mod, but his post–hippy undergraduate cousin who'd just written a thesis on comparative religion may have thought Roger had a point. After all, the same had happened to certain Greek, Roman and Norse festility gods as well as King Arthur, Harold Godwinsson, William Rufus, Charles I – beheaded in his climacteric seven–times–seventh year – and President Kennedy. The Victim's awareness of the role is irrelevant. The crux was that the common people – some of them anyway – believed that he had been slaughtered for them and their land. It was written in *The Golden Bough*, and it had been viewable on general release in *The Wicker Man*, a 1973 B–feature that Moon had probably seen, in which a far–flung Scottish island reverts to pagan ways in hope of rich harvests.

Yeah, well... a full–time regrouping of Daltrey, Entwistle, Townshend and a new drummer was seen then as probable by even the most marginal outsider. Yet if Pete was the mind; John, the heart, and Roger, the flesh and blood, Keith was surely the soul of The Who. There was hearsay, however, that, as their biggest liability – a wellspring of vexation rather than humour by then – he was also going to be their Pete Best – or, more pertinently, their Dennis Wilson – but that his death had spared one of a deputation of the other three from marshalling his words and daring the speech that everybody knew had to be made.

Rather than accept such a decision – if it was ever on the cards – gracefully, and allow an unsettled chapter in the group's career to close, Keith's last service to The Who was to gild their legend by satisfying most of the qualifications of a doomed rock hero: self–absorption; gargantuan intake of stimulants and sex; a visual appearance that remains modern; an aura of either fascinating depravity or cartoon scariness, depending on a given observer's credulity – and, to round it off, the 'beautiful sadness' of an early extinction. Finally, despite the unquiet nature of his thirty–two years on this planet, Keith had just about retained a boy's face, a look of fated youth, albeit one with a lot of miles in the eyes.

Through the cigarette smoke at the Peppermint Park, they'd met those of Paul McCartney. Keith assured Paul that he had every intention of keeping a promise to be among the cast on Tuesday 3 October 1978 at Abbey Road for two tracks, 'Rockestra Theme' and 'So Glad To See You Here', intended for the next Wings album, *Back To The Egg*. This latest manifestation of McCartney's cocksure talent was to be preserved on celluloid because of arrangements that Cecil B. de Mille might have approved had he been a late 1970s record producer with the biggest names in British rock only a telephone call away. John Bonham alone sent the console's decibel metre into the red, but he was but one sixth of a percussion battalion that also included Kenney Jones from The Faces.

'Keith Moon was going to turn up too, but unfortunately he died a week before,' (*sic*) explained Paul. [8] Nonetheless, fingering unison riffs were the two incumbent guitarists in his Wings plus Pete Townshend, Hank B. Marvin and Pink Floyd's Dave Gilmour. Jeff Beck was meant to be there too, but he suffered from tinnitus [9] – which 'So Glad To See You Here' and 'Rockestra Theme' might have worsened when even Bonham's Led Zeppelin cohort, John Paul Jones, one of no less than three bass players, fought to be heard amid the massed guitars, drums, keyboards and horns.

While they made outmoded monophonic Dansette record–players shudder, the numbers weren't the flat–out blasts you may have imagined on top–of–the–range stereo – though, had he been able to make it, Keith Moon might have made perhaps a faintly discernable difference.

Notes

1. *The Beat*, March 2005.
2. *New Musical Express*, 27 July 1974.
3. In 1985, Frank Zappa's 'We're Turning Again' (on *Frank Zappa Meets The Mothers Of Prevention*), was to include nihilistic 'joking' about the behaviour that led to the deaths of Moon, Hendrix, Mama Cass, Janis Joplin and Jim Morrison. He also muses about going back in time to undo the circumstances that ended their lives. Tommy Mars, Zappa's keyboard player, found 'We're Turning Again' mean–spirited and tasteless.
4. Collators of macabre coincidences in pop might note that on 7 April 1981, Kit Lambert, Meadon's successor as The Who's manager – and also prone to serious substance abuse – also died after tumbling down a flight of stairs in his mother's London home, having squandered most of his wealth too.
5. *Not Like A Proper Job: The Story Of Popular Music In Sheffield, 1955– 1975* by J. Firminger and M. Lilleker (Juma, 2001).
6. Who was to collapse with 'exhaustion' during a Led Zeppelin concert in Europe, and, following sixteen vodkas during a pub luncheon in Windsor – and a few more after chucking–out time – he'd be poured on to a bed in Jimmy Page's house to sleep it off. By the next morning, he'd turned blue, and given up the ghost.
7. 'The wish to be cured is the first step towards health'.
8. *Rolling Stone*, 12 December 1979.
9. As Pete Townshend had, apparently, since the incident on *The Smothers Brothers Comedy Hour* in 1967.

Phil Nixon remembers Keith Moon: 'I was playing bass in a group called Lorelei at Wokingham Rock Club, and a support band was arranged by the venue. After the soundcheck. we went for a pint – as the place was not licenced – and came back in time to see these youngsters finishing their set.
What struck me was the size of the drummer's kit. It was a thirteen–piece Premier, which was a bit out of the usual to say the least. In the changing room, I asked the drummer where he had got the kit from. He said his father had been given it by Keith Moon – and then I found out I was talking to thirteen–year–old Zak Starkey.'

Epilogue: The Good's Gone

'No–one could ever take Keith's place, and we're not even going to try to replace him – but we're more determined than ever to carry on'
– Pete Townshend [1]

Keith Moon's drumming had been as good as it would ever get around the time of *Who's Next,* and the repercussions of all he'd done artistically up to this point – particularly his contributions to The Who's first run of chart strikes – yet resound. However, having left such a mark on pop, the short years left to him were bestowed with a debatable irrelevance, regardless of latter–day windfalls such as the astonishing *Quadrophenia*, parts of *Who By Numbers* and even the group's 'Who Are You' – title track of a new album slipping into the domestic Top Twenty on the back of the first rumblings of a 'Mod Revival', and doing likewise in the States. As Keith might have wished, this single was still in both charts on the day he passed away. The LP entered the British list that weekend.

Already, Daltrey, Entwistle and Townshend were taking stock. Cemented together by the common jubilations and ordeals of their heyday – and the opportunity to make an easy fortune – it was decided, after much debate, that, though blood ties had counted for less than membership of The Who once upon a time, they were going to risk offending purists by augmenting what was left of the group with a horn section, a keyboard player – and a new drummer.

When the news leaked out, hopefuls from cruise ships, night clubs, nice–little–bands, pit orchestras, ceilidh outfits, hotel lounge combos, you name it, were stirred into action. Not a postal delivery to The Who's office would go by without a deluge of packages containing tapes and supplicatory letters thumping onto the doormat. Tongue–tied callers who'd found out the ex–directory number would beg for their cases to be fast–tracked. Fingers calloused by drum–sticks pressed the bell constantly. They didn't have a prayer between them.

Among established names that could have been considered were Mitch Mitchell and Aynsley Dunbar, but the only one sounded out by The Who, purportedly, was Kenney (formerly Kenny) Jones of the now–sundered Faces, who had sprung from The Small Faces, The Who's Mod sparring partners in the 1960s. His two–bar round–the–kit clatter had kicked off their 'Whatcha Gonna Do About It' chart debut seven months after 'I Can't Explain' intruded upon the Top Fifty. Moreover, Kenney's contribution to 'It's Only Rock 'N' Roll', the title song and spin–off single from the 1974 Rolling Stones album had so passed muster that a holidaying Charlie Watts hadn't been required to layer his own drumming onto the invested rhythm and tempo.

Though he went with the flow, Roger had misgivings about Kenney, nutshelling them years later like a Shepherd's Bush Socrates: 'It's like a room of four walls. If you lose one, the room can be any size you want it, but we built another wall.' [2] Despite his doubts, it was announced on 22 December 1978 – slightly over three months since Keith's death – that Kenney Jones was a full–time member of The Who. Not merely a hired hand, he was the *beau ideal*, acceptable to both Who traditionalists and more open–minded fans expecting the group to loosen the straitjacket of the old regime. 'Their manager told me "The Who haven't considered, and will not consider, anybody else",' Jones informed *Modern Drummer*. [3] As if in acknowledgement, his maiden stage appearance with The Who at London's Rainbow Theatre the following May prompted a glowing *Melody Maker* review, beaming about a 'joyous experience of rock 'n' roll excellence' [4].

Such approbation, nevertheless, was not reflected in the day–to–day mundanities of selling records, most immediately, the follow–up to "Who Are You". "Long Live Rock" – taped with Moon in 1972 –had served as a useful demo for Billy Fury's contribution to the *That'll Be The Day* soundtrack. After the group's version fell from its UK peak of Number Forty–Eight in 1979 – and a re–issue of The High Numbers' 'I'm The Face' from one short of the same position – things went quiet until 1981 when 'You Better You Bet' with a now road–drilled Kenney Jones – slipped into global Top Twenties – with Roger Daltrey believing that industry politics prevented it from rising higher than Number Nine at home. Its album, *Face Dances*, sold well too, even if its very makers didn't think it embodied the truism to be articulated by John McNally of The Searchers: 'You don't have to be young to make good records.' [5]

Jones remained with The Who for further recordings – including the ominously–titled in–concert offering, *Who's Last* – as well as several tours and one–off charity and awards ceremony events. Within his limits, Kenney was a skilled and respected musician, and he'd been as animated as the other Faces in their trademark knockabout stage routines. However, while listeners grew used to it, the pulse of interaction with the other fellows in The Who wasn't as appealingly loose as it had been in Keith's day in which the concept of the guitarists and singer being controlled *en bloc* by tempos defined by bass and drums had always been a misnomer. It had depended just as much on Townshend's chord–slashing and the way in which Daltrey placed the lyric on the beat – with Moon thwacking or implying the snare off–beat perhaps a fraction of a second behind – or in front, but never at exactly the same time – and Entwistle somewhere in between.

As well as not quite belonging musically, Jones had been, perhaps predictably, at frequent loggerheads with Daltrey. Besides, as the 1990s approached, The Who weren't much of a group any more. This had been painfully obvious to Mick Jagger when he walked in on a backstage tongue–lashing that seemed bereft of any underlying affection: 'I learned a lesson from The Who being on the road when they were not getting on. It embarrassed me and made me feel sad.' [6]

In 1989 however, they went the distance of a trek round North America and a shorter one in England with Simon Phillips, a session shellback of younger vintage than Clem Cattini, Bobby Graham and Lloyd Ryan. Among his more illustrious clients had been Jeff Beck, Jack Bruce, Roxy Music and the latter–day Walker Brothers. With The Who, he studiously avoided confrontation, collected his pay and, while he didn't look the part, was rated by Ryan as the most outstanding drummer who'd ever trodden the boards with the group. This praise for his combination of precise time–keeping and a close approximation of Moon's idiosyncracies was however countered , 'but he didn't have the magic, the showmanship or the flair that Keith had, as far as the public was concerned anyway.'

The job done, Simon returned to the retractable sphere of the studio, and The Who downed tools as a working group for nigh on seven years before rematerialising like ghosts from the recent past with a new recruit who, unlike Kenney and Simon, wasn't a pop methuselah – though he was the eldest child of one. A young face in an old group wasn't uncommon post–Live Aid – particularly if he had a rafter–raising affinity to a deceased former member. In 1993, The Troggs had gone ahead with an engagement in Germany having resolved uniquely the quandary of their usual drummer being indisposed. Introduced as 'someone special' by Reg Presley, the substitute was none other than Darren Bullis, son of the now late Ronnie Bond, and very much a chip off the old block behind the kit, just as the similarly placed Jason Bonham had proved to be when enlisted into a briefly reunited Led Zeppelin five years earlier.

As his father, Ringo Starr, had scorned drumming lessons, Zak Starkey was restricted to just one tutorial 'then he just told me to listen to records and play along with them'. [7] Given a free choice, Zak preferred to pound along to The Who rather than The Beatles.

While his self–taught drumming continued to improve, the same could not said of certain subjects taught at the private academy Zak attended in London. His dad's gallivanting absences in California and elsewhere setting no good example, Zak's truancies and general misbehaviour were causing anxiety. With an open invitation to bolt to the 'safe house' of 'Uncle' Keith Moon's West End apartment when retribution was imminent, what chance did the unhappy youth have? 'See, during my puberty, Moonie was always there with me,' he elucidated, 'while my old man was far away in Monte Carlo or somewhere.' [6]

As well as taking after his father facially and in his manner of speaking, Zak was also partial to a drink or two. The worst for it once, he was barred from a Bracknell pub for menacing demands that the staff change a tape of Beatles hits thar had started piping from the sound system the minute he entered the building. 'Being Ringo's son is a total pain,' he'd scowl, 'I'm always written about as Ringo's son, always classed with him in every single thing I try to do.' [7]

Among these had been membership of The Next and Monopacific, otherwise unsung post–punk outfits – though Zak's connections with Keith Moon – whose picture adorned the wall of his bedroom – gained Monopacific a manager in Moon's former personal assistant, Peter 'Dougal' Butler. As a result, the unit also attracted the attention of Entwistle, Daltrey – and Townshend, who considered young Starkey's 'the most accurate emulation of Keith's style,' [7] qualifying this with 'luckily Zak also has a style of his own, but many have been moved, when listening to his explosive solos, to say "My God! It's him!" [7] Obviously, Starkey's shadowing of Moon hadn't been wasted for, at the few venues Monopacific played before going the way of The Next, his performance, if as animated as Keith's, had a disciplined exactitude equalling that of both his sire and Simon Phillips. 'His time–keeping was more accurate,' agreed Lloyd Ryan, 'and the fills were cleaner.'

As enthusiastic about Zak's playing as Ryan and Townshend, John Entwistle found time to produce the lad's next ensemble, Nightfly. Furthermore, largely through John, Starkey was employed for what he did rather than who he was on many lucrative sessions – notably for Denny Laine's *Lonely Road* and – its title track a nod to Zak's mentor – Daltrey's *Under A Raging Moon*. In conjunction with ageing keyboard *wunderkind* Eddie Hardin – who, in 1967, quit A Wild Uncertainty for The Spencer Davis Group – Zak recorded his first album, the *Musical Version O Wind In The Willows*. Zak sat in too with his father's All–Starr Band, and, though he had more contemporary fish to fry with Ice, the group that came after Nightfly, he'd be at the kit throughout the older outfit's North American expedition in 1992.

In the line–up too was John Entwistle, thrumming bass and giving 'em 'Boris The Spider' amongst Billy Preston, Felix Cavaliere from the Young Rascals, Grand Funk Railroad's Mark Farner, Randy Bachman of Bachman–Turner Overdrive and others in the constant flux of mainly middle–aged personnel making up value–for–money numbers in this peddling of trans–continental nostalgia.

In 1998 however, Jack Bruce was to replace Entwistle, who was involved once more in ongoing Who projects – as was Zak Starkey, whose adolescent aspiration was to assert its old power in once unimaginable abundance when he began a longer tenure with the group than Simon Phillips and even Kenney Jones at a Prince's Trust Benefit concert in Hyde Park's natural amphitheatre one Saturday in June 1996. In reciprocation, if he wasn't a biological duplicate or with the same self–immolatory tendencies of someone they daren't forget, The Who had in Starkey the supreme replacement that they'd despaired of ever finding [8].

Since then, while filling stadiums to overflowing – with revivals of *Tommy* and *Quadrophenia* as well as more orthodox recitals and a two–song slot in July 2005's *Live 8* spectacular in London, The Who have continued to struggle in the charts. Nevertheless, their spectre hovered over Britpop – as exemplified by Birmingham trio Dodgy's 'In A Room', notable in a 1996 Top Twenty boiling over with drum machines for the scampering tom–toms and unpredictable cymbal crashes of their Matthew Priest. That year too, the spirit of 1996 faced the ghost of 1966 when Dodgy supported The Who, who were perhaps more the patron saints of Britpop than any other self–contained Swinging Sixties beat group. Brand–leaders Oasis demonstrated that their hearts were in the right places via an eventual revival of 'My Generation' in the teeth of tidy–minded (or lazy) journalists finding 1960s 'opposite numbers' to contemporary groups, arguing that, however superficially, Oasis were a modern counterpoise to, first, The Rolling Stones and then The Beatles.

Yet the overall chart climate at the turn of the century begged the question: who wants proper songs anymore or, at least, someone singing a song as opposed to producing a production? Though I was furious at the time, the 1965 week that Ken Dodd's schmaltzy 'Tears' kept 'My Generation' from the top was seen through a rosy haze by the turn of the millenium when, if you caught me in full philistine rant about virtually all the major rap executants, *Pop Idol* winners and any new 'boy band', I sounded just like some middle aged Dad, *circa* 1965, going on about The Who.

Nevertheless, if I'd gone to a latter–day Who recital, what would I have wanted to hear? While they might continue to attract a remarkably young crowd that, not wanting its 1960s medicine neat, mouth the words of the later stuff and occasional obscurity as accurately as the ancient smashes, the group are unlikely to become serious contemporary challengers again, partly because most other fans, old and new, will always clap loudest for the sounds of yesteryear, available on compact discs of such clarity that, straining your ears just a little, you could almost make out the impact of dandruff falling from Keith Moon's split ends – and you could certainly hear the quieter passages of *Tommy* that used to disappear in crackle and hiss.

The objects of yesteryear have continued to be valued too – in every sense. A pair of yellow cotton trousers that had once hung round Moon's legs, and his floor tom–tom with images of 'Pictures Of Lily' postcard Victoriana painted round its shell drew high bids at pop memorabilia auctions where they'd been displayed and put under the hammer as solemnly as if they'd been splinters from the True Cross. Cash for lesser treasures changed hands at the Who fan conventions that are now annual fixtures in cities throughout the world with guest speakers, archive films, exhibitions and sets by clone groups with big–nosed guitarists, blonde lead vocalists and so forth.

Shortly before John Entwistle's sudden demise, all three of the surviving genuine articles had been present in the Charing Cross Road disco that hosted a comparatively recent launch party for yet another stage version of *Tommy*. Hired for the cabaret was a Wild West character with a lasso, a whip and a rifle. Using a mirror, he attempted to aim over his shoulder at three balloons hanging behind him. He missed all of them, but plugged and severely injured the disc–jockey. In the ensuing panic, some inflammable liquid to be used in a fire–eating act was set alight, and a snake charmer's nearby basketful of singed and enraged reptiles ran amok.

Within a few minutes, therefore, there'd been a near–fatal shooting, a blaze, seething snakes wreaking havoc, and the summoning of police and a fire engine. After having their eyeful of unscheduled spectator sport, some of the celebrity guests ambled up the road to the Astoria theatre where there was now a Keith Moon Bar, to guffaw that this could have happened only at a function organised by The Who. Do you remember that end–of–tour party when Moon...?

As the old, old stories unfolded once again, some may have ruminated that when the graph of the late drummer's life had given a sharp upward turn in 1965, he'd blossomed as if made for the success that, in the long term, denied him maturity. Instead, an industry in which sales figures and bums–on–seats were arbiters of progress, brought him a fortune that he spent in much the same way as had many another ordinary lad who'd won the Lottery. With the autocracy of the bluest–blooded grandee, he behaved as if the Rolls, the fancy clothes, the champagne, the curvaceous model, the tax exile *et al* had been his heritage since birth.

He spent less time statistically on anything constructive than on just larking about. Towards the end, if mentally–ill–arious still, Moon was in danger of delighting us for too long. Indeed, the entertainment he provided, official and otherwise, had long developed more than a hint of fever, deteriorating too frequently into behaviour that made the tabloids for the wrong reasons – and, at worst, got boring or boring *and* revolting.

No–one liked to mention anything – well, not outright – about his personal stagnation – or that he had toppled from his perch and, as swiftly, had admitted tacit defeat. Everything that was weak in him had come to the fore. He disintegrated not because he wished The Who had never happened but because he wished they were still happening. No matter what he said to the contrary, he, far more than the other three, would have most liked to do it all again. Instead, he made do with trying to relive the old days as best he could as his life settled into what has become almost the set pattern for famous 1960s pop musicians: the years of struggle, the climb to fame, the consolidation, the decline, the 'wilderness years'.

They'd try to suppress the thought, but, to certain of his fans – and maybe professional associates too – it had been Keith's ill luck to live on after he'd outlived his social purpose and dumped his artistic load. Luckily for them – and possibly himself too – he died seconds before he could have become pathetic.

Notes

1. *NME Rock 'N' Roll Years* ed. J. Tobler (BCA, 1992)
2. *The Guardian*, 28 January 2005
3. Quoted in *Happy Boys Happy: The Small Faces And Humble Pie* by U. Twelker and R. Schmitt (Santuary, 1997)
4. *Melody Maker*, 12 May 1979
5. 10. *Sunday Times*, 5 May 1990
6. *Rolling Stone*, 5 November 1987
7. *The Sun*, 23 September 1982
8. Starkey was still with The Who in 2005, though his stint with Oasis that year delayed the release of The Who's first album without John Entwistle.

COMPLETE DISCOGRAPHY OF RECORDINGS
FEATURING KEITH MOON

The author and editors believe this to be the most complete discography of recording to feature Keith Moon ever compiled. However, should any reader detect omissions or have other comments, please write to Chrome Dreams at PO Box 230, New Malden, Surrey, KT3 6YY, UK or email to info@chromedreams.co.uk. This will enable future editions to be corrected. Any assistance will be greatly appreciated.

The discography uses UK releases unless noted otherwise.

With regards reissues we have only noted these when they contain material not on the original editions or are significant for other reasons. In the compilations section we have included titles which contain previously unreleased material or which contained tracks not available on album at the time the compilation was originally released.

ALBUMS

My Generation
Out In The Street / I Don't Mind / The Good's Gone / La La La
Lies / Much Too Much / My Generation / The Kids Are Alright /
Please, Please, Please / It's Not True / The Ox / A Legal Matter /
I'm A Man
LP – Brunswick (1965)
Re–issue
2CD – Polydor (2002)
Bonus Tracks:
Disc 1 I Can't Explain / Bald Headed Woman / Daddy Rolling
Stone
Disc 2 Leaving Home (Alternate) / Lubie (Come Back Home)
/ Shout And Shimmy / (Love Is Like A) Heatwave (Alternate)
/ Motoring / Anytime You Want Me / Anyway, Anyhow,
Anywhere (Alternate) / Instant Party Mixture / I Don't Mind
(Full Length Version) / The Good's Gone (Full Length Version)
/ My Generation (Instrumental Version) / Anytime You Want Me
(Acapella Version)

A Quick One
Run, Run, Run / Boris The Spider / I Need You / Whiskey Man /
Heat Wave / Cobwebs And Strange / Don't Look Away / See My
Way / So Sad About Us / A Quick One While He's Away
LP – Reaction (1966)
Re–issue
CD – Polydor (2003)
Bonus tracks:
Batman / Bucket T / Barbara Ann / Disguises / Doctor, Doctor /
I've Been Away / In The City / Happy Jack (Acoustic Version) /
Man With The Money / My Generation and Land Of Hope And
Glory (Medley)

The Who Sell Out
Armenia City In The Sky / Heinz Baked Beans / Mary–Anne With
The Shaky Hands / Odorono / Tattoo / Our Love Was / I Can See
For Miles / I Can't Reach You / Medac / Relax / Silas Stingy /
Sunrise / Rael
LP – Track (1967)
Re–issue
CD – Polydor (1998)
Bonus tracks:
Rael 2 / Glittering Girl / Melancholia / Someone's Coming /
Jaguar / Early Morning / Cold Taxi / Hall Of The Mountain King
/ Girl's Eyes / Mary–Anne With The Shaky Hand (Alternate
Version) / Glow Girl

Tommy
Overture / It's A Boy / 1921 / Amazing Journey / Sparks /
Eyesight To The Blind (The Hawker) / Christmas / Cousin Kevin
/ Acid Queen / Underture / Do You Think It's Alright? / Fiddle
About / Pinball Wizard / There's A Doctor / Go To The Mirror
/ Tommy Can You Hear Me? / Smash The Mirror / Sensation /
Miracle Cure / Sally Simpson / I'm Free / Welcome / Tommy's
Holiday Camp / We're Not Gonna Take It
2LP – Track (1969)
Re–issue
2 CD – Polydor (2004)
Bonus Tracks
Disc 1 See Me Feel Me – Listening To You
Disc 2 I Was / Christmas (Out–Take 3) / Cousin Kevin Model
Child / Young Man Blues (Version 1) / Tommy Can You Hear
Me? (Alternate) / Trying To Get Through / Sally Simpson (Out–
Take) / Miss Simpson / Welcome (Take 2) / Tommy's Holiday
Camp (Band's Version) / We're Not Gonna Take It (Alternate
Version) / Dogs (Part 2) / It's A Boy (Alternate) / Amazing
Journey (Alternate) / Christmas (Out–Take 2) / Do You Think It's
Alright? (Alternate) / Pinball Wizard (Alternate)

Live At Leeds
Young Man Blues / Substitute / Summertime Blues / Shakin' All
Over / My Generation / Magic Bus
LP – Track (1970)
Re–issue
2 CD – Deluxe Edition Polydor (2001)
Bonus Tracks:
Disc 1 Heaven And Hell / I Can't Explain / Fortune Teller / Tattoo
/ Happy Jack / I'm A Boy / A Quick One While He's Away
Disc 2 Overture / It's A Boy / 1921 / Amazing Journey / Sparks
/ Eyesight To The Blind (The Hawker) / Christmas / The Acid
Queen / Pinball Wizard
/ Do You Think It's Alright? / Fiddle About / Tommy Can You
Hear Me

Quadrophenia
I Am The Sea / Real Me / Quadrophenia / Cut My Hair / Punk
And The Godfather / I'm One / Dirty Jobs / Helpless Dancer / Is It
In My Head / I've Had Enough / 5.15 / Sea And Sand / Drowned /
Bell Boy / Dr Jimmy / Rock / Love Reign O'er Me
2 LP – Track (1973)
Re–issue
CD – Polydor (1996 – No Bonus Tracks)

Two Sides Of The Moon (Keith's only solo album)
Crazy Like A Fox / Solid Gold / Don't Worry Baby / One Night
Stand / The Kids Are Alright / Move Over Mrs. L / Teenage Idol /
Backdoor Sally / In My Life / Together
LP – Polydor (1975)
Re–issue
CD – Repertoire (1997)
Bonus Tracks: US Radio Spot / I Don't Suppose / Naked Man
/ Do Me Good / Real Emotion / Don't Worry Baby (US Single
Version) / Teenage Idol (US Single Version) / Together 'Rap'

The Who By Numbers

Slip Kid / However Much I Booze / Squeeze Box / Dreaming
From The Waist / Imagine A Man / Success Story / They Are All
In Love / Blue Red And Grey / How Many Friends / In A Hand Or
A Face

LP – Polydor (1975)

Re–issue

CD – Polydor (1998)

Bonus Tracks: Squeeze Box (2) (Live) / Behind Blue Eyes (Live)
/ Dreaming From The Waist (2) (Live)

Who Are You

New Song / Had Enough / 905 / Sister Disco / Music Must
Change / Trick Of The Light / Guitar And Pen / Love Is Coming
Down / Who Are You

LP – Polydor (1978)

Re–issue

CD – Polydor (1998)

Bonus Tracks: No Road Romance / Empty Glass / Guitar And
Pen (2) (Olympia '78 Mix) / Love Is Coming Down (2) (Work In
Progress Mix) / Who Are You (2) (Lost Verse Mix)

SINGLES

I'm The Face (as the High Numbers)
I'm The Face / Zoot Suit
Year Of Release – 1964
Formats – 7"
Label – Fontana

I Can't Explain
I Can't Explain / Bald Headed Woman
Year Of Release – 1965
Formats – 7"
Label – Brunswick

Anyway, Anyhow, Anywhere
Anyway, Anyhow, Anywhere / Daddy Rolling Stone
Year Of Release – 1965
Formats – 7"
Label – Brunswick

My Generation
My Generation / Shout And Shimmy
Year Of Release – 1965
Formats – 7"
Label – Brunswick

Substitute (first issue)
Substitute / Instant Party
Year Of Release – 1966
Formats – 7"
Label – Reaction

Substitute (second issue)
Substitute / Circles
Year Of Release – 1966

Formats – 7"
Label – Reaction

Substitute (third issue)
Substitute / Waltz For A Pig (Performed By 'The Who Orchestra'
whose true identity was The Graham Bond Organisation)
Year Of Release – 1966
Formats – 7"
Label – Reaction

A Legal Matter
A Legal Matter / Instant Party
Year Of Release – 1966
Formats – 7"
Label – Brunswick

Ready Steady Who EP
Disguises / The Batman Theme/ Circles / Bucket "T" / Barbara
Ann
Year Of Release – 1966
Formats – 7"
Label – Reaction

The Kids Are Alright
The Kids Are Alright / The Ox
Year Of Release – 1966
Formats – 7"
Label – Brunswick

I'm A Boy
I'm A Boy / In The City
Year Of Release – 1966
Formats – 7"
Label – Reaction

The Good's Gone
The Good's Gone / La La La Lies
Year Of Release – 1966
Formats – 7"
Label – Brunswick

Happy Jack
Happy Jack / I've Been Away
Year Of Release – 1966
Formats – 7"
Label – Reaction

Pictures of Lily
Pictures of Lily / Doctor, Doctor
Year Of Release – 1967
Formats – 7"
Label – Track

The Last Time
The Last Time / Under My Thumb
Year Of Release – 1967
Formats – 7"
Label – Track

I Can See For Miles
I Can See For Miles / Someone's Coming
Year Of Release – 1967
Formats – 7"
Label – Track

Dogs
Dogs / Call Me Lightning
Year Of Release – 1968

Formats – 7"
Label – Track

Magic Bus
Magic Bus / Dr. Jekyll And Mr. Hyde
Year Of Release – 1968
Formats – 7"
Label – Track

Pinball Wizard
Pinball Wizard / Dogs Pt. II
Year Of Release – 1969
Formats – 7"
Label – Track

The Seeker
The Seeker / Here For More
Year Of Release – 1970
Formats – 7"
Label – Track

Summertime Blues
Summertime Blues / Heaven A nd Hell
Year Of Release – 1970
Formats – 7"
Label – Track

Won't Get Fooled Again
Won't Get Fooled Again / I Don't Even Know Myself
Year Of Release – 1971
Formats – 7"
Label – Track

Let's See Action
Let's See Action / When I was A Boy
Year Of Release – 1971
Formats – 7"
Label – Track

Join Together
Join Together / Baby Don't Do It
Year Of Release – 1972
Formats – 7"
Label – Track

Relay
Relay / Waspman
Year Of Release – 1972
Formats – 7"
Label – Track

5:15
5:15 / Water
Year Of Release – 1973
Formats – 7"
Label Track

Don't Worry Baby (Keith's only UK solo single)
Don't Worry Baby / Together
Year Of Release 1975
Formats – 7"
Label – Polydor

Squeeze Box
Squeeze Box / Success Story
Year Of Release – 1976
Formats – 7"
Label – Polydor

Substitute (reissue this was the first 12" single ever to be released in the UK)
Substitute / I'm A Boy / Pictures Of Lily
Year Of Release – 1976
Formats – 7", 12"
Label – Polydor

Who Are You
Who Are You / Had Enough
Year Of Release – 1978
Formats – 7"
Label – Track

SELECT COMPILATIONS

Direct Hits
Bucket "T" / I'm A Boy / Pictures Of Lily / Doctor, Doctor / I Can
See For Miles / Substitute / Happy Jack / The Last Time / In The
City / Call Me Lightning / Mary–Anne With The Shaky Hands /
Dogs
LP – Track (1968)

The Ox (budget compilation of tracks composed by John Entistle)
Heinz Baked Beans / Heaven and Hell / Dr. Jekyll and Mr. Hyde /
Fiddle About / Cousin Kevin / Doctor, Doctor / Medac / Boris the
Spider / I've Been Away / Whiskey Man / In the City / Someone's
Coming / Silas Stingy
LP – Backtrack (1970)

Meaty, Beaty, Big and Bouncy
I Can't Explain / The Kids Are Alright / Happy Jack / I Can See
For Miles / Pictures Of Lily / My Generation / The Seeker /
Anyway, Anyhow, Anywhere / Pinball Wizard / A Legal Matter /
Boris The Spider / Magic Bus / Substitute / I'm A Boy
LP – Track (1971)
Re–issue
CD – Polydor (2001 No Bonus Tracks)

30 Years of Maximum R&B
Disc 1 I'm The Face / Here 'Tis / Zoot Suit / Leaving Here / I
Can't Explain / Anyway, Anyhow, Anywhere / Daddy Rolling
Stone / My Generation / The Kids Are Alright / The Ox / A Legal
Matter / Substitute (Live At Leeds, 14 Feb. 70) / I'm A Boy /
Disguises / Happy Jack / Boris The Spider / So Sad About Us / A
Quick One, While He's Away / Pictures Of Lily / Early Morning
Cold Taxi / The Last Time / I Can't Reach You / Girl's Eyes / Call
Me Lightning

Disc 2 I Can See For Miles / Mary–Anne With The Shaky Hands / Armenia City In The Sky / Tattoo / Our Love Was / Rael 2 / Sunrise / Jaguar / Melancholia / Fortune Teller / Magic Bus / Little Billy / Dogs / Overture / Acid Queen / Underture (Live At Woodstock, 16 Aug. 69) / Pinball Wizard / I'm Free / See Me, Feel Me (Live At Leeds, 14 Feb. 70) / Heaven And Hell / Young Man Blues (Live At Leeds, 14 Feb. 70) / Summertime Blues (Live At Leeds, 14 Feb. 70)

Disc 3 Shakin' All Over (Live At Leeds, 14 Feb. 70) / Baba O' Riley / Bargain (Live At Civic Center, San Francisco, 12 Dec. 71) / Song Is Over / Pure And Easy / Behind Blue Eyes / Won't Get Fooled Again / The Seeker / Boney Maronie (Live At Young Vic, London, Apr. 71) / Let's See Action / Join Together / The Relay / The Real Me (1979 Studio Version With Kenney Jones) / 5:15 / Bell Boy / Love Reign O'er Me

Disc 4 Long Live Rock / Life With The Moons (#1 From BBC) / Naked Eye (Live At London, '71) / University Challenge (From BBC) / Slip Kid / Poetry Cornered (From BBC) / Dreaming From The Waist (Live At Swansea, 12 June 76) / Blue, Red And Grey / Life With The Moons (#2 From BBC) / Squeeze Box / My Wife (Live At Swansea, 12 June 76) / Who Are You / Music Must Change / Sister Disco / Guitar And Pen / You Better You Bet / Eminence Front / Twist And Shout (Live At Toronto, 82) / I'm A Man (Live At New York, 89) / Saturday Night's Alright (For Fighting)

4CD – MCA (1994)

Odds & Sods
Postcard / Now I'm A Farmer / Put The Money Down / Little Billy / Glow Girl / Pure & Easy / Faith In Something Bigger / I'm The Face / Naked Eye / Long Live Rock
LP – Track (1974)
Re–issue
CD – Polydor (1998)

Bonus Tracks:
Leaving Here / Baby Don't You Do It / Summertime Blues /
Under My Thumb / Mary–Anne With The Shaky Hand / My
Way / Young Man Blues (Studio Version) / Cousin Kevin Model
Child / Love Ain't For Keeping / Time Is Passing / Too Much Of
Anything / We Close Tonight / Water

The Kids Are All Right (Soundtrack)

My Generation (Live On Smothers Brothers Show, 1967) /
Anyway, Anyhow, Anywhere (Live) / Happy Jack (Live At Leeds,
14 Feb. 70) / Young Man Blues (Live At London Coliseum, 16
Dec. 69) / I Can See For Miles / I Can't Explain / Long Live
Rock / Magic Bus / My Wife (Live At Kilburn State Theatre,
Dec 77) / Baba O'Riley (Live At Shepperton Film Studios, May
78) / A Quick One While He's Away (Live At Rolling Stones
Rock 'N' Roll Circus) / Tommy Can You Hear Me / Sparks (Live
At Woodstock) / Pinball Wizard (Live At Woodstock) / See Me,
Feel Me (Live At Woodstock) / Join Together (Live At Pontiac
Silverdome, 6 Dec 75 (Not On CD)) / Roadrunner (Live At
Pontiac Silverdome, 6 Dec 75 (Not On CD)) / My Generation
Blues (Live At Pontiac Silverdome, 6 Dec 75 (Not On CD)) /
Won't Get Fooled Again (Live At Shepperton Film Studios, May
78)
2LP – Polydor (1979)
Re–issue
CD – Polydor (1993 No Bonus Tracks)

The Story Of The Who
Magic Bus / Substitute / Boris The Spider / Run, Run, Run / I'm
A Boy / Heat Wave / My Generation / Pictures Of Lily / Happy
Jack / The Seeker / I Can See For Miles / Bargain / Squeeze Box
/ Amazing Journey / The Acid Queen / Do You Think It's Alright

/ Fiddle About / Pinball Wizard / I'm Free / Tommy's Holiday
Camp / We're Not Gonna Take It / Summertime Blues (Live At
Leeds, 14 Feb. 70) / Baba O'Riley / Behind Blue Eyes / Slip Kid /
Won't Get Fooled Again
2 LP – Polydor (1976)

Rarities Vol. 1
Instant Party / Batman / Bucket T / Barbara Ann / In the City /
I've Been Away / Doctor, Doctor / The Last Time / Under My
Thumb / Someone's Coming / Mary–Anne With The Shaky Hands
/ Dogs / Call Me Lightning / Dr. Jekyll and Mr. Hyde
LP – Polydor (1983)

Rarities Vol. 2
Join Together / I Don't Even Know Myself / Heaven And Hell /
When I Was A Boy / Let's See Action / Relay / Waspman / Here
For More / Water / Baby Don't You Do It (Live At SF Civic
Center, 12 Dec. 71)
LP – Polydor (1983)
Re–issue
Rarities Vol 1 & 2
2CD – Polydor (2000)

GUEST APPEARANCES

Jeff Beck
Truth (Album)
KM: drums on 'Beck's Bolero'
LP – Columbia (1968)
CD – EMI (2005)
'Beck's Bolero' also released as b–side to 'Hi Ho Silver Lining'
7" Columbia 1967

Screaming Lord Sutch
Hands Of Jack The Ripper (Album)
KM: drums on unspecified tracks
LP – Atlantic (1972)
CD – Wounded Bird (2005)

Topo D Bill (Pseudonym for 'Legs' Larry Smith from Bonzo Dog Band)
Witchi Tai To (Single)
KM: drums and backing vocals on Witchi Tai To (a–side)
7" – Charisma 1970

John Entwistle
Smash You Head Against The Wall (Album)
KM: percussion on 'Number 29' backing vocals on 'I Believe In Everything
LP – Track (1971)
CD – Castle (2005)

Mike Heron
Smiling Men With Bad Reputations (Album)
KM: drums on 'Warm Heart Pastry'
LP – Island (1971)
CD – Fledgling (2003)

Viv Stanshall And Gargantuan Chums
Suspicion (Single)
KM: drums and producer on 'Suspicion' (a–side) and 'Blind Date'
(b–side credited to BiG GRunt)
7" – Fly (1971)

Scaffold
Do The Albert (Single)
KM: drums on 'Do The Albert' (a–side)
7" – Parlophone (1971)

Patches
Living In America (Single)
KM: Keith Moon played drums on some studio takes of this
recording. It is unsure whether he is featured on the released
version.
7" – Warner Bros. (1972)

Dave Carlsen
A Pale Horse (Album)
KM: drums on 'Death On A Pale Horse'
LP – Spark (1973)
CD – Unavailable

Roy Harper
Valentine (Album)
KM: drums on 'Male Chauvinist Pig Blues'
LP – Harvest (1974)
CD – Science Friction (2002)
'Male Chauvinist Pig Blues' also released as b–side to (Don't You
Think We're) Forever 7" Harvest (1974)

Flashes From The Archives Of Oblivion (Album)
KM: drums on 'Too Many Movies', 'Male Chauvinist Pig Blues',

'Home'
2LP – Harvest (1974)
CD Resurgence (2000)
'Home' also released as a–side 7" Harvest (1974)

Michael Bruce
In My Own Way (Album)
KM: drums on 'As Rock Rolls By'
LP – Warner Brothers (1974)
CD – Burning Airlines (2002)

Bo Diddley
20ᵗʰ Anniversary of Rock n' Roll (Album)
KM: tambourine on 'Bo Diddley Jam'
LP – RCA (1976)
CD – Edsel (1992)

Various Artists
Flash Fearless Versus The Zorg Woman Parts 5 and 6 (Album)
KM: narration (as Long John Silver – at last!) on 'Space Pirates'
tympani on 'Supersnatch'
LP – Chysalis (1975)
CD – RPM (1995)

All This And World War 2 (Album)
KM: Voals on 'When I'm 64'
2LP – 20ᵗʰ Century (1976)
CD – Unavailable

DVD

30 Years Of Maximum R&B (Live)

Anyway, Anyhow, Anywhere / So Sad About Us / A Quick One, While He's Away / Happy Jack / Heaven And Hell / I Can't Explain / Water / Young Man Blues / I Don't Even Know Myself / My Generation / Substitute / Drowned / Bell Boy / My Generation Blues / Dreaming From The Waist / Sister Disco / Who Are You / 5:15 / My Wife / Music Must Change / Pinball Wizard / Behind Blue Eyes / Love Reign O'Er Me / Boris The Spider / I Can See For Miles / See Me, Feel Me
DVD – MCA (2000)

The Who – Live At The Isle Of Wight Festival 1970

Heaven & Hell / I Can't Explain / Young Man Blues / I Don't Even Know Myself
Water / Shakin' All Over / Spoonful / Twist & Shout / Summertime Blues / My Generation / Magic Bus / Overture / I'm A Boy / Eyesight To The Blind / Christmas / Acid Queen / Pinball Wizard / Do You Think It's Alright / Fiddle About / Go To The Mirror / Miracle Cure / I'm Free / Were Not Gonna Take It / Tommy Can You Hear Me
DVD – Warner Vision (2000 – Also available as a double–LP with the same track listing)

The Kids Are Alright

My Generation / I Can't Explain / Shout And Shimmy / Young Man Blues / Substitute / Anyway, Anyhow, Anywhere / Magic Bus / Pictures Of Lily / See Me, Feel Me / Pinball Wizard / Happy Jack / A Quick One, While He's Away / Baba O'Riley / Won't Get Fooled Again / (I'm A) Road Runner / Barbara Ann / Who Are You
DVD – Pioneer (2003)

That'll Be The Day / Stardust

DVD – Warner Brothers (2003)

Tommy
2 DVD Special Edition – Odyssey Video (2004)

The Rolling Stones Rock 'N' Roll Circus
2 DVD – Island / Universal (2004)
The Who perform 'A Quick One, While He's Away' in it's
entirety, one of the stand out performances of the show.

The Who 1964–1968 Under Review; A Critical Analysis
This documentary is an independent critical review of The Who's
music and career between 1964 and 1968. It features footage
previously unreleased on DVD and rare recordings from the same
era.
DVD – Chrome Dreams (2005)